VAN AND

COLOURGUIDE
Second Edition

Edited by Constance Brissenden
Photography by Hamid Attie

FORMAC PUBLISHING COMPANY LIMITED
HALIFAX

CONTENTS

For photo credits and acknowledgements, see page 216.

CONTENTS

National Library of Canada Cataloguing in Publication

Vancouver and Victoria colourguide / edited by Constance Brissenden ; photography by Hamid Attie. — 2nd ed.
(Colourguide travel series)
Previous ed. published under title: Vancouver and Victoria : a colourguide.
Includes index.
ISBN 0-88780-618-X
1. Vancouver (B.C.)—Guidebooks. 2. Victoria (B.C.)—Guidebooks.
I. Brissenden, Connie, 1947- II. Attie, Hamid III. Series: Colourguide
Series.
FC3847.18.V34 2004   917.11'33045   C2004-900178-7

Formac Publishing Company
5502 Atlantic Street
Halifax, Nova Scotia B3H 1G4
www.formac.ca

Printed and bound in China

Distributed in the
United States by:
Casemate
2114 Darby Road, 2nd Floor
Havertown, PA 19083

Distributed in the
United Kingdom by:
Portfolio Books Limited
Unit 5, Perivale Industrial Park
Horsenden Lane South,
Greenford, UK UB6 7RL

▲ GREATER VANCOUVER MAP

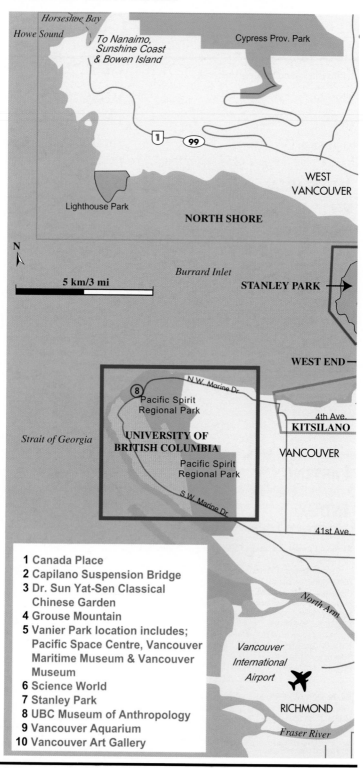

1 Canada Place
2 Capilano Suspension Bridge
3 Dr. Sun Yat-Sen Classical Chinese Garden
4 Grouse Mountain
5 Vanier Park location includes; Pacific Space Centre, Vancouver Maritime Museum & Vancouver Museum
6 Science World
7 Stanley Park
8 UBC Museum of Anthropology
9 Vancouver Aquarium
10 Vancouver Art Gallery

1. 900 West Sea & Steakfood Restaurant
2. Bacchus Ristorante
3. Bin 941 Tapas Parlour
4. C
5. Café de Paris
6. Chartwell
7. Cioppino's Mediterranean Grill
8. Diva at the Met
9. Earl's Restaurants
10. Ezogiku Noodle Café
11. Five Sails Restaurant
12. Fleuri Restaurant
13. Floata Seafood Restaurant
14. Hon's Wun Tun House
15. Imperial Chinese Seafood Restaurant
16. Il Giardino di Umberto
17. Kirin Mandarin Restaurant
18. Le Crocodile
19. Liliget Feast House
20. Musashi Japanese Restaurant
21. Nottes Bon Ton Bakery and Confectionary
22. Piccolo Mondo
23. Raincity Grill
24. Rodney's Oyster House
25. Shanghai Chinese Bistro
26. Steamworks Brewing Co.
27. Subeez
28. Villa Del Lupo
29. White Spot Triple O
30. Won More Szechuan Cuisine

▲ VANCOUVER ACCOMMODATION MAP

1. Best Western Chateau Granville Hotel
2. Best Western Downtown Vancouver
3. Blue Horizon Hotel
4. Bosman's Hotel
5. Century Plaza Hotel and Spa
6. Crowne Plaza Hotel Georgia
7. Days Inn Vancouver Downtown
8. Empire Landmark Hotel — Downtown Vancouver
9. Executive Hotel Downtown Vancouver
10. Fairmont Hotel Vancouver
11. Four Seasons Hotel Vancouver
12. Georgian Court Hotel
13. Greenbrier Hotel
14. Hampton Inn & Suites
15. Holiday Inn Hotel & Suites
16. Howard Johnson Hotel
17. Hyatt Regency Vancouver
18. Listel Vancouver
19. Lord Stanley Suites on the Park
20. Marriott Pinnacle Hotel
21. Metropolitan Hotel
22. Opus Hotel
23. Pacific Palisades Hotel
24. Pan Pacific Hotel Vancouver
25. Quality Hotel Downtown
26. Ramada Inn & Suites Downtown Vancouver
27. Renaissance Vancouver Hotel Harbourside
28. Robsonstrasse Hotel
29. Rosedale on Robson
30. Sheraton Vancouver Wall Centre Hotel
31. St. Regis Hotel
31. Sutton Place Hotel
33. Sylvia Hotel
34. Terminal City Club Tower Hotel
35. Waterfront Centre Hotel
36. Wedgewood Hotel
37. Westin Bayshore Resort & Marina Vancouver
38. YMCA Hotel
39. YWCA Hotel

ABOUT THIS GUIDE

This guide has been written to help you get the most out of your stay in Canada's favourite West Coast destinations — Vancouver, Victoria and the surrounding areas including Whistler and the Gulf Islands. It will enrich your stay by directing you to the top attractions as well as to places off the beaten track. The contributors to this book are people who know and love these destinations and want to share their knowledge with you.

The guide is divided by city with the Vancouver section beginning on page 11 and the Victoria section on page 125. The Vancouver section offers nine chapters focusing on top attractions and activities. It also offers nine chapters dedicated to some of Vancouver's most exciting neighbourhoods.

The Victoria section of the guide includes general information, a brief history of the city, the top things to see and do and chapters on shopping and dining.

Following the section on Victoria, the guide explores Whistler, the Gulf Islands and the Sunshine Coast. Listings are carried at the end of the book. City and neighbourhood maps, as well as maps showing the locations of restaurants, hotels and attractions, appear at key points throughout the guide.

Like the other books in the Colourguide series, this is an independent publication. No payments or contributions have been solicited or accepted by the creators or publishers of this guide.

While every effort was made to ensure that the information was up to date when it went to press, things do change over time. It is always wise to phone ahead to confirm that the information presented here is still current.

Brief biographies of the contributors follow.

KEVIN BARKER (Sunshine Coast) is a business writer and long-time resident of the Sunshine Coast.

MELANEY BLACK (Victoria Shopping) is a contributing writer for Victoria's *Monday Magazine*.

SHAWN BORDOFF (Entertainment) is an actor, scriptwriter and a TV producer who teaches for the Vancouver School Board.

CONSTANCE BRISSENDEN (editor; Exploring

VANCOUVER AT NIGHT

Vancouver; Whistler) is a Vancouver writer and editor with seven books and hundreds of magazine articles about Vancouver to her credit.

GAIL BUENTE (Vancouver's Top Attractions; Annual Events) has written for many magazines and publications, with a special emphasis on the arts and music.

CHUCK DAVIS (A Brief History of Vancouver) has shared his in-depth knowledge Vancouver history in many books and articles, including *Chuck Davis' Guide to Vancouver* and *Vancouver, An Illustrated Chronology*.

PATRICIA FRASER (Vancouver Shopping) is the coordinator for international programming, Fairchild Radio, and covers shopping for *Vancouver* magazine.

MARIAN GILMOUR (Kids' Stuff) is the manager of one of Vancouver's most beautiful historic buildings, Heritage Hall.

GARY HYNES (Victoria Dining) is a veteran food critic and publisher of *EAT* (Epicure and Travel).

LESLEY KENNY (Victoria's Top Attractions) is a researcher and writer who has organized tours for conference delegates and visiting business people.

ALMA LEE (Granville Island and False Creek) is the producer of the Vancouver International Writers Festival.

BOB MACKIN (Sports) is a sports reporter for the *North Shore News* and the author of *Baseball Trivia*.

GARY MCFARLANE (Commercial Drive) is a writer who lives and works in the Commercial Drive neighbourhood.

KELSEY MCLEOD (Kitsilano) is a Vancouver historian and member of the B.C. Historical Society.

MARG MEIKLE (Parks and Gardens) is the author of *Garden City: Vancouver*, as well as numerous other fact-based books and children's books.

JAMES OAKES (West End) is a veteran journalist and the former editor of a West End business newsletter.

CHRIS PETTY (UBC), a UBC graduate and historian, edits the *UBC Chronicle* alumni magazine.

JOANNE POON (Chinatown) has a degree in Chinese social history from UBC and works in Chinatown.

D. C. (DENNIS) REID (Exploring Victoria; A Brief History of Victoria) is a Victoria resident, published poet and historical novelist.

ANN ROSENBERG (Galleries), a retired art teacher, is now an independent curator and art critic.

LEANORE SALI (Gastown) is the director of the Gastown Business Improvement Society.

ANNE SMART (Gulf Islands) is the author of *All About Salt Spring Island*.

BARBARA TOWELL (Downtown Vancouver) has a BA in Art History and an MA in Archival Studies from the UBC.

ROCHELLE VAN HALM (North Shore) was born, raised and still lives on the North Shore; she is a veteran freelance writer.

KASEY WILSON (Vancouver Dining) is Vancouver's leading food writer and broadcaster; she is the author of the highly successful *Best of Vancouver*.

VANCOUVER

EXPLORING VANCOUVER

CONSTANCE BRISSENDEN

Always a popular destination, Vancouver's confirmed status as host to the 2010 Olympic and Paralympic Winter Games (sharing the honour with Whistler) is infusing the city with renewed energy.

Visitors will benefit from improvements that are already reshaping an urban centre known as one of the best in the world both to

TOP: CANADA PLACE

INSET: VIEW OF DOWNTOWN VANCOUVER

live in and to visit. For the Greater Vancouver area, the news will mean $2 billion in road and transit improvements, including a faster link from downtown to the Vancouver International Airport. At least another $86 million has been spent renovating Vancouver venues and building new facilities. All of Vancouver's tourism infrastructure is bound to benefit as existing businesses spruce up their services to promote the city as a world-class destination worthy of the winter Olympics. That's good news for visitors who already enjoy a high degree of service, mobility and safety in the Pacific Rim city.

AN IDEAL CITY

Vancouver is a superbly livable place. The weather is moderate, as befits a coastal rain forest, the grass is always green and flowers bloom twelve months of the year. The Coast Mountains make the perfect backdrop to the Pacific

Ocean, especially in winter when they are brushed with a fresh coat of snow. All in all, it's an ideal environment, which explains why Canadians flock here to live and to visit. In the past fifteen years, the Greater Vancouver area has grown by more than half a million people.

Growth is good news for Vancouver's tourism attractions, services and infrastructure. What was once a small provincial town is now a cosmopolitan Pacific Rim player, with excellent hotels, impressive restaurants and plenty to see and do year-round. The mix of people here is unique, a blend of West meets East, with 30 per cent of the population of Asian descent. Vancouver also has a high First Nations contingent. Their influence is evident in the city's galleries, museums, at special events like powwows and even in stores, which often feature clothing and jewellery by native designers.

LIONS GATE BRIDGE

While some residents complain about traffic, getting around the city is easy for visitors. Public transit is provided by the SkyTrain, a light rapid-transit system, the SeaBus, which crosses Vancouver harbour, or by bus. With a TransLink day pass, you can visit the North Shore cities of West Vancouver and North Vancouver, or head south to explore the historic Steveston fishing village where the Gulf of Georgia Cannery National Historic Site is housed. For real efficiency, call TransLink's Customer Information number: 604 953-3333 for routes and schedules. You don't even need a car to travel the 120 kilometres (75 miles) to Whistler: transportation is available by Greyhound Canada, tour companies and by air. If you prefer driving, however, the roads in and around Vancouver are good, although rush hours can be slow.

**MIDDLE: STANLEY PARK CYCLIST
BOTTOM:
GRANVILLE ISLAND
MARKET STALL**

FAVOURITE SPOTS TO EXPLORE

Ask any Vancouverite, and they'll enthuse about their favourite things to see and do in the city. For some, it's a walk along English Bay to Stanley Park. Depending on how ambitious you are, you may want to walk around the park's ten-kilometre (seven mile) seawall perimeter, passing under the Lions Gate Bridge and past Brockton Point with its array of totem poles. Or you may simply want to stop at a park bench and watch the world stroll, skate or bike by. Granville Island, with its busy market,

13

HARBOUR CENTRE

SEAWALL AT STANLEY PARK

multitude of small arts and crafts shops and hustle and bustle, is completely different from Stanley Park. Yet here, too, you can find quiet spots and quiet moments. On a clear day, you may even see towering Mount Baker to the south in Washington State from your Granville Island viewpoint.

Across the water, on the North Shore, the pace of life slows back down, with strolls along Ambleside Beach or days spent hiking on Seymour Mountain. Rivers have carved deep canyons through the many lush forests on the North Shore. These canyons can be viewed at several spots, the best known of which is the Capilano Suspension Bridge.

To get to know the Vancouver area quickly, contact a local tour company. If you'd like to tour and explore at the same time, the Vancouver Trolley Company's "jump on, jump off" bus is ideal. Many other types of tours are available, from horse-drawn wagons through Stanley Park to boats up Howe Sound.

Unique and informative walking tours are available in several of the city's neighbourhoods. If you're interested in history, Walkabout Historic Vancouver opens windows to downtown, Gastown and Granville Island from mid-March to mid-November. Gastown and Chinatown also have free walking tours. Note that some excursions are not available year-round. For an overview of the city and the North Shore, visit The Lookout! atop Harbour Centre Tower. The revolving observation deck is 167 metres (547 feet) up via outside glass elevators.

For both Vancouver and Victoria, also included in this guide, you will find detailed information on climate, travel arrangements, currency, customs, accommodation, emergency care and other vital data in the Listings section at the end. In the "Top Attractions" sections, you will find in-depth descriptions of the main attractions of both cities. Please refer to the Listings for telephone numbers and other key information. Other chapters take readers through a variety of each city's fascinating neighbourhoods. Shopping and dining are also covered. For more on Victoria, see the "Exploring Victoria" section.

The Vancouver Tourist InfoCentre is extremely helpful. Its website, www.tourismvancouver.com, provides lots of great information. If you visit in person, the staff will make reservations for you at B.C. hotels. You can also book your hotel on-line. For current information on entertainment, attractions and dining, check the Thursday editions of *The Province*, *Vancouver Sun* and the free weekly *Georgia Straight*.

A BRIEF HISTORY

CHUCK DAVIS

There are several accounts relating to Vancouver's origins, but a favourite involves the 1792 meeting between a Spanish exploration party and some of the local Salish people. (An earlier expedition, a 1791 visit by Don José Marie Narvaez, marked the first contact between Europeans and native people in this area.) It happens that 1792 was the same year Captain George Vancouver was exploring these waters. In fact, Vancouver met Dionisio Galiano, the leader of the Spanish expedition, here and the two men hit it off and became friends. Vancouver gave the name Spanish Banks to the area where that meeting occurred, and it bears that name more than 200 years later. Aside from Indian Arm, an arm of the Burrard Inlet (today the city's harbour), Vancouver bestowed no native-inspired names, even though he had the Musqueam, the Squamish, the Kwantlen, the Tsawwassen and many other groups to choose from. Some of these groups were seasonal, coming down from the interior to the mouth of the Fraser River when the salmon were running.

Simon Fraser made a very brief visit in 1808 before being chased back up the river by angry Musqueam men. Nearly sixty years were to pass before the white people returned ... this time to stay. What attracted them first were the area's magnificent trees. The forest industry then attracted other kinds of enterprise.

ABOVE: INUIT SCULPTURE IN STANLEY PARK

TOP LEFT: CAPTAIN GEORGE VANCOUVER

15

STATUE OF GASSY JACK IN GASTOWN

ORIGINS

September 30, 1867 marks the arrival in what is now Vancouver of John "Gassy Jack" Deighton. The Yorkshire-born Deighton, with a complexion, according to a chum, of "muddy purple," rowed into the Burrard Inlet with his native wife, her mother, her cousin, a yellow dog, two chairs and a barrel of whiskey. A busy sawmill stood where Gassy landed on the south shore of the inlet. A busier, bigger one existed on the North Shore. A kilometre or so to the west through the trees three fellows derisively nicknamed the "Three Greenhorns" (for paying the exorbitant price of $1 an acre for their land) were trying to make bricks from a vein of clay.

Gassy, retired from his career as a riverboat captain, jovially greeted the men who worked at the mill. He knew that the nearest drink for these thirsty fellows was a five-kilometre row east along the inlet to the North Road, then a long walk along a rude trail built by the Royal Engineers to New Westminster through the forest, the elk and the bears. A saloon near the mill on the South Shore was an ideal business opportunity. Gassy avowed that if the mill workers helped him build a bar, they could have all they could drink. The Globe Saloon was up within 24 hours.

The Globe is gone now, but it stood in the heart of what is now Vancouver's Gastown. The voluble Mr. Deighton, who well deserved his nickname because he never shut up, chose his location more wisely than he knew. The new country of Canada had been formed just two months earlier. British Columbia would soon join this Confederation, lured by the Canadian Pacific Railway's promise that it would link B.C. to Eastern markets. If they had known it would take fifteen years to arrive, they might not have agreed so readily. But in 1871, B.C. signed on, and now British Columbians were also Canadians. The population grew and Gassy Jack thrived. So did the Greenhorns. Their landholdings are today's apartment-crammed West End.

By the spring of 1886 there were enough people in Vancouver to form a city. The little ramshackle collection of tents and wooden shacks was incorporated on April 6. A little more than two months later, on June 13, the whole thing was destroyed by fire. A freak wind sprang up while some CPR workmen were burning brush, and in less than 45 minutes the town disappeared. "Vancouver didn't burn," one of the survivors said, "it exploded." The heat was so intense

STEAM CLOCK IN GASTOWN

that the bell at St. James Anglican Church melted into a puddle. You can see it today at the Vancouver Museum. The survivors began to build, more solidly this time, while the ashes were still smoking.

THE RAILWAY

The CPR's first train arrived on July 4, 1886 at Port Moody. Contrary to expectations, it didn't stop there: the railway extended the line to Coal Harbour, what is now part of the Vancouver waterfront. That enraged the speculators who had bought land at Port Moody based on the CPR's promise to put a terminal there. It turns out that the water at the end of the inlet wasn't deep enough for the oceangoing ships that were part of the CPR's plans to establish links to China and other Far Eastern points.

Complaints were useless; the CPR was a hard-nosed firm, led by a single-minded, stocky, bearded bull of a man named William Van Horne, who ran his railway his way. Van Horne named Vancouver. It was originally named Granville, for the colonial secretary of the time, but Van Horne declared no one would ever know where "Granville" was. But "Vancouver," now that was a different matter. Everyone knew of Captain George Vancouver's famous Pacific Coast explorations. Van Horne had his way. He nearly always did.

William Van Horne was an American. Americans have played an important part in Vancouver's past: William Shaughnessy, a later CPR president and the man for whom the city's old-money neighbourhood is named, was an American. So was Benjamin Tingley Rogers, who built the huge B.C. Sugar Refinery company. L.D. Taylor, the man elected mayor of Vancouver eight times, more often than anyone, was from Michigan.

INSET: WILLIAM VAN HORNE

BOTTOM: FIRST CPR TRAIN ARRIVES IN VANCOUVER

The first thing Vancouver's first city council did in 1886 was petition the federal government to lease it a 1,000-acre military reserve at the entrance to the harbour. The heavily forested reserve had been established as a potential defense point just in case the bumptious Americans tried to take over the area. That's how Vancouver got Stanley Park, one of the world's great city parks.

The railway, which had received thousands of acres of free land in return for coming into Vancouver, established a hotel named Hotel Vancouver some distance south of Gastown that, in effect, pulled the city's downtown around it. When Van Horne arrived in the city and saw the hotel, he confronted the architect: "So you're the damned fool who made it look like a hospital!" You see today the third Hotel Vancouver. This imposing, green-turreted landmark (now Fairmont Hotel Vancouver) has hosted royal guests since 1939, beginning with King George VI and Queen Elizabeth, later the Queen Mother.

One very tangible result of the Great Depression of the 1930s is still visible in Vancouver: the Lions Gate Bridge. This big, splendid and beautiful bridge opened in 1938, paid for and built by the Guinness Brewing Company of Ireland. The brewers had bought, at distress Depression prices of less than $19 an

TOP: THE SECOND HOTEL VANCOUVER ABOVE: FAIRMONT HOTEL VANCOUVER TODAY

acre, a vast tract of land on the wooded slopes of the North Shore and began to sell the property. They built the bridge to encourage traffic, and buyers, to come on over. It worked. British Pacific Properties is still the most affluent neighborhood in Greater Vancouver. The residents in one of its postal zones have the highest per capita income in the country.

NEW GROWTH

After some years of relative quiet, Vancouver began to show signs of growth in the 1950s. A handsome office building erected on Burrard Street in 1955 by B.C. Electric was the first skyscraper built south of downtown. Much of what has been built since is distinctive, too. The city has given Canada some important architects, including Ron Thom, Bing Thom, Bruno Freschi, C. B. K. Van Norman and, pre-eminently, Arthur Erickson. Erickson's unique buildings dot the metropolitan area, and his provincial courthouse complex still draws admiring crowds in the city's downtown heart. His MacMillan Bloedel Building (no longer occupied by the giant forest company) is a striking and lofty landmark, noted for its immensely deep windows. Simon Fraser University, also his creation, in the suburb of Burnaby to the east, provided an apt setting for the hotbed of student revolt in the 1960s. Erickson's magnificent Museum of Anthropology on the University of British Columbia campus to the west is further evidence of

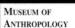

the work of this globally famous architect.

Vancouver inherited a reputation as "Lotus Land" in the swinging 1960s and 1970s. More global attention was heaped on it in 1986 with the terrifically successful Expo 86, a world exposition that attracted more than 20 million paying visitors. The Expo lands were sold to Hong Kong financier Li Ka-Shing at a bargain-basement price and spawned a high-rise boom. In the past decade, Lotus Land has been superseded by the same frenetic energy that has infected cities worldwide. Today the up-and-coming live in lofty "smart" high-rises, bristling with high-tech features. What remains are the breathtaking views of the city, the harbour and the looming Coast Mountains.

MUSEUM OF ANTHROPOLOGY

INFLUX OF NEWCOMERS

Suburban growth continues to this day, and so does the number of newcomers: over the last couple of decades, there has been a huge influx of Asian immigrants: Hong Kong Chinese (many of whom decided to leave Hong Kong in advance of the 1997 takeover by China), Vietnamese, Korean, Thai, Filipino and other South Asians. They've established neighbourhoods: suburban Richmond is one-third Chinese; suburban Surrey has attracted thousands of East Indian residents. By opening shops and restaurants and participating in the business, social and community lives of the region, these newcomers have added verve to the Lower Mainland.

Besides the jolt to the economy the newcomers provide, Vancouver and its suburbs are thriving because of their fervent embrace of high technology. The slow decline of resource-based industries like forestry, mining and fishing is being counterbalanced by the growth in biotechnology and computer-related companies, new media, film, television and related trades. Tourism is now one of the pillars of B.C.'s economy, and Vancouver is consistently ranked as one of the world's most liveable cities. Its centre is alive with people who live and work downtown, notably in the West End where examples of late nineteenth-century houses still nestle among the high-rise towers overlooking English Bay. The census of 2001 revealed that the city's population has grown by more than 20 per cent since 1996.

BOTTOM: ENGLISH BAY

It's still climbing rapidly, now topping 572,000 for the City of Vancouver and 2.1 million for the Greater Vancouver region. "Our city," says Larry Beasley, a Vancouver city planner,"is emerging as an unbelievably unique place. We have tens of thousands of citizens who have elected to move into the city. Most of North America has an anti-urban philosophy. But here, people want to move into the downtown."

TOP ATTRACTIONS

GAIL BUENTE

TOTEMS IN STANLEY PARK	There are many attractions in Vancouver that a visitor should not miss. Here are the top destinations and sites to see while you are in the city.
	### STANLEY PARK
	Ask any Vancouverite to recommend one must-see attraction, and the answer will be Stanley Park. Everyone from the born-and-raised local to the newest arrival agrees, Vancouver just wouldn't be Vancouver without the park. At twenty times the size of New York's Central Park, it is North America's third-largest urban park. Its location, almost entirely surrounded by the Pacific Ocean and adjacent to the city centre and the West End, makes Stanley
STANLEY PARK'S MINIATURE TRAIN	Park unique. While paid parking is available, the best way to get to the park is by TransLink city bus, or on foot

through the West End. A free shuttle bus operates inside the park on summer days.

In 1889, Governor General Lord Stanley dedicated Stanley Park "to the use and enjoyment of people of all colours, creeds and customs for all time." If His Lordship could see the park now, he'd be amazed at how prophetic his dedication was. With an estimated 8 million visitors a year, this 405-hectare (1,000-acre) urban wilderness is treasured by all. At any time of the year, the trails and footpaths buzz with the sounds of dozens of languages, spoken by people of all ages, races and beliefs.

Back in Lord Stanley's day, a visit to the park was a dignified affair, culminating with a posed snapshot of the family inside the Hollow Tree. Today, people still visit the giant cleft tree located near Third Beach off Stanley Park Drive, but a day in the park now includes much more. Vancouver has grown and changed and so has the park. It has come to symbolize all the traits of this vibrant city: informality, naturalness, energy and diversity. But the century-plus since it became a park is only a brief moment in the life of this ageless patch of earth.

Stanley Park is full of geological hints of a past far older than the high-rise buildings around it. Siwash Rock, according to legend, is a Squamish Indian warrior turned to stone by the gods. In fact, it is an ancient deposit of lava. Fossils found in the park indicate that semitropical palms and sequoia trees once thrived here many millions of years ago. Where today visitors feed friendly squirrels, cougars and other wildlife thrived in the not-so-distant past. Remnants of Indian middens, ancient piles of sea shells and cultural debris, tell of thousands of years of native habitation when villagers hunted, fished and held potlatches on the peninsula. Today's Lumberman's Arch was once the site of the Squamish village of Whoi Whoi. Deadman's Island, now a military base and not publicly accessible, once provided a secluded funeral ground for these early peoples.

Visitors to Stanley Park soon

SPRING FLOWERS IN STANLEY PARK

THE HOLLOW TREE

discover that there are really two distinct parks: an outer rim, which is tamed, developed and well-used, and a wilder inner heart, where the noise and hustle of the city seem light years away. The outer portion is circled by the ten-kilometre-long (six-mile) seawall. Started in

TOP: LOST LAGOON
INSET: CYCLISTS ON SEAWALL

1917 and completed in 1980, the seawall surrounds all of the park's extensive recreational attractions: Vancouver rowing and yacht clubs, the Vancouver Aquarium and Marine Science Centre, cricket and rugby fields, a petting farm and miniature railway for the kids, picnic areas, two swimming beaches and a children's water park, a cultured

rose garden, a pitch-and-putt golf course, lawn bowling and tennis courts, Malkin Bowl (home to the open-air Theatre Under the Stars musical theatre on summer evenings) and Lost Lagoon. Along the way, in-line skaters and cyclists glide by. Walkers can stop at any of a variety of concessions and restaurants: The Teahouse at Ferguson Point, Prospect Point Café, the Fish House Restaurant or the Stanley Park Pavilion. Among this array of amusements, all sorts of other activities take place spontaneously. On weekends, for example,

STANLEY PARK
ROWING CLUB

THE TEAHOUSE AT
FERGUSON POINT

budding as well as professional artists set up their easels and display their works at an impromptu gallery on the grass.

STANLEY PARK TOTEM

As the seawall winds around the rim of the park, it passes numerous structures of historic and cultural interest. A walk along the path will take you past the *Girl in a Wetsuit* sculpture, Brockton Point Lighthouse, the huge wooden Lumberman's Arch monument and Vancouver's unique acoustic landmark, the Nine-O'Clock Gun, at Hallelujah Point. Except for a brief stretch during the Second World War, the cannon has been fired at precisely nine p.m. since 1894. Originally, the gunshot helped mariners in setting their chronometers, but nowadays it continues simply out of affection for tradition. Nearby, sightseers and picture takers stop at the Brockton Point Totem Park to inspect a historic grouping of nineteenth-century original poles and replicas, by carvers of the Haida, Kwakwaka'wakw and Nuu-chah-nulth nations. A little farther along the seawall is another favourite with photographers, the lookout at Prospect Point. From here, the highest point in the park, you can survey all of Burrard Inlet and the North Shore.

Other crowd pleasers along the seawall are the sandy beaches. Second Beach is a city beach par excellence, sporting a saltwater swimming pool, children's playground, baseball diamonds and picnic areas. All summer, the air rings with laughter, radios and the thwack of baseball bats. On weekend nights, the sounds of ethnic folk dancing fill the air. The aroma of deep-fried fish and chips, a Stanley Park tradition, wafts across the grass. On warm afternoons, every log becomes a pillow for a sunbather.

Lost Lagoon is perhaps the most representative feature of the "outer park." Once a rough tidal basin off Coal Harbour, the lagoon was a favourite canoeing spot for poet Pauline Johnson, the daughter of a Mohawk chief, who named the lagoon for the way it disappeared at low tide.

THIRD BEACH

STANLEY PARK CYCLISTS CONSULT MAP

Today, pedestrians stroll along its banks or stop to feed swans and ducks in the shade of willow trees.

The interior park, in contrast, is overgrown and wild. For the most part, it is densely forested, with a network of bike and foot paths crisscrossing beneath fir and cedar boughs. These trails follow the routes of the skid roads used for logging many years ago. For a time, Deadman's Island was home to a sawmill. Beaver Lake, the inner park's freshwater counterpart to Lost Lagoon, is a natural-state pond, edged with cattails and teeming with frogs croaking from water lilies. You'll also find, without too much effort, that the boggy soil around the lake is teeming with skunk cabbage, a large, graceful plant with a pungent perfume that is, well, not to everyone's liking.

When venturing from the park's civilized exterior into its wilder interior, don't be led astray by the apparently easy-to-follow trailways. It's quite possible to get lost in the maze, and many first-time visitors have found themselves walking in circles before they discover the exit path. Walkers unfamiliar with the trails should take a map if they want to get back in time for dinner.

DISCOVERING MARINE LIFE AT THE AQUARIUM

In many ways, Stanley Park's two sides reflect the contrasting attitudes about its future. Vancouverites fall generally into two camps. Half of them want to continue to develop the park "for the use and enjoyment of all people." Just as many would like to see it kept as natural and untouched as possible. The controversy is dynamic and healthy, and continues to remind Vancouver of just how passionately involved it is with its very own urban wilderness.

VANCOUVER AQUARIUM MARINE SCIENCE CENTRE

Since 1956 when it opened in Stanley Park, 30 million visitors have been entertained and amazed by the Vancouver Aquarium Marine Science Centre. Life-and-death marine dramas are brought to life in 167 aquatic displays.

In the steamy jungle environment of the Amazon Rainforest gallery, two caimans, second cousins to the crocodile, set the tone. Every hour, "rainstorms" are created inside this space. Giant freshwater Amazon fishes that play a vital role in the survival of the rainforest, Scarlet Ibises and a pair of sloths add to the atmosphere.

Once a day in the Tropic Zone Gallery, a research naturalist dives with the sharks. Twice a week the diver feeds the sharks and the result is very dramatic. The waters literally thrash as the sharks gulp down their food. Overall, the gallery mimics a tropical reef at Indonesia's Bunaken National Marine Park, including black-tipped reef sharks, stone fish and rainbow-coloured tropical species.

Six beluga whales in the Arctic Canada presentation

area can be viewed through an underwater gallery. The newest member of the beluga clan is young Tuvaq, born in July 2002. Nearby, three sea otters, Mylo, Nyac and Elfin, keep company. The sea otters, like the belugas, are under constant study. Even the sea otters' feces provide scientific data on reproductive hormone and cortisol levels. Nyac is the oldest living female sea otter survivor of the Valdez Alaska oil spill of 1989.

In the Pacific Northwest area, local waters are the focus. Search in the watery habitats for playful sea otters, elusive wolf eels and giant Pacific octopi. Meet Spinnaker, the Pacific white-sided dolphin. Stellar sea lions, like the other residents here, are not only entertaining but are significant for public education and scientific observation. In all, more than 60,000 aquatic creatures live at the aquarium.

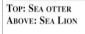

TOP: SEA OTTER
ABOVE: SEA LION

As a privately operated, self-supporting, non-profit organization, the aquarium is dedicated to promoting conservation through display and interpretation, education, research and direct action. It was the first public aquarium in Canada and is now considered by leading professionals to be among the top five facilities in the world. It is internationally recognized for its successful Marine Mammal Rescue and Rehabilitation Program, and it was the first aquarium in Canada to incorporate professional naturalists on-site. The Vancouver Aquarium is recognized for its stunning displays and its innovative programming, such as the immensely popular sleepovers. After the Aquarium has closed its doors for the night, school or

MEETING A BELUGA

family groups are invited to bring their sleeping bags and join in an overnight adventure with snacks, an up-close-and-personal look at sea creatures, and fun educational activities. Then, after an attempt at sleep, the young guests are served a light breakfast and given souvenir pillowcases to remind them of their special after-hours visit.

After the galleries, visitors can relax with a latte and sandwich in The UpStream Café, adjacent to the beluga whale habitat. At the colourful ClamShell Gift Shop, souvenirs from soapstone whale carvings to local postcards come in many price ranges. Not surprisingly, anything with a killer whale image is an instant bestseller.

SCIENCE WORLD/ALCAN
OMNIMAX THEATRE AT SCIENCE WORLD

Science World is housed in an Expo 86 legacy building. Originally the Expo Centre, it was affectionately called "the golf ball" during the 1986 world exposition. Three years later, the silver ball reopened as Science World, with Queen Elizabeth II on hand for the ceremonies. By day, the mirror-like exterior reflects the waters of nearby False Creek. At night, the geodesic dome sparkles with 131 exterior lights.

Science World is now a hugely popular family attraction. More than 400,000 people visit each year to enjoy its permanent and evolving exhibits. A healthy 62,000 are students on school trips. Science World is designed as a hands-on experience for the hoards of energetic kids who visit daily. They run, scream, laugh and frolic. In other words, they love it here.

Adults and children come to Science World to be dazzled by science as entertainment. It certainly works. Hundreds of creative exhibits ensure that even science dropouts can find something intriguing and new. One exhibit makes your hair stand on end; another lets you blow square bubbles. In the main gallery's Matter and Forces area, physics is made simple (if that's possible) with ample demonstrations. Five additional galleries round out the offerings, featuring everything from Kidspace, an evolving environment for children three to six years of age, to Mine Games, focusing on the province's mining industry. If that doesn't grab you, check out Visual Illusions and play with optical tricks that leave you puzzling over what's real and what's not. In the Sara Stern Search Gallery, natural history is taught through hands-on "discovery boxes."

The Alcan OMNIMAX Theatre is found inside the centre's multi-million-dollar geodesic dome. Everything about the Alcan OMNIMAX Theatre is big and loud. The steeply raked, 500-seat theatre boasts one of the world's largest domed screens, capable of projecting an image nine times larger than a conventional movie. Sound pumps out of twenty-eight digital sound speakers backed by ten tons of equipment. The most comfortable viewing experience is near the top of the amphitheatre.

The 50-minute documentaries vary in subjects from dolphins to the mysteries of Egypt to Olympic glories. The images are shot to make the most of the OMNIMAX technology. Don't be surprised if you duck when a flying dolphin appears to leap right out of the screen onto your lap. While most children enjoy the visual surround-and-sound combination, some may find the huge moving images overpowering. The theatre presents five shows each weekday, with an additional show at five p.m. on weekends and holidays. An additional fee is charged for Alcan OMNIMAX shows.

After taking in Science World, relax over snacks at the Bytes Cafeteria overlooking False Creek. Before you leave, drop by the Science World Gift Shop where you'll find some of the more amusing souvenirs of the city. Even plastic dinosaurs have a place. Among the better choices are science books for kids, including one that features "really gross experiments." Science experiment kits and ingenious toys are also sold here.

TOP: MUSEUM OF ANTHROPOLOGY GREAT HALL
MIDDLE: HOUSE POSTS CIRCA 1906 AT THE MOA

HAIDA DANCERS AT THE MOA

THE UBC MUSEUM OF ANTHROPOLOGY (MOA)

The University of British Columbia Museum of Anthropology's research collection of approximately 230,000 artifacts includes ethnographic and archeological materials from Europe, Africa, the Americas, Asia and the South Pacific. There is everything from ceramics to Asian textiles, but the high point of the museum is its collection of Kwakwaka'wakw, Nisga'a, Gitksan, Haida and Coast Salish art. Experts agree it is one of the finest collections of Northwest Coast First Nations art anywhere in the world.

In the Great Hall of the museum, sunlight streams in through 13.7-metre high picture windows. Immense totem poles, graceful cedar canoes and many other First Nations artifacts appear as they might have in remote coastal villages. The spirits of ancient carvers seem to hover in the air above a cluster of visitors and their tour guide.

While the artifacts are given the careful treatment necessary for historic objects, they are also appreciated as works of art. The MOA feels like a gallery, displaying its artifacts elegantly and with as much natural light as

possible. Only the most fragile items are kept encased in darkness, and even those are accessible to visitors through an innovative approach called "visible storage." By keeping the objects in glass-topped drawers, over 90 per cent of the permanent collection is visible to the public. Most museums display about 2 to 5 per cent of their collections.

The museum was a pioneer in both the visible storage system and the use of natural light, a concept that has since been incorporated into the design of the National Gallery in Ottawa. Both these innovations, now widely copied, were considered controversial back in 1976 when the museum opened its doors, leading to citations for both best design and worst design.

The architecture, evoking the plank houses of the Northwest Coast First Nations, was designed by Vancouver's Arthur Erickson. His challenge was unique: to create a building to house a group of already-existing artifacts. From its humble beginning in 1949, with a small collection of oceanic materials housed in the basement of UBC's Main Library, the holdings had grown over many years and the collection was well established. The new museum is magnificent, a building worthy of its subject matter and its majestic location overlooking Howe Sound.

WOVEN BASKET, PRE-1916, AT THE MOA

In the Visible Storage galleries, row upon row of Kwakwaka'wakw dance masks stare out in an eerie display of variations on a theme. Forty-three black raven heads with wild cedar-bark manes raise their red beaks defiantly, appearing to watch the passing crowds through steely, white-rimmed eyes. Those masks see, and are seen by, more than 170,000 visitors yearly. In the Masterpiece Gallery, exquisitely carved jewellery and small sculptures of argillite, silver, gold and bone take the viewer back to an age when there was enough time for craftsmanship.

HAIDA BEAR SCULPTURE (MIDDLE); BILL REID, *RAVEN AND THE FIRST MEN* (BOTTOM); BOTH AT THE MOA

In the museum's central rotunda, a skylight illuminates Bill Reid's sculpture *Raven and the First Men*, a highlight of the contemporary collection. The massive yellow cedar carving portrays Raven, the magical trickster, as he discovers the first humans in a clamshell and coaxes them out into the world. According to legend, the Haidas are descended from these shell people. The Museum of Anthropology's collection of Bill Reid art is the largest assemblage anywhere of works by this influential artist whose unique creations fused modern design with traditional Northwest Coastal native forms. An outdoor exhibit features two Haida houses designed by Bill Reid and Doug Cranmer and totem poles by some of the finest contemporary carvers of the coast.

Back in the Great Hall under the towering totems, the history of the coast's first people is recorded in red cedar. There are sturdy boxes made by steaming a single plank and used for everything from cooking to cradles to coffins for the dead. Bowls and feast dishes take the form of mythical beings like T'sonoqua, the wild woman of the woods. Carved canoes were used for fishing and whaling off the rugged British Columbia coast. The boxes, bowls and feast dishes conjure images of huge potlatches, traditional ceremonies essential to the survival of native coastal communities. At the potlatches, hereditary names and privileges were passed from generation to generation, and social status was publicly affirmed. Lavish feasts were served and gifts exchanged. From 1884 to 1951, the Canadian government banned the potlatch in an attempt to control and destroy a culture it did not understand or approve of. The potlatch has re-emerged as a significant symbol of the contemporary resurgence in First Nations identity.

The MOA is truly a living museum, proud of its training programs and its record of hiring students, who will be its future conservators, anthropologists and archeologists. As the largest teaching museum in Canada, it has built a reputation for successfully integrating research with public access.

VANCOUVER ART GALLERY

The Vancouver Art Gallery houses British Columbia's largest collection of artworks, from classical museum pieces to the latest works of the avant-garde. Established in 1931, it moved into its present location, a neo-classical-style heritage building, in 1983. Formerly used as a provincial courthouse, the building was redesigned by renowned local architect Arthur Erickson to accommodate an additional 3,716 square meters of exhibition space. The internationally recognized gallery touches all the bases, with exciting touring exhibits alongside an

TOP: EMILY CARR, *A SKIDEGATE POLE,* AT THE VAG ABOVE: EMILY CARR, *UNTITLED,* AT THE VAG

outstanding permanent collection of close to 7,000 works.

In its mission statement, the Vancouver Art Gallery calls itself a place "to inspire and please through visual art," and that describes it well. Visit the four floors of exhibition space and you'll find numerous delightful surprises: one-person and group shows by established and emerging artists, exhibits arranged thematically and travelling exhibitions from other museums. You may see an exhibit of familiar paintings by Impressionist masters, or a show of vibrant new works by up-and-coming local artists.

Yet for many guests, the highlight of the gallery is the permanent collection of works by B.C. artist and writer Emily Carr. Now well known in Canada and internationally, for most of her life Carr was neglected by both the public and the art establishment. Though highly regarded by other painters, including members of Canada's influential Group of Seven, many regarded her solely as an eccentric Victoria boarding house keeper with a penchant for pet dogs and monkeys. Her treks in a dilapidated caravan took her into the province's remote corners in search of subject matter for her sensuously beautiful and spiritual paintings. This dowdy, down-to-earth, observant woman carted her paint box and canvases to isolated First Nations settlements. Her forays took her deep into the ancient forests to capture the essence of coastal British Columbia.

When success finally did arrive, the modest artist was unprepared for it. Several major galleries began to acquire her work. When in 1937 the Vancouver Art Gallery purchased its first Carr painting, *Totem Poles, Kitseulka*, she wrote in her diary that "this sudden desire to obtain 'Emily Carrs'" made her afraid that the attention might "knock me into conceit." The Vancouver Art Gallery's Carr holdings, including 150 paintings and 100 works in other media, constitute the most important single Carr collection. About fifty works, the core of the collection, were donated by the artist herself shortly before her death in 1945. Among them are some of her most famous works, including *Big Raven, Tree Trunk* and *Scorned as Timber, Beloved of the Sky*.

Tours and gallery talks add to the enjoyment of the Carr and other permanent exhibits at the Vancouver Art Gallery, and accompany many of the touring exhibitions. As well, demonstrations, lunch-hour concerts, hands-on interpretive centres, art-making studios and a wealth of other innovative programs make learning about art fun for everyone in the family. Finish your visit by browsing for quality posters, books and artist-made gifts in the Gallery Shop before making a relaxed stop at the licensed Gallery Café and patio.

VANCOUVER MUSEUM, H.R. MACMILLAN PACIFIC SPACE CENTRE, H.R. MACMILLAN PLANETARIUM, VANCOUVER MARITIME MUSEUM

Four Vancouver gems are found on the south shore of English Bay in Kitsilano near the Burrard Bridge. The Vancouver Museum, H.R. MacMillan Pacific Space Centre, H.R. MacMillan Planetarium and Vancouver Maritime Museum are all located in Vanier Park. En route to the park, you'll pass through several blocks of the "Kits Point" neighbourhood, with its lovely houses, just minutes from the beach.

Some say the Vancouver Museum resembles a First Nations woven hat; others liken it to a spaceship. Outside the museum, George Norris's stainless steel sculpture, *The Crab*, is a longtime favourite for picture taking.

The museum got its start in the mid-1880s, when a group of Vancouver's founding citizens

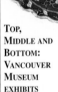

held a show of paintings and curios, including purchased Northwest Coast artifacts, in a rented space on Granville Street. A stuffed trumpeter swan was the collection's first donation. By 1905, the museum settled into the top floor of the Carnegie Library at Main and Hastings streets, now a community centre for the downtown eastside. The collection moved to its present site in 1968, becoming the largest administered and interpreted permanent collection of any Canadian civic museum. What you see as you wander through the many exhibits equals only 2 per cent of the museum's entire holdings. The rest is stored in a football field-sized storage vault.

The museum's special mission, according to its curators, is to tell the story of Vancouver, and collect and interpret the objects that embody those stories. It's also a place where visitors can learn about the wider world through high-quality visiting exhibits on places such as Egypt, China and Japan.

All museums are time machines, and this one is no exception. The curators bring the past to life with seven permanent walk-through exhibits relating to the history of Vancouver. The first is a recreation of a fur-trading post. Step over the piles of fur as you move on to the below-the-decks steerage bunks of an immigrant ship. The room is dark, the ceiling low, and you can hear the creaking of the wooden ship against the wind, a nice touch provided on tape. Move ahead through Vancouver's lumbering days when its huge, valuable Douglas firs made it the envy of the world. Gastown, a riotous enclave of rabble-rousing men, is next, complete with saloon keeper Gassy Jack's famed trunk. It's said that when he came ashore, the trunk was all he had, yet within a day his saloon was built and opened. Walk on until the last exhibit, an Edwardian household, complete with parlour, bedroom and a detailed kitchen and pantry. The furniture, curtains, bed coverings, even the kitchen scrub board were all donated in the spirit of the trumpeter swan. One look at the pre-electric kitchen and you will bless your dishwasher.

TOP, MIDDLE AND BOTTOM: VANCOUVER MUSEUM EXHIBITS

Vancouver's history is also highlighted with special temporary exhibits, such as City Lights, the history of neon. The museum recently renovated its temporary exhibits' gallery and added an orientation gallery to help visitors better understand Vancouver. You can access the H. R. MacMillan Pacific Space Centre from the same foyer as the Vancouver Museum. Launched in October 1997, twenty-nine years after the venerable H.R. MacMillan Planetarium opened, the space centre features many styles of programming. Here's the place where the wonders of space come down to earth with innovative programs like the Cosmic Courtyard hands-on gallery. Visitors can discover the ups and downs of travelling the solar system, including the chance to touch a real moon rock or play state-of-the-art computer games.

Daily multimedia shows such as The Universe Tonight, ZSKY: Radio Station of the Stars and Laser Kid Power are fun for all ages. Groundstation Canada is the place to learn the latest about space in a multimedia mission control theatre. Live demonstrations include Space Update, featuring current space and astronomy news, and Rocket Lab, which teaches the principles of rocketry. In Inventions, Planets & Probes, Canadian innovation is explored, along with a comparison of Earth and Mars and a study of space exploration. Evening laser shows, the staple of the H.R. MacMillan Planetarium, continue to be a major draw.

ZEISS STAR PROJECTOR, H.R. MACMILLAN PLANETARIUM

GROUNDSTATION, CANADA THEATRE AT H.R. MACMILLAN PACIFIC SPACE CENTRE

Donated by one of the province's lumber barons in 1967 as a Canadian centennial gift to the City of Vancouver, the planetarium is a city icon. These days, the famed multimedia shows are presented in the renovated Star Theatre. Its dome, Zeiss star projector and theatre interior have been fully upgraded and a large-format video, new laser projection and other technological enhancements added. Sit back — well, lay back really — in the comfortable lounge chairs and view the night sky unfolding overhead.

A short five-minute walk from the museum and planetarium, you'll find the Vancouver Maritime Museum

VANCOUVER MARITIME MUSEUM

BOTTOM:
RCMP SCHOONER
***ST. ROCH* AT THE VANCOUVER MARITIME MUSEUM**

at the foot of Cypress Street on the waterfront. Permanent exhibits as well as temporary feature exhibits bolster the Maritime Museum's most famous display, the RCMP schooner *St. Roch*, the first ship to cross the treacherous Northwest Passage in both directions, as well as the first ship to circumnavigate North America.

The Pacific Northwest's seagoing heritage dates back to the First Nations people who voyaged along the coast in sturdy seagoing canoes. European contact was made by Juan Perez of Spain in 1774. The Man the Oars and Map the Coast exhibit pays tribute to Captain George Vancouver, after whom the city is named, even though Vancouver was a latecomer who didn't arrive until 1792.

Today's coastal waters are plied by tankers, fishing boats, pleasure craft and a host of other vessels. Fireboats, another exhibit, goes back more than sixty years to honour these essential coastal work boats. Outside the museum, Heritage Harbour provides a closer look at heritage vessels of all types, including a small boat-building and repair workshop. Kids will also enjoy the Children's Maritime Discovery Centre with its full-scale replica tugboat wheelhouse and remote-controlled underwater

CANADA PLACE

robot, as well as the area known as Pirates!, complete with a treasure chest, pirate weapons and costumes and the pirate ship *Shark* .

CANADA PLACE/CN IMAX THEATRE AT CANADA PLACE

Built for Expo 86, Canada's 1986 world exposition, Canada Place was designed to give the stylish Sydney, Australia, Opera House a run for the money. With its five white, Teflon-coated "sails" echoing a nautical theme, the Canada Place complex may not entirely live up to its designer's goal, but it does stand out against the high-rise hotels of Vancouver's waterfront. Today Canada Place is a popular tourist destination, home to a cruise ship terminal, the CN IMAX Theatre, Vancouver Trade and Convention Centre and the World Trade Centre. The domed Pan Pacific Hotel is one of several major hotels in the area.

The complex resembles an immense ocean-going vessel, stretching three city blocks into Burrard Inlet. From the open-air promenade around Canada Place, you have one of the best views of busy Port Vancouver. Pleasure craft, working vessels, SeaBuses and seaplanes make the promenade a great place to sit and have lunch.

Luxury cruise ships, en route to Alaska, dock at Canada Place, as well as the nearby Ballantyne Pier. More than 220 cruise ship stopovers are recorded every year in Vancouver. Between May and October, close to 1 million passengers

CRUISE SHIP PASSING UNDER LIONS GATE BRIDGE

depart Vancouver to enjoy the famed Vancouver-Alaska cruise, the third most popular cruise destination in the world.

Whether trekking at the top of Everest or walking in the footsteps of dinosaurs, CN IMAX Theatre film presentations are designed to dazzle viewers with sound and images. IMAX technology is the largest film format in motion picture history, ten times that of conventional 35-mm film. The 440-seat, steeply pitched amphitheatre features a towering five-storey screen and six-channel IMAX Digital wraparound sound. Some shows even require the donning of IMAX 3D glasses for more intense "you are there" sensations. Open daily, for afternoon and evening features, shows at CN IMAX Theatre are approximately 40 minutes long.

CAPILANO SUSPENSION BRIDGE

CAPILANO
SUSPENSION BRIDGE

What an adventure it must have been in the late nineteenth century when George Mackay's buddies, calling themselves the Capilano tramps, would trudge to the pioneering Scotsman's secluded cabin on the north shore of Burrard Inlet. Seventy metres (230 feet) above the Capilano River canyon, George had suspended a rickety rope-and-cedar bridge for what certainly must have been a petrifying crossing. Today, the Capilano Suspension Bridge is recognized by Attractions Canada as British Columbia's best outdoor attraction. Built of sturdy steel cables, the 140-metre-wide (450-foot) bridge is certainly safer and more accessible, but the lush forest property is no less breathtaking than it was in Mackay's time.

The bridge's swaying span attracts 800,000 visitors each year. It's the world's longest and highest suspension footbridge. Since 1899, when the original bridge was built, the attraction has been improved and enhanced by each of its six successive owners. The Story Centre traces the history of the bridge and the development of the city around it. An English country garden planted with rhododendrons and azaleas, the Living Forest interactive ecology display, a tranquil Nature Park and a gift shop all add to guests' enjoyment. An especially popular attraction is the Totem Park, a display of locally carved poles collected since the 1930s. In the nearby Big House, visitors can watch First Nations carvers at work and ask them about their techniques. Tours, displays and special activities are designed to give guests a glimpse into the historic and botanical roots of the area. As well, the full-service Bridge House restaurant and two casual eateries serve hungry visitors with fresh West Coast-style cuisine. The décor is turn-of-the-century (the nineteenth century, that is). The park is a twenty-minute drive from downtown Vancouver.

GROUSE MOUNTAIN

It takes a maximum of eight minutes for the Grouse Mountain Skyride to climb 1.6 km to 1,128 metres above sea level. That's the only disappointing part of the Grouse Mountain experience because on a clear day, the panoramic view of Vancouver, the Strait of Georgia and far-off Vancouver Island is unsurpassed. You simply want the ascent to last longer.

Grouse Mountain, part of the Coast Mountain range, was named after the blue grouse. Located at the top of North Vancouver's Capilano Road, the mountain was one of the first ski areas developed near Vancouver. Noted for being the smallest and closest of the local mountains, the first skier on Grouse is reputed to be a Swede, Rudolph Verne, in 1911. Today, hardy types still prefer to make their way to the top the old-fashioned way with a strenuous hike known as the Grouse Grind. The Grind is a badge of honour for many, including an eighty-five-year-old man who is said to make the climb twice a day.

The majority of visitors prefer the more sedate Skyride. Once at the top, try downhill skiing, snowboarding, snowshoeing, sleigh rides and a mountaintop ice-skating pond. Ski lessons and equipment rentals are available. For summer visitors, try hiking on your own or with a guide in the alpine meadows. Helicopter and mountain bike tours,

TOP AND MIDDLE: GROUSE MOUNTAIN ACTIVITIES

VIEW FROM GROUSE MOUNTAIN

logger sport shows and tandem paragliding with a certified instructor are available. Peak Chair rides to the summit at 1,366 metres are another summer activity.

If you're not the outdoorsy type, you can spend your time at the top enjoying the free Theatre in the Sky show. The theatre features the high-definition video presentation, *Born to Fly,* as part of your Skyride pass.

At the First Nations-developed hiwus feasthouse atop the mountain, enjoy a five-course traditional feast amidst native carvings and totems.

SKYRIDE AT GROUSE MOUNTAIN

Members of the local Squamish Nation and Sechelt Band ensure the authenticity of this dining experience, enhanced with live dances, songs and legends performed in traditional regalia. To get to the longhouse, a First Nations guide leads visitors through the Alpine forest to the shores of Blue Grouse Lake.

To make the most of the view, try fine dining in The Observatory (advance reservations allow you to ride the Skyride free). Also open daily are the Bar 98 Bistro, a casual dining area with a large outdoor rooftop patio, and Lupin's Cafe for fresh, self-service food. Panoramic views, the specialty of the house, are provided by all.

DR. SUN YAT-SEN CLASSICAL CHINESE GARDEN

In Vancouver's Chinatown, families in search of the freshest vegetables mingle with visitors exploring medicinal herb shops. Traffic inches alongside throngs of pedestrians crowding the sidewalks. In the midst of all this kinetic energy, it would be easy to miss the tranquil Dr. Sun Yat-Sen Garden tucked away in a quiet corner a few steps off Main Street. But you won't want to miss this peaceful "Refreshment for the Heart."

DR. SUN YAT-SEN GARDEN

Enter the garden near the intersection of Pender and

Carrall streets, through a whitewashed wall behind the Chinese Cultural Centre. As soon as you pass through the doorway marked Yi Yuan, or Garden of Ease, you'll find yourself relaxing and slowing your step as you enter another time and place.

Classical Chinese gardens are an ancient art form, perfected over the course of twenty centuries. The most famous of these are in the city of Suzhou in China's Chiang-Su province. These contemplative "scholar's gardens" have influenced garden design worldwide. In 1986, the Dr. Sun Yat-Sen Garden became the first full-scale classical Chinese garden constructed outside China, and the first of these gardens to be built in nearly 500 years. Once inside, you could be in Suzhou, it is so authentic. In less than half an acre, this microcosmic world is cleverly laid out to maximize its intricacy and complexity. Framed by round moon gates and lacy latticework, glimpses of exquisite vistas emerge, disappear and reappear to create infinite visual space.

DR. SUN YAT-SEN GARDEN

Built in Ming Dynasty style, the garden reflects nature through the four elements of rock, water, plants and architecture. Everything within its walls conforms to the Taoist principle of yin and yang. Shadow is always matched by light, smooth surfaces by rough, so that all elements remain in perfect equilibrium. A gnarled pine grows side-by-side with a delicate gingko.

The overall design of the garden echoes features of the renowned examples that inspired it, right down to the painstaking adherence to tradition with which it was crafted. More than fifty skilled Chinese artisans came to Vancouver to build the garden using centuries-old techniques, ancient tools and authentic building materials. The Yun Wei Ting gazebo, for example, perches atop a miniature mountain built of a unique rock found only on the bottom of Lake Tai in Suzhou. China shipped some 450 tons of the rare limestone for use in the garden. But the garden is also an original, incorporating local plants and innovations. Not a relic of the past, it comes alive with year-round events, commemorating special occasions from Chinese New Year to the autumn Harvest Moon Festival. On summer nights, the Enchanted Evening series of concerts features Asian music. When your visit to the Dr. Sun Yat-Sen Classical Chinese Garden comes to an end, you're sure to step back into the twenty-first century with nerves calmed, eyes delighted and heart refreshed.

STATUE OF DR. SUN YAT-SEN

Admission to the Dr. Sun Yat-Sen Classical Chinese Garden includes tea and a tour. The garden offers special family and group rates and rental for private events. The gift shop features Vancouver's largest selection of English-language books about Chinese culture.

DINING

KASEY WILSON

Vancouver's culinary reputation is built on fresh food and fresh flavours. The variety of dining experiences continues to grow each year, with some of the country's finest chefs devoted to creating food that is innovative and, in many cases, unique to the West Coast.

If there is a quintessential West Coast food, it is wild salmon. It comes in five varieties: sockeye, pink, coho, spring and chum, and can be cooked in a multitude of ways. The original inhabitants, First Nations people both on the Pacific as well as the inland rivers, barbecued or baked it. Local restaurants sometimes feature traditional delicacies such as alder-grilled salmon, with First Nations-style pan-fried oolichans, toasted seaweed and bannock (an unleavened bread).

With some 30 per cent of Vancouver's population of Asian origin, it's not surprising that Oriental cooking is plentiful throughout the city. No matter where you go within Vancouver or its neighbouring suburbs — Burnaby, New Westminster, the North Shore or Richmond — you'll find the diversity of Asia represented in the kitchens. With a light touch, the chefs offer up a tasty mix of texture and colour, flavour and flair.

These days, dining in Vancouver encompasses a great many nationalities: French, Italian, Lebanese, Hungarian, Swiss, Persian, Portuguese and Spanish are but a few examples. No matter what the style, cooking on the coast is buoyed with top-quality ingredients, brought in from the individualistic farms and ranchers of the hinterlands.

The perfect complement to fine dining in Vancouver are the internationally recognized icewines grown in the Okanagan Valley. Canada is now recognized as the world's leading producer of icewine. Unlike any other dessert wine, frozen icewine grapes are harvested by hand in the Okanagan during the nights in December and January when the temperature reaches –8° C (18° F) or colder. Just as wonderful are the ales, beers and stouts from local micro-breweries. And don't forget the coffee. It's not just a pick-me-up but a way of life in the multitude of coffee bars that dot the city's streets.

B.C. SALMON DINNER

CHINESE

Chinatown is, of course, the first place to go in search of Chinese food.

Getting a table at the Floata Seafood Restaurant on Keefer Street shouldn't be hard, even at the notoriously busy dim sum hour. With 1,000 seats, it is immense. The ease and skill evident in the service and cooking, however, belie its size. A second Floata Seafood serves Richmond. A bit further along Keefer Street is Hon's Wun Tun House, an institution revered for fast, inexpensive servings of Cantonese-style rice and noodle dishes and vegetarian dim sum.

HON'S WUN TON HOUSE

Just outside Chinatown, the Pink Pearl on Hastings Street is crowded with discriminating Chinese families, especially between 11 a.m. and 2 p.m. on weekends, when dim sum is a tradition. Lunch-time dining is easy here for visitors: servers urge you to make choices from the dishes displayed on their carts. Coming for dinner instead? You could catch a glimpse — and get an earful — of a Chinese wedding banquet, usually a boisterous affair.

The Chinese food experience doesn't end at Chinatown's border. Across the Oak Street Bridge in Richmond are a number of Asian-style malls, complete with eateries. The Yaohan Centre's food courts offer a wide range of Asian street eats at bargain prices. Next to the

41

DIM SUM AT SUN SUI WAH

Yaohan Centre, the Radisson President Hotel harbours the Richmond Mandarin Chinese Restaurant, distinguished by its creative dim sum menu and masterful repertoire of Cantonese dishes.

Between the new Asian centre of Richmond and the pioneering region of Vancouver's Chinatown are literally hundreds more Chinese restaurants. The popularity of humble Hon's, for instance, has translated into additional venues in downtown Vancouver, Richmond, New Westminster and Coquitlam. Hon's has also spawned a thriving trade in frozen potstickers, buns and dim sum, as well as won ton noodles and chili oil. Most every visiting food writer dines at Sun Sui Wah, designed by noted B.C. architect Bing Thom; owner Simon Chan developed the Cantonese-style menu of dim sum specialties. The Won More Szechuan Restaurant serves reasonably-priced hot and sour soup, potstickers and other dishes, mainly spicy, in a crowded, upstairs space in West End Vancouver and bigger, slightly more expensive digs in Kitsilano. At the Shanghai Chinese Bistro, a skein of noodles makes its first appearance as a rope of dough, undergoes a fascinating ritual of twisting and stretching, and ends up on your plate as Tan Tan noodles with peanut sauce. Szechuan cuisine reappears in a slightly costlier incarnation at the Szechuan Chongqing Seafood Restaurant with locations in both Vancouver and Burnaby. Both restaurants showcase cooking from the Chongqing region and specialize in seafood.

The Imperial Chinese Seafood Restaurant brings Chinese fine dining with a view to the downtown business

BEEF AND MIXED VEGGIES AT HON'S

district. Its serene atmosphere frequently breaks down in the face of giggles from its younger patrons. It's equally likely to be shattered by the adults, whose unsuppressed admiration for a perfect, glistening rock cod, whole and

KIRIN MANDARIN

steamed with ginger and scallions, is often hearty and spontaneous. Look to the elegant Kirin Mandarin, also downtown, for specialties such as Shanghai smoked eel, Beijing duck and Szechuan hot and spicy scallops.

JAPANESE

The popularity of teriyaki, teppan and especially sushi has taken Japanese food far from the small stretch of Powell Street known as Japantown. At Tojo's, in central Fairview, the privileged and prudent few who reserved a place at the ten-seat sushi bar are treated to a show of Hidekazu Tojo's consummate skill with sushi. Tojo's edible masterpieces are the main draw for the knowing Japanese businesspeople, filmmakers and celebrities that crowd the establishment, but a wide range of non-sushi dishes round out the somewhat pricey menu.

The West End's Musashi Japanese Restaurant offers more sensibly priced sushi and sashimi. Its menu includes the usual soups, salads, tempura, teriyaki chicken and beef, as well as rice and noodles, many assembled nicely into combination dinners. Yuji's Japanese Tapas offers a unique menu of Japanese appetizer dishes perfect for snacking and socializing at reasonable prices.

Gyoza King has a much narrower focus. While noodle dishes and inexpensive specials do appear on the menu, there's no sushi to be seen in this West End eatery. The place is crammed with locals and tourists alike, who consume one plateful of plump meat, seafood or vegetable gyozas after another. And for ramen in all its forms — regular (pork), miso and soy — try Ezogiku Noodle Cafe, a short walk away, where little else, only a fried rice dish, a fried noodle dish, a curry and gyozas, are offered. There's a second Ezogiku near the Vancouver Public Library.

TOJO'S RESTAURANT

SOUTH ASIAN

In many parts of Greater Vancouver, South Asian restaurants are easy to find. Vij's Restaurant showcases B.C.-influenced Indian curries and other specials. The West Side's Maurya has an incredible wine list and the tandoori quail served over spinach and chickpea cakes is a must. There's a lunch buffet for $9.95 — a bargain you can't afford to pass up. Both places are modern, high-profile eateries. In contrast, the more mature Rubina Tandoori is located on a busy East Side street. The dowdy façade hides a contemporary heart and the deft hand of Krishna Jamal,

43

matriarch and chef. Look for Rubina Grill takeout spots on Granville Island and in the Capilano Mall Food Court in North Vancouver.

THAI AND OTHER ASIAN

Thai restaurants represent yet another sector of the city's multi-faceted Asian community. Montri's Thai in Kitsilano is hot, in every sense of the word (but you can ask for milder). Often cited as the city's best Thai, Montri's presents authentically-spiced dishes that make the scaled heat ratings — from one chili (mildest) to five chilies (hottest) — required reading. The Phnom Penh is family-run, with a focus on Vietnamese and Cambodian food with some Chinese dishes. While the surroundings may be rather plain, the hot and sour soup, tender flash-fried squid tubes and fresh-oyster omelettes are anything but.

MONTRI'S THAI

FRENCH AND ITALIAN/MEDITERRANEAN

For French dining, look to Le Crocodile. Located downtown, it offers roomy, luxurious surroundings with a patio, and French wines and Alsace regional dishes that are well worth the expense. Owner and chef Michel Jacob's Alsatian onion tart has been hailed as the best in Vancouver. For a bistro experience, try Café de Paris in the West End. The warm dark woods, wine racks and lace curtains instantly bring to mind a Paris bistro. The menu includes moderately-priced classics: duck confit, steak tartare and cassoulet; all are served with the pommes frites that have become legend in the city. A table d'hôte, as well as original contemporary French creations, is available. Bistro Pastis also produces solid country fare. Look for an outstanding cheese plate and, in cooler weather, satisfying braises, cassoulets and roasts. The Smoking Dog Bar and Grill will sate a hunger for uncomplicated food such as coq au vin, steak au poivre, duck à l'orange, and salade niçoise. On a sunny afternoon, watch the Kitsilano crowd from the patio.

In West Vancouver, the unpretentious La Régalade is winning awards for no-nonsense country cooking inspired by the neighbourhood bistros in France. Don't miss the escargots or the homemade pâtés. Italian, French and Spanish flavours meld at Cioppino's Mediterranean Grill, where chef and owner Pino Posteraro infuses his philosophy of "cucina naturale" into light, fresh dishes. In the same Yaletown area, Villa Del Lupo delivers a generous and contemporary menu of excellent pastas and favourites such as lamb shank osso buco.

LE CROCODILE

Another bit of Italy resides in Il Giardino di Umberto, a seaside villa recreated on Hornby Street. The Tuscan menu emphasizes pasta and game. Traditional northern Italian cooking rules at the West End's Piccolo Mondo, where the soups are outstanding. And at Quattro on Fourth and Gusto di Quattro, the rooms are mosaic-tiled and mahogany-trimmed. Quattro prepares some unusual Italian pastas; the combination plate provides a good overview. Across the Lions Gate Bridge, The Beach Side Cafe in West Vancouver has deck dining to capitalize on views of Stanley Park and Kitsilano across the water. A strong wine list and Italian food preparation characterize the restaurant.

QUATTRO ON FOURTH

PACIFIC NORTHWEST

The Pacific Northwest's original First Nations cuisine cannot be ignored. The Liliget Feast House occupies a stunning longhouse near the beach in the West End. There are wood walkways, pebbled floors, cedar plank tables and walls hung with contemporary native art. A feast, or potlatch, platter ensures a wide sampling; it includes bannock, baked sweet potato with hazelnuts, alder-grilled salmon, toasted seaweed with rice, steamed fern shoots and barbecued venison.

IL GIARDINO DI UMBERTO

Plentiful, readily available seafood is a characteristic of Pacific Northwest cuisine. At Rodney's Oyster House in Yaletown, oysters are the main attraction: a dozen or so varieties lie on ice, in long stainless steel beds, while customers line the oyster bar. Other fresh seafoods, chowders and slapjacks are also popular. Search out the Cannery, isolated among the Burrard Inlet wharves. The interior is lined with seafaring memorabilia and, fittingly, the Cannery always makes good on the seafood promises offered by the "daily fresh" sheet. The Beach House, on the other side of the Burrard Inlet, is also especially strong on seafood. It also offers a marvellous view of the West Vancouver waterfront.

At the Raincity Grill, near English Bay, the menu changes according to whatever fresh, local ingredients are

LILIGET FEAST HOUSE

on hand. Wine is available by the glass from an extensive, award-winning wine list. The West Coast theme is upheld by a trio of hotel restaurants as well. At 900 West Restaurant, the well-travelled menu includes everything from USDA prime rib to an ahi tuna tower. Many of the wines on their much-lauded list can also be ordered by the glass.

The Five Sails at Canada Place presents a menu that also focuses on imaginative presentations such as pan-seared

STILTON
CHEESECAKE AT
DIVA

halibut crusted with fine herbs and a watercress emulsion. To top it off, diners enjoy a spectacular harbour view. Diva at the Met optimizes an airy, natural space with multi-tiered seating, and out of its Waldorf-style open kitchen come both stylish, contemporary items such as potato-crusted wild salmon, cinnamon-smoked duck and perhaps the best desserts in the city by internationally-recognized pastry chef Thomas Haas.

The Fish House at Stanley Park has an enviable location, surrounded by trees, tennis courts, and lawn bowling greens in one of the world's best urban parks. Flaming prawns are one of the Fish House's most popular dishes, and Chef Karen Barnaby's ahi tuna steak Diane with mashed potatoes has become a classic.

ABOVE: SMOKED
BLACK ALASKA COD
FROM SEASONS
RESTAURANT IN
QUEEN ELIZABETH
PARK
BOTTOM: THE
TEAHOUSE
RESTAURANT IN
STANLEY PARK

Bishop's location streetside in Kitsilano, away from the harbour and the beach, lets you fully appreciate master host John Bishop's superlative standards of service and cuisine. Should your attention stray to the modern Canadian art gracing the walls, the smoked sablefish with truffle brandade cake and herb horseradish sabayon or the crème brûlée (which may be cappuccino, roasted pear, or sun-dried cherry) will easily recapture your interest. The Pear Tree in Burnaby lures Vancouver visitors and residents out to the suburbs with the promise of Scott Jaeger's reasonably priced and inventive menu, which might, for example, offer a braised lamb shank with seared scallops and roasted pear risotto.

In the midst of all the West Coast innovation, a bit of tradition stands firm. Patrons at the Teahouse Restaurant at Ferguson Point in Stanley Park won't allow traditional favourites such as the Teahouse's stuffed mushroom caps off the menu. Seasons in the Park, in Queen Elizabeth Park, also has a conservative menu which focuses mostly on fish and poultry. The restaurant overlooks a beautiful quarry garden, the mountains and the Vancouver skyscape.

UPSCALE AND HOTEL DINING

West recently received a gold award as restaurant of the year by *Vancouver Magazine*'s Critics' Poll for its outstanding decor, food, service and deep wine list. Try Chef David Hawksworth's foie gras and chicken liver parfait, but be sure to leave room for original and beguiling desserts.

C RESTAURANT

At Lumière, talented chef Rob Feenie has found the perfect balance between classic French and contemporary presentations. Feenie introduced tasting menus to the city. His vegetarian tasting menu is superb and his wine bar is perfect for a martini and an appetizer. Next door is Feenie's, his casual dining bistro. C, located on the downtown perimeter, has extravagant caviars, a private wine cellar and a patio with a million-dollar marina view. C's chef creates distinct dishes that taste as intriguing as they sound: seared octopus, bacon-wrapped diver scallops and any of the items from their menu tasting.

Some of the city's best restaurants are ensconced within downtown hotels, including the Five Sails, 900 West Restaurant and Diva at the Met (see Pacific Northwest). Fleuri may be tucked away at Sutton Place, yet it is widely known for its Chocoholic Bar, afternoon teas, Sunday brunch, seafood buffet and ever-changing, always excellent, menu. Chartwell, inside the Four Seasons Hotel, is a classic choice for Vancouverites and their visitors. The dining room's rich wood panelling and fireplace are as conducive to successful business dealings as they are to soothing dining. The Bacchus Restaurant in the small, exclusive Wedgewood Hotel is a beautifully and discreetly lit room that unfailingly delivers fine food.

SPECIALTY

The Hart House in Burnaby is remembered as much for its Tudor-style, heritage-home setting as it is for its service and food. Award-winning Chef Carol Chow's cooking ranges from daring dishes like B.C. spot prawns with sauce provençal and citrus basmati rice to the more traditional rack of lamb with rosemary Yukon gold potatoes. The desserts have a traditional streak as well: a Belgian chocolate espresso mousse tower and a warm apricot-ginger cake.

WEST COAST HALIBUT

Vegetarians and non-vegetarians seek out Habibi's for bargain-priced dishes of perfectly prepared traditional Lebanese home cooking, including falafels and vegetarian

TEXAS FLANK STEAK AT BIN 941

dishes. Hon's (see Asian) has a dedicated vegetarian cooking facility at its downtown Robson Street location and can fashion vegetarian versions of dim sum and almost any dish you can think of, even vegetarian goose (actually bean curd skin rolls filled with dried Chinese mushrooms). Planet Veg, close to Kitsilano Beach and Vanier Park, cooks up East Indian, Mexican and Mediterranean vegetarian fast foods. Lineups are fairly frequent but takeout is always an option. Order ahead or at the door (no home delivery available). There's no vegetarian fare at Memphis Blues Barbeque House on West Broadway and Commercial Drive. All the favourites — pulled pork, ribs, beef brisket and their signature cornish game hens — are beautifully prepared with sides of baked beans, coleslaw and cornbread.

Tapas are served at Bin 941 downtown, a warm, close room where the tasting bowls are generously filled and reasonably priced. A similar concept operates at Bin 942. The room is larger, but has much the same atmosphere and offers repeats of many of the menu items.

For many families, Earl's, which has several Vancouver locations, is the restaurant of choice. The service is fast and the food is fresh and healthy. It has an enviable wine list, and many of the locations have patios. For even faster service, look for White Spot Triple O's for fries, milkshakes and Vancouver's favourite burgers with the legendary Triple O sauce. Tomato Fresh Food Cafe distinguishes itself from other diners with healthy, colourful comfort food such as BLTs, turkey sandwiches, tomato and pesto sandwiches and vegetarian chile. The very hip Subeez with its thirty-speaker sound system fits in well with its Yaletown neighbours. Don't miss the killer fries with garlic mayo, chicken and brie burger or any of the vegetarian dishes.

NOTTE'S BON TON PASTRY AND CONFECTIONARY

The Dockside Brewery on Granville Island fuses a casual restaurant with a micro-brewery and pub. In summer, the smashing outdoor patio is open for business. The large open kitchen is versatile, alternating between pub grub and up-market fare. The lounge offers a full bar of spirits and a range of lagers and ales from their highly regarded brewery. However, some say the best beer in town flows from the custom-designed taps at Steamworks, an extraordinary Yaletown brew pub with a wide-ranging brunch, lunch and dinner menu.

Visit Notte's Bon Ton Pastry and Confectionary, an institution since the 1930s, for tea and traditional French pastries. The Diplomat Cake is a tempting concoction made up of three layers of puff pastry, sponge cake, butter cream and rum. Patisserie Lebeau (near Granville Island) has fine Belgian waffles, delicious pastries and a selection of French breads and croissants for pâtisserie-purists. A few doors down at Les Amis du Fromage, mother and daughter team Alice and Allison Spurrell supply you and many top chefs with more than 400 cheeses at affordable prices. Comfort food takeout is also available from their freezer.

SHOPPING

PATRICIA FRASER

Stand at the corner of Granville and Georgia streets and you'll find yourself at the centre of Vancouver life. Look up, and see the skyscraping towers of commerce. Below the streets, the SkyTrain light rail transit whisks travellers to the suburbs. Georgia Street travels west to Stanley Park and the ocean. Look north along Granville and see the North Shore mountains — this is the heart of this cosmopolitan city. It's also the starting point for some serious shopping. No matter which direction you take, you'll find major malls (Pacific Centre) or mini-malls (Sinclair Centre), shopping promenades (Robson Street) or boutiques specializing in antiques or locally designed fashion (Gastown).

ROBSON STREET AT NIGHT

GEORGIA AND GRANVILLE

On the northeast corner of Georgia and Granville streets is the Hudson's Bay Company, known as "The Bay." Established in 1824 as a network of fur-trading posts, it's Canada's sole national department store, and a handy stop for everything from scarves to soup plates. The other corners of Georgia and Granville streets hold the downtown Sears and Vancouver's own London Drugs, an institution in its own right.

Head downstairs through the Bay to the underground Pacific Centre Mall. Running north from Georgia Street, this large and comfortable mall holds chains such as the very posh Canadian store, Holt Renfrew, as well as The Gap, Baby Gap, Club Monaco, Banana Republic, The Museum Store, Fairweather, Eddie Bauer and Jacob. It also provides easy access to the SkyTrain beneath the Bay.

Back above ground, walk west along Georgia and you'll pass the Vancouver Art Gallery, with a gallery shop well stocked with quality arts and crafts, books and games. Keep going west until you come to Burrard Street. You could go underground again to the Royal Centre and Bentall Centre malls, or turn south for a block and head up to Robson Street.

ROBSON STREET

TOP: ITEMS AT THE VANCOUVER ART GALLERY SHOP
MIDDLE: DESIGNER SHOPS ON ROBSON STREET

Once a quiet street once known as Robsonstrasse for its European-style delis and coffee shops, Robson Street is now lined with youth-oriented chains such as The Gap, Roots, Banana Republic and Mexx, interspersed with a special blend of coffee shops. Walk west along Robson to Denman Street and you're in the depths of the West End. The shopping area here is more residential than Robson Street, with flower stores and framers, fish-and-chip shops and beachwear (being minutes from English Bay).

WATER STREET

GASTOWN

Built after the Great Fire of 1886, this former warehouse area is chock-a-block with tourist shops and restaurants in refurbished heritage buildings along the waterfront. The former Canadian Pacific Railway station is now the terminus for the SkyTrain and connecting station for the SeaBus to the North Shore. Take the SeaBus for a 15-minute waterborne jaunt across Vancouver harbour for a visit to Lonsdale Quay Market on the North Shore. You can buy lunch and hand-crafted souvenirs at the same time at the quay, which is located right at the SeaBus dock.

GRANVILLE ISLAND

Granville Island, on the south side of False Creek, is a former industrial peninsula reclaimed by the city and reborn as a shopping and arts centre. The Kids Only Market, housed in original warehouses, is home to over 20 different shops for children. The huge Granville Island Market is a collection of vendors of gourmet food items, fresh produce and hand-crafted jewellery and gifts. In the Net Loft, another large building packed to the gunwales with boutiques, find Edie's Hats (a Vancouver fashion landmark), Nancy Lord's handwoven clothes and accessories, El Greco Jewellery and a multiplicity of artists' studio shops, galleries and gift stores.

ANTIQUES AND COLLECTIBLES

Vancouver loves antiques. Shops and galleries are concentrated in three areas: West 10th Avenue by the University of British Columbia (Canada West Antiques Co. and Folkart Interiors,); Granville Street between West 6th and West 14th Avenues (Small Comforts, William Robert, Hampshire Antiques, Carmen Boré and Farmhouse Collections); and Main Street between 12th and 29th Avenues (Second Time Around, Deeler's, Ages Ago, Blue Heron and Baker's Dozen).

BOOKSTORES

If you've seen the movie *You've Got Mail*, you know all about the battle of the bookstores, between the mega-stores and the little corner shops. The big guys are represented by the three Chapters (downtown, South Granville and Metrotown), each with its own Starbucks coffee shop, children's story times and comprehensive database of books in print. The little guys include the Granville Book Company downtown, Duthie Books on 4th Avenue, the new-age Banyen Books on West 4th Avenue and gay lit Little Sister's Bookstore in the West End. Also Kidsbooks on West Broadway is a must-see with young readers.

KIDS ONLY MARKET ON GRANVILLE ISLAND

CANADIAN CLOTHING DESIGNERS

Western style starts here: First Nations fashion maven Dorothy Grant uses her Haida background as inspiration for clothing based on "button blanket" design. Zonda Nellis on South Granville has developed a worldwide following for her subtly coloured, elegant hand-loomed designer wear. Canadian RozeMerie Cuevas has created the coolly classical Jacqueline Conoir Line for Esmode Boutique on South Granville. Nancy Lord produces handwoven fashions and accessories from her loom on

Granville Island, while in swank Kerrisdale, Margareta Design offers clothing that is conservative and classic. A-Wear is the house label for a team of local designers at Leone in Sinclair Centre. For hard-wearing, attractive sportswear, visit Tilley Endurables Adventure Clothing on South Granville.

THE TOYBOX ON WEST BROADWAY

CHILDREN'S STORES

Clothing for the well-dressed tot can be found at Bobbit's for Kids! on West 4th, Bratz on South Granville, Isola Bella in Kerrisdale and Please Mum on West Broadway. As for toys and games, sure we have Toys R Us (on West Broadway and in every single suburb in North America) but for more individual attention, you can check out Kaboodles on West 10th and The Toybox on West Broadway. As well, the Kids Only Market on Granville Island is a collection of more than twenty shops, including one devoted to kites.

CHINA AND CRYSTAL

Apart from the Bay, which has everything, you can find what your heart desires at Atkinson's at West 6th and Granville. The whole store sparkles. Chintz and Company in Yaletown boasts "entertaining tablewares." W. H. Puddifoot & Co. is a favourite in Kerrisdale.

DESIGNER BOUTIQUES

Not only will you find favourite labels at Vancouver's many designer boutiques, but petites will be pleasantly surprised at the selection. Nearly one-third of Vancouver's population is of Asian heritage and sizes are appropriately geared to the market. Most shops are temptingly close to major downtown hotels. There's Chanel on Burrard Street;

Leone Boutique, Escada Plaza and Gianni Versace Boutique at Sinclair Centre; Enda B, Edward Chapman's Ladies Shop, Bacci's and Boboli on South Granville; Boutique Zolé, Romeo Gigli and Instante on Hornby Street; and Dyanna's on Howe Street.

FIRST NATIONS ARTS AND JEWELLERY

Vancouver offers a fine selection of authentic First Nations art and jewellery. In Gastown, Hill's Native Art on Water Street (formerly Hill's Indian Crafts) stocks carved jewellery and chunky, virtually indestructible wool Cowichan sweaters. The Inuit Gallery, around the corner on Cambie Street, is a respected gallery for collectors of quality Inuit and First Nations carvings and prints. Marion Scott Gallery on Howe Street has Inuit sculptures. The

Lattimer Gallery on West 2nd Avenue near Granville Island offers masks, jewellery, prints and drums. The Eagle Spirit Gallery on Maritime Mews on Granville Island also carries Haida-carved argillite. The Museum of Anthropology at the University of British Columbia has a good selection of jewellery, books, prints and sculpture, including soapstone, a traditional local material.

HOME FURNISHINGS

Cosmopolitan Vancouverites enjoy their interiors as well as their city's great natural settings. Near the corner of Broadway and Granville streets, decorators will find retro-chic Restoration Hardware, classic Jordan's Interiors, rustic Country Furniture, and urbane Industrial Revolution. Upholstery Arts on Burrard Street near West Eighth Avenue offers a huge selection of soft furnishings made to order, and UpCountry, down in Kitsilano, is modern to the max.

GIFT SHOPS

You will find well-designed objects from pottery to jewellery at Circle Craft on Granville Island and the Vancouver Art Gallery, on Robson between Hornby and Howe. And for birthday/wedding/anniversary gifts for every budget and occasion, try Chachkas on Robson, Lightheart and Co. on Howe, Moulé on West 4th and Park Royal Mall in West Vancouver, and The Museum Company in Park Royal.

JEWELLERY

In Vancouver, as in every other major Canadian city, the Grand Dame of jewellery stores is Birks, now presiding at the corner of Hastings and Granville. Toni Cavelti, a major local designer noted for combining precious stones in startling presentations, is now distributed exclusively through Birks. Other long-respected jewellers are Georg Jensen and Tiffany in Holt Renfrew, both in the Pacific Centre. Other sparkling stars are Karl Stittgen for gold and precious metals in clean, modern lines and the internationally recognized Martha Sturdy for jewellery and home fashion accessories in unexpected fabrications and organic forms (both on South Granville).

LEATHER

Those who are, as they say, "into" leather will find a wonderful selection of ready-made and custom apparel at Mack's Leather's Inc. on Granville Street. But more prosaic choices may be made at Castle Milano in the Sinclair Centre, Danier in the Pacific Centre and on Robson, Neto on East 4th Avenue, and Marquis of London on Beatty Street.

MUSIC

Vancouver has some of the best CD prices in the world, and it's all due to A & B Sound's downtown and other locations. They keep the

JOHN FLUEVOG BOOTS AND SHOES

prices down, but they have plenty of competition. Sam the Record Man is right beside them on Seymour Street, and HMV and the Virgin Megastore are nearby on Robson. For those hard-to-find eclectic recordings, try Black Swan on West Broadway, D & G Collectors on East Hastings, Highlife Records on Commercial and the Magic Flute and Zulu Records on West 4th Avenue.

MEN'S CLOTHING

High-end establishments well worth a visit include Boboli on South Granville, Harry Rosen, Boys' Co. and Holt Renfrew in the Pacific Centre, E. A. Lee on Pender Street, Leone in the Sinclair Centre, Mark James on West

BOBOLI ON SOUTH GRANVILLE

Broadway, Enda B. on 10th Avenue, S. Lampman in Kerrisdale, and Chevalier Creations on Seymour Street for custom-mades. For a sportier look, try Eddie Bauer in the Pacific Centre, Roots on Robson Street and Tilley Endurables Adventure Clothing on Granville.

SHOE STORES

Save your shoe leather for a walk along Robson Street, where you'll find Salvatore Ferragamo, Simard & Voyer Shoes and Stephane de Raucourt. Over at the corner of Robson and Granville streets, John Fluevog creates perfectly outré styles strictly for those willing to put their funkiest foot forward (the store also carries a wide range of Doc Martens). Visiting Hollywood stars have fallen head over heels for Dayton Boots — rugged and dependable as the workers they were originally made for, they're now available for the rest of us on Granville Street. Ingledew's is also on Granville, offering quality dress, casual and walking footwear.

ENTERTAINMENT

SHAWN BORDOFF

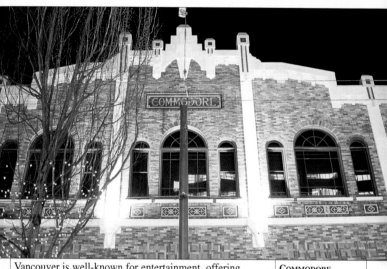

Vancouver is well-known for entertainment, offering everything from big-name performers to talented amateurs. If you enjoy music, ranging from folk to classical, and live theatre or dance, you'll find events happening every night of the year. The after-hours scene is lively with most clubs now open until 4 a.m. on weekends. Vancouver clubs offer something for all ages and persuasions. Most performing arts productions sell tickets in advance. Ticketmaster has a monopoly in this area, with a telephone line dedicated to arts events.

COMMODORE BALLROOM

BOTTOM LEFT: **NICOLA CAVENDISH** AS *SHIRLEY VALENTINE* **PETER HUCK IN** *SINGING IN THE RAIN*

LIVE THEATRE

The Vancouver Playhouse (part of the Queen Elizabeth Theatre complex) is one of the best regional theatres in Canada. Plays presented here employ the top actors, directors, designers and craftspeople from across Canada. The theatre has been home to the Vancouver Playhouse Theatre

Company since 1962, a company that often premieres award-winning Canadian plays. A terrific example of this is *The Overcoat*, conceived by

Morris Panych and Wendy Gorling, a unique play without words that tells the moving story of a man whose life is transformed when he finds a colourful coat.

In the 1930s, the Stanley Theatre on Granville Street near Broadway was the place for vaudeville. It later became an excellent movie theatre but eventually closed in the heyday of multiplex madness. In 1997, the Arts Club Theatre completed lengthy and difficult renovations to transform the dilapidated but distinguished cinema into a first-class professional theatre. Today it's a delightful 650-seat venue with a charming interior, home to many of Vancouver's most entertaining productions, including many smaller musicals. The plays are just as good at the Arts Club's 450-seat mainstage theatre on Granville Island. A string of hits, including homegrown and international plays, contribute to the Arts Club's longevity. Having run the Arts Club since it opened in 1972, artistic director Bill Millerd is the most respected, and probably most decorated, theatre practitioner in the country.

If you thought that Granville Island was just for shopping, you'll be surprised at how many live theatres coexist here. Across the walkway from the Arts Club's mainstage theatre is its Revue Theatre. This cabaret-style venue hosts the Vancouver Theatresports League, offering comic improvisation fine-tuned to a science. If you haven't seen a live improv show, catch one of the regular early-evening performances. Vancouver Theatresports is suitable for the entire family. The Waterfront Theatre is another Granville Island venue, noted for performances of new Canadian plays.

For some adult comedy improvisation on the edge, the Urban Well Restaurant and Lounge hosts hilarious shows every Monday night. And if merely watching an improv is not enough and you want to get involved in a show, consider some interactive theatre. Since 1995, people have been raving about Tony and Tina's Wedding, a dinner theatre show with a twist. You start off at a "church wedding" at St. Andrew Wesley's Church in the West End and end up flirting at the "dinner reception" a few blocks away. The audience member initially too embarrassed to respond to the actors usually ends up being the star of the show. For an alternate opportunity to get involved, drop by Doll & Penny's Cafe on a Friday evening. Crowds at this entertaining drag show often spill into the street.

Constructed in a former fire hall, the Firehall Arts Centre on East Cordova is just two blocks from Vancouver's troubled Main and Hastings corner. Devoted to new plays, performance art

NICOLA CAVENDISH AS MAE WEST IN DIRTY BLONDE

*MIDDLE: FIREHALL ARTS CENTRE
BOTTOM: NICOLA CAVENDISH AND ALLAN MORGAN IN DIRTY BLONDE*

BRAMWELL TOVEY CONDUCTING THE VSO

and dance, the Firehall has a loyal audience. In addition to its professional theatres, Vancouver has several good community theatres. Presentation House in North Vancouver is as good as most professional venues. Metro Theatre in South Vancouver's Marpole area has mastered the art of dry British comedy. At the Jewish Community Centre's Norman Rothstein Theatre, a state-of-the-art auditorium seats 318 people in luxury.

If you're looking for a New York-style Broadway production at Vancouver prices, the Queen Elizabeth Theatre is the place to go. Throughout the year, large musicals with elaborate sets and all the trimmings stop by to dazzle Vancouver audiences at the "QE." The City of Vancouver built the Queen Elizabeth Theatre in 1959 — by West Coast standards, that makes it a historical monument. Nevertheless, the building is perfect for Broadway shows. The stage is 23 metres wide with a proscenium arch; the seats are plush and the décor is elegant.

Another elegant theatre that brings in large Broadway shows like *42nd Street*, *Fosse* and *Hamlet* is the Centre for the Performing Arts. This huge, state-of-the-art theatre opened in the early 1990s as the Ford Theatre for the Performing Arts. It closed due to financial difficulties but re-opened in 2002 under new management.

MUSIC

Vancouver has a strong musical history. The Vancouver Symphony Orchestra (VSO) has existed since 1919, and now performs more than 130 concerts annually. Over the years, the VSO has welcomed many outstanding artists, among them Sir Yehudi Menuhin, Maureen Forrester, Isaac Stern, Dame Janet Baker, Yo-Yo Ma and even Bobby McFerrin. You'll usually find the symphony at the historic Orpheum Theatre, built in 1927. The

KATHLEEN BRETT AND THOMAS GERTZ IN *LA BOHÈME* AT THE VANCOUVER OPERA

Orpheum, like the Stanley Theatre, opened as a vaudeville house. At the time, it was one of the largest and most impressive theatres on the West Coast. Later, it dwindled into a movie house. In 1977, after five years of extravagant renovations, the City of Vancouver reopened the Orpheum as home to the Vancouver Symphony Orchestra. It still impresses with its classic ambiance of old-time elegance.

Like the symphony, the Vancouver Opera grew out of historic roots, with the first opera performances in the city in the late 1880s. The Vancouver Opera company was launched in 1960, with a performance of Bizet's *Carmen*. Today, Vancouver Opera is one of the largest performing arts organizations in BC, with a strong commitment to the development of Canadian talent. While the opera hires

LA BOHÈME, **VANCOUVER OPERA**

The Fabulous COMMODORE Ballroom

principle singers of international fame, preference is given to Canadians. The company also employs its own orchestra and chorus made up of local musicians and singers. There is plenty for the traditional opera fan, from *Don Giovanni* to *Madama Butterfly*. All performances are at the Queen Elizabeth Theatre.

One of Vancouver's newest musical venues is the Chan Centre for the Performing Arts at the University of British Columbia. This 1,400-seat facility was designed to have optimum acoustics. The UBC Opera Society performs here a few times a year, as does the Vancouver Symphony Orchestra. If you want to hear something really special, look for the Vancouver Cantata Singers performing at the Chan Centre. This 40-voice award-winning choir is recognized as one of Canada's foremost ensembles.

One of the most enjoyable places for an informal concert is the Commodore Ballroom on Granville Street downtown. Once a fancy black-tie room, the Commodore gradually deteriorated into little more than a beer hall. For years, the main attraction remained its bouncy, horsehair-sprung floor. The floor eventually gave out from years of hard dancing. In the mid-1990s, the club closed, was renovated and reopened. Although the floor was repaired, there is still a bit of bounce left in for fun. Check in advance to see who's playing because the Commodore is very eclectic. Artists have included Anthrax, the Powder Blues, Kim Mitchell, and even Dal Richards and his Big Band Orchestra.

The best place to see jazz is the Purple Onion in Gastown. Relax to some swing or more mellow sounds in its intimate lounge. There's also a large dance room that caters to a younger crowd on weekends. For rocking blues, the Yale (near the Granville Bridge on the downtown side) boogies on in one of the oldest buildings in Western Canada. When the Yale was built in 1889, it was a place for miners and loggers to get a drink. They still serve beer, but it's now one of the best blues bars in the world. Dress casually and enjoy.

DANCE

For modern dance, the Vancouver East Cultural Centre on Venables is BC's most diverse performance space. "The Cultch" opened on October 15, 1973 with a two-week run of the locally based Anna Wyman Dance Theatre. Today the Cultch offers a marvellous array of unique dance performances and performing arts. Beware of the balcony though. It's terrific to look at but not a good place to sit. Sight lines are best from front row centre on the lower level. You may want to keep an eye out for Kokoro Dance, an innovative troupe that performs here and at various other venues throughout the city. Dance Arts Vancouver also presents several festivals, the most popular being the annual KISS Project. This mid-winter event began in 1994 and has developed a real

ACACIA SCHACHTE AND EDMOND KILPATRICK IN BALLET B.C.'S PRODUCTION OF *THE WINTER ROOM*

following. The KISS Project can be seen at Performance Works on Granville Island.

For classical and modern dance, Ballet British Columbia has built an international reputation for artistic excellence. The company first performed on April 11, 1986 and was quickly recognized for its combination of talent and creativity. You can see the ballet at the Queen Elizabeth Theatre.

CLUBS

For star watchers, the bar of choice is the Gérard Lounge. Located on the first floor of the Sutton Place Hotel, the Gérard is one of Vancouver's trendiest lounges. It is also exquisitely furnished, luxurious, and the bar prices reflect the surroundings. It's not uncommon to spot some of Hollywood's most memorable faces here. Vancouver is known for its politeness, so please be discreet. If you're

more intent on meeting someone available, attractive and of the opposite sex, Richard's on Richards is the place to go. The crowds at this big dance club tend to be in their late twenties and early thirties. On the weekend, the music leans towards hip-hop and house.

A few blocks from Richard's, you'll find one of the country's most sophisticated night clubs. Skybar, at the corner of Granville and Smythe streets, is Vancouver's new, exclusive, three-level dance club. Friday and Saturday nights the minimum age is 25.

Au Bar is the place to be seen. The club has a line outside most every night from Thursday through Saturday. Another place to dress up for and be seen is the lounge at the new Opus Hotel in Yaletown. In Vancouver, the downtown clubs with the least amount of attitude are the gay clubs. The Odyssey, geared toward alternative dance music, has always been a popular club with a loyal gay crowd. If

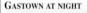

PUMPJACKS GAY LEATHER BAR

you're looking to meet a gay man while you're in town, your best bet is Numbers. It's the gay equivalent to Richard's on Richards. Pumpjacks is a gay leather bar where fetish enthusiasts come to play. Vancouver is also home to Honey Lounge, a cool bar with a good percentage of Lesbian patrons. Next door to Honey is a women's-only nightclub called Lick.

The biggest problem with Vancouver clubs are the lineups. Any place worth going to usually has a lineup after 9 p.m. Smoking is not permitted inside public buildings, so be prepared to smoke outside.

FETISH

Vancouver's fetish scene has been growing steadily over the last dozen years. Two events are open to the public each month, both with strict dress codes enforced. No casual wear, jeans, business attire or usual nightclub clothes are permitted. Patrons must wear something sexy, kinky or creative, although full nudity is not permitted as the events are held in public places. The original fetish party, the Bettie Page Social Club, is now called the Body Perve Social Club and takes place on the last Saturday night of every month. The parties are held at the Lotus Club and at Lick (this is one event where men are allowed in Lick and the patrons are mixed).

On the second Saturday of every month Vancouver celebrates Sin City. This party is held at Club 23 West. Even though it hasn't been around as long as the Body Perve Social Club, it's still very popular and you should arrive before 10 p.m. to avoid waiting in line. Sin City is open until 4 a.m., so you can make up the time if you do get caught in line.

You may want to do a little shopping before heading out to a fetish night. Cameron Banks of MOR (Made of Rubber) is perhaps the best rubber designer in the country and will make custom-fit outfits on requests. Gastown's

GASTOWN AT NIGHT

Cabbages and Kinx sells new and vintage fetish wear including some great accessories such as silver finger armour.

GALLERIES

ANN ROSENBERG

In 1961, the New Design Gallery, co-operated by Abraham Rogatnick and Alvin Balkind, was the first Vancouver gallery to show leading-edge contemporary art. Now, more than forty years later, 150 galleries in Greater Vancouver exhibit vanguard works from all parts of the world reflecting British Columbia's cultural diversity and the sophistication of gallery audiences and consumers. In the past, the importance of First Nations contributions went unacknowledged. Now, however, there are twelve galleries in various city locations presenting museum-quality Native art and creating a worldwide commerce in Northwest Coast, Inuit and Plains art and artifacts.

MARCHESSAULT-ARCETRI-HIRES AT BAU-XI GALLERY

BURGERS' *BEYOND THE BOUNDS* AT BAU-XI GALLERY

SOUTH GRANVILLE

"The Row" is an impressive strip of twenty galleries. Akin to Soho in New York, The Row begins on Granville Street near West 16th Avenue with Catriona Jeffries' Gallery, where several of Canada's most leading-edge artists are shown. It continues north down the hill, with venues dotting either side, to Uno Langmann's elegant antique gallery close to the Granville Street Bridge.

West of Langmann's between West 5th and West 7th Avenues, are other outlets that consider themselves part of The Row, and are often included in walkabout tours of this

DIANE FARRIS GALLERY

multi-gallery area. The most famous of the off-Granville galleries is Diane Farris, located on West 7th Avenue. Several of the galleries on, and off, Granville Street give insight into the history of Canadian art. First Nations art and artifacts may be discovered in Douglas Reynolds and Spirits of the North. The Heffel Gallery specializes in nineteenth century and Group of Seven paintings. The Harrison and the Art Emporium show landscapes with rich colours that Tom Tomson would have enjoyed.

The Bau-Xi serves many senior Canadian artists including Jack Shadbolt, who was the titan of Canadian art until his death. The Atelier represents musician and collagist Al Neil and painter Robert Yonge. The Equinox courts Governor-General's award winners Gathie Falk, Liz Magor and Takeo Tanabe, among a group which also includes pre-eminent senior artist Gordon Smith.

Monte Clark Gallery deals with younger art stars like Generation X's Douglas Coupland. Upcoming local artists in several media may be viewed at Tracey Lawrence, Petley Jones, Anthony-Canasia and Elissa Cristall. Finally, art by French-speaking Canadians is on display at Le Centre Culturel Francophone de Vancouver. Douglas Udell Gallery represents Prairie artists, including the popular Joe Fafard.

JE T'AIME BY ANNA BONIFACHO AT BAU-XI GALLERY

Flavours of the exotic may also be found on The Row. The Jacana and Tensho galleries both show Oriental as well as Canadian contemporary work. Simon Patrich's Latin American connections give his exhibition program a unique twist. The Kurbatoff exhibits works by international artists, often with European backgrounds.

GRANVILLE ISLAND

A few minutes from South Granville is Vancouver's highly successful Granville Island. The site houses dozens of artist's studios like New-Small and Sterling Studio Glass, with its crowd-pleasing demonstrations of glass blowing, as well as traditional galleries selling local and international artworks.

Charles H. Scott is the most important gallery on Granville Island. It features a rotation of exhibitions designed to complement the Emily Carr Institute of Art and Design's curriculum. Malaspina Printmakers and the Dundarave Print Workshop show limited edition prints created by their members. Circle Craft Gallery and Crafthouse both exhibit juried selections of BC craftspersons' art in media as diverse as knitted ware and

CHARLES H. SCOTT GALLERY

original furniture. The Gallery of BC Ceramics serves, as you might expect, the best of the province's pottery. In addition to shops where certain small items of Northwest Coast design may be purchased, the New Eagle Spirit Gallery offers ceremonial objects for sale.

Adjacent to Granville Island, closer to Burrard Street, is another cluster of attractive galleries. Chief is The Waterfall, designed by world-famous architect Arthur Erickson, which encompasses four galleries (the Cascada, Elliot Lewis, Aaron Ross and Studio Blue) on West 2nd Avenue. Nearby is the Leona Lattimer Gallery, which specializes in Northwest Coast art and limited edition prints. The Third Avenue Gallery stresses experimental art by emerging artists.

GASTOWN

The oldest intact commercial district in Vancouver is Gastown, an area of century-old buildings housing both elegant, established galleries as well as souvenir-type shops with works by less-experienced Canadian and First Nations artists. Three of the best quality galleries are Spirit Wrestler, Images for a Canadian Heritage and the Inuit Gallery. These mostly exhibit museum-quality First Nations.

There is a great deal of variety in Gastown's many galleries. Among the most intriguing are Access and Artspeak, two non-profit spaces exhibiting experimental and conceptual work. Beautifully curated shows are staged at the Bfly Atelier. Industrial Artifacts presents unique, even odd, furniture while Honjo hosts Japanese art.

TOP: SPIRIT WRESTLER ART ABOVE: KILLER WHALES PLAQUE AND HAWKMAN SUN MASK AT THE APPLETON GALLERY BOTTOM: SCULPTURE AT BUSCHLEN MOWATT GALLERY

YALETOWN

In, or near, Yaletown is another cluster of galleries which make a pleasant half-day's exploration. The Exposure and onepointsix galleries are photo-based venues. The Elfsar Collection is also unusual for Vancouver in its specialty of animation cells. The Contemporary Art Gallery and the OR Gallery are committed to leading-edge Canadian and international art. The Phthalo brings international art to Vancouver while Centre A focuses on Asian art.

DOWNTOWN

A few of the galleries in downtown Vancouver are relatively close together but most are far-flung. A walk from the Buschlen Mowatt Gallery on West Georgia Street, with its leading-edge contemporary art, to the Appleton on Hornby where Northwest Coast and Inuit art is on display, would wear out your walking shoes.

But it is possible to spend an informative day, without too much walking, if you begin with the Vancouver Art Gallery's permanent collection and current exhibits. Just across West Georgia Street in the HSBC Building is the Pendulum Gallery. Its foyer shows are open to the public from the start of the business day. Contemporary Canadian or Southeast Asian art at the nearby Winsor can be followed by African art at the Howe Street Gallery of Fine Art. Nearby are the Marion Scott Gallery with its magnificent Inuit works, Dorian Rae's African and Asian selections, more First Nations art at Sharing the Spirit, and jade sculptures in the Sopel Gallery near Canada Place.

PARKS AND GARDENS

MARG MEIKLE

VANDUSEN GARDENS
(TOP AND BOTTOM)

It will come as no surprise to visitors that gardening is currently the number one outdoor leisure activity in Vancouver. It has always been in the top five — and it shows. The combination of a mild climate, plenty of precipitation and very diverse immigration to this area makes for a wide variety of gardening styles. From the abundant crops of the Chinese vegetable gardens around Chinatown to the amazing tomatoes and grapes of the Italian community around Commercial Drive, from the seemingly out-of-place palm trees on Beach Drive in the West End to the colourful perennial borders in many other neighbourhoods, there is much to enjoy around here. Vancouver is also one of the few cities in the world blessed with two botanical gardens: VanDusen Botanical Garden and the University of British Columbia (UBC) Botanical Garden are both superb living research libraries.

VANDUSEN BOTANICAL GARDEN

Lush VanDusen is a 22-hectare (55-acre) garden conveniently located on the edge of Shaughnessy, a well-heeled, historic section of Vancouver. But remarkably, the lush, mature VanDusen Botanical Garden was only built on a former golf course in the early 1970s. At any time of the year you can find plants, trees and shrubs in bloom. This garden also contains many theme areas, including the Chinese Medicinal Garden, Children's Garden, Fragrance Garden, Meditation Garden, Rose Garden and a Sino-Himalayan Garden. There's also a maze, a rhododendron walk, a Canadian Heritage garden and a fern dell.

Many popular special events are held here including the

Festival of Lights at Christmas, the VanDusen Plant sale in April, the VanDusen Flower and Garden Show in June and various other club shows and sales throughout the spring and summer. There is a lovely gift shop, a fledgling plant shop and a very civilized restaurant called Shaughnessy's.

RHODODENDRON IN FULL BLOOM AT VANDUSEN GARDENS

UBC BOTANICAL GARDEN AND OTHER UBC GARDENS

The UBC Botanical Garden sits on the ocean edge of the campus, overlooking the Strait of Georgia. Open to the public for wandering, breathing in that fresh sea air and those gorgeous scents, this 28-hectare (70-acre) theme garden is also used for teaching and research. The various gardens include: Alpine Garden, Asian Garden, Winter Garden, B.C. Native Garden, Physick Garden (herbs), Food Garden and Perennial Borders. The 25-hectare (61-acre) David C. Lam Asian Garden has a huge variety of woody Asian plants, maples, clematis, roses, rhododendrons, azaleas, magnolias and rare Oriental plants. In addition to a wide variety of outdoor experiences available, the Shop-in-the-Garden offers a good selection of gardening books and a particularly great nursery, including plants developed through the UBC plant introduction program and unusual plants propagated by members of the Friends of the Garden.

BELOW: MAZE AT VANDUSEN
BOTTOM: POND AT VANDUSEN

Of special interest at UBC is the classical Japanese Nitobe Memorial Garden designed, with a very West Coast view, by Japanese landscape architect Kannosouke Mori. He used many native trees and shrubs, training and pruning them in traditional Japanese fashion. Within this one-hectare (2.5-acre) garden are many more: the Tea Garden with a Tea House, the Nightingale Fence, the Tenth Bridge, several water crossings and a stroll garden.

QUEEN ELIZABETH PARK AND BLOEDEL CONSERVATORY

Second only to Stanley Park, Queen Elizabeth Park is located on Little Mountain, the highest point in Vancouver. It offers a terrific view of the city and the North Shore's Coast Mountains. June is a particularly showy month for the 52-hectare (130-acre) Queen E. Park, as the locals call it, because the roses

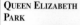

QUEEN ELIZABETH PARK

are in full bloom. But any time is worth a wander through the Quarry Garden at the peak of the mountain. It was created in the 1960s and there are similarities to Butchart Gardens near Victoria, which was created 60 years earlier, also in a quarry.

There is public art of note throughout Queen Elizabeth Park. A Henry Moore sculpture, *Knife Edge-Two Piece*, is close to the Bloedel Conservatory. The conservatory is a huge climate-controlled Plexiglas dome that holds a large variety of tropical, desert and exotic plants as well as more than 100 tropical birds. It is a particularly great destination on a rainy day, for inside this very warm and dry dome is a jungle of palms, banana trees and orchids, among other species.

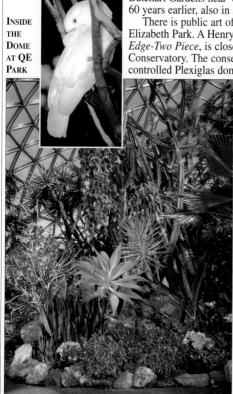

INSIDE THE DOME AT QE PARK

DR. SUN YAT-SEN CLASSICAL CHINESE GARDEN

The Dr. Sun Yat-Sen Classical Chinese Garden, opened in 1986, is the first authentic full-sized classical Chinese garden built outside China. In a serene environment behind a wall in the middle of Chinatown, you will find tranquil ponds, natural rock sculptures, courtyards and an interesting variety of plants. The garden reflects the Taoist philosophy of accentuating harmony in contrasts. Every stone, pine and magnolia flower in the garden has been placed purposefully and carries a symbolic meaning. The Garden offers guided tours, which provide perspectives on Chinese culture, life during the Ming dynasty, architecture and plants. A popular program offered at the Garden is the Enchanted Evening series in July and August. Visitors sip a cup of complimentary tea, enjoy a one-hour Chinese music program and then stroll through the garden. This is an especially nice place to go on a rainy day, as the walkways are covered and the tips of the eave tiles are designed to let the drops fall from them in a particularly gentle way.

DR. SUN YAT-SEN CLASSICAL CHINESE GARDEN

STANLEY PARK'S GARDEN DELIGHTS

The 404-hectare (1,000-acre) heavily-wooded Stanley Park has many attractions, including a variety of gardens. Of special interest in June and July is the Rose Garden, which features hundreds of roses divided in beds by colour. Also noteworthy, particularly in April and May, is the Ted and Mary Grieg Rhododendron Garden containing not only rhododendrons, but also camellias, magnolias, maples and azaleas. The park boasts many trails throughout the forested area. (See Stanley Park map, page 6)

STANLEY PARK

CENTURY GARDENS AT DEER LAKE PARK

If you like rhododendrons, Burnaby's official flower, this is the place to see a lot of them. Located on the grounds of the Burnaby Art Gallery, this garden was created in 1967 for Canada's centennial. The garden, which overlooks Deer Lake, also has a good collection of roses and azaleas.

CYCLING IN STANLEY PARK

PARK & TILFORD GARDENS

Created in 1968 by a privately owned distillery, these North Vancouver gardens have been preserved despite re-zoning and other changes in the area. The owners and merchants of the nearby Park & Tilford Shopping Centre now fund the gardens, which consist of separate theme gardens or outdoor rooms devoted to roses, herbs, rhododendrons and West Coast native plants as well as the White Garden (perennials), Asia Garden, Townhouse Garden, Yellow Garden, annual display gardens, hanging baskets, a Victorian greenhouse and a Florentine pergola covered in vines.

The gardens display plants suitable for the West Coast climate and are developed with organic methods and integrated pest management. Park & Tilford works with Capilano College's horticultural students and staff to create a unique, hands-on experience.

BELOW: STANLEY PARK

TREES GALORE

Vancouver has more flowering trees than any other city in Canada. Trees have been the lifeblood of the economy and define this place. Vancouverites are truly passionate about their trees. Tens of thousands of flowering cherry, plum, magnolia and dogwood trees make spring a delight throughout the city. As well as the tree collections in the public gardens listed here, consider a free tour of the Riverview Lands Davidson Arboretum. This collection of about 1,800 trees on the 244 acres of the Riverview Hospital grounds contains more than 150 varieties. It was one of the first arboreta in Canada, created around 1905.

In the Shaughnessy area is a round park in the middle of "The Crescent," one of the most prestigious addresses in town. This park has a collection of unusual trees, some of which are more than 100 years old. See if you can spot the Japanese Snowbell, Winged Euonymus, Pyramidal Blue Lawson Cypress or Eddie's White Wonder Dogwood, the latter developed right here in Vancouver. For a complete map, a listing, and much more on trees, see Gerald Straley's *Trees of Vancouver.*

Sports and Activities

Bob Mackin

Dragon boat race

In which North American city can you start the day on the golf course, go in-line skating at midday, hit the ski slopes or marina before sunset, then unwind at a professional hockey or football game? If you answered Vancouver, you're right. The city is a four-season destination for those who enjoy the sporting life as an observer, participant or both.

Baseball

Vancouver tried hard to get a Major League Baseball franchise in the 1980s, a main reason why BC Place Stadium was built. At the end of the 1990s, the city lost its Triple-A team, the Canadians, when a new owner moved it to Sacramento, California. The "Cs" broke a lot of hearts when they won the Pacific Coast League championship in their final home game and, a week later, won a North American championship.

A new minor league team, also named the Canadians, was launched in the summer of 2000. These Cs play at Nat Bailey Stadium, the same ballpark as their predecessors. The old-style stadium was built in 1951 in the shadow of Little Mountain and was originally called Capilano Stadium. It was renamed in 1978 for the late founder of White Spot Restaurants and owner of the Vancouver Mounties, a team that played there in the 1950s and 60s. The Vancouver Canadians' season runs from June to Labour Day. Tickets are priced from $7.50 to $11.25.

Dragon boat race

BC LIONS

FOOTBALL

The BC Lions are the only major sports tenant at the 60,000-seat BC Place Stadium. The Canadian Football League franchise, founded in 1954, moved from the outdoor Empire Stadium in East Vancouver to the downtown dome in 1983. Since then, the Lions' fortunes have fluctuated. It's always a struggle to bring the crowds indoors in summer, partly because the air-supported dome wasn't built with air conditioning. Action always intensifies after Labour Day, when the CFL's eight teams begin to jockey for playoff berths. (CFL games are played on larger fields than traditional American football and have three downs rather than four.) The most exciting moment in the Lions' history took place here in 1994. With no time left on the clock, veteran kicker Lui Passaglia kicked the winning field goal to win the Grey Cup. The season runs from June to November. Tickets range from $20 to $60.

HOCKEY

Vancouver has a rich hockey history. Its Millionaires played at the long-gone Denman Arena near Stanley Park and won the Stanley Cup in 1915.

    The National Hockey League's Vancouver Canucks haven't been so lucky. Founded in 1970, they lost in the Stanley Cup finals in both 1982 and 1994. In 1994, the playoffs went seven games until the New York Rangers came out on top. The team is rebuilding in the post-Pavel Bure era, and in 2003 was one of the top teams in the NHL — making their way to the semi-finals. The Canucks moved from their original rink, the Pacific Coliseum, in 1995 to the $160-million General Motors Place downtown (known locally as The Garage). It's next door to B.C. Place Stadium and nestled between the Georgia and

VANCOUVER CANUCKS

Dunsmuir viaducts. The Stadium SkyTrain station is across the street and False Creek and Chinatown are both a short walk away. Ticket prices at GM Place range from $35.25 to $144.50 including service charges and GST.

Beginning in fall 2001, hockey returned to the Pacific Coliseum in the form of the Vancouver Giants of the Western Hockey League, a major junior circuit throughout Western Canada and the US Pacific Northwest. Co-founded by hockey legends Gordie Howe and Pat Quinn, the team offers a glimpse of future NHL stars at a modest price. Tickets are between $15 and $17.

VANCOUVER CANUCKS

HORSERACING

Vancouver punters have the option of watching thoroughbreds or standardbreds race live, or via satellite feeds from racetracks around Canada, the US, Australia and Hong Kong. Hastings Racecourse on the Pacific National Exhibition grounds has perhaps the most scenic view of any track anywhere, with Burrard Inlet and the North Shore's Coast Mountains in the distance. Thoroughbred racing runs April through November with ample nearby paid parking and plenty of covered and indoor seating. Races from other tracks are simulcast year round. New owners, Woodbine Entertainment Group from

HASTINGS RACECOURSE

Ontario, have added considerable improvements in the past few years.

Surrey's Fraser Downs Raceway is located on the Cloverdale Fairgrounds 45 kilometres (28 miles) from Vancouver. Harness racing runs from September to May. A popular buffet restaurant with a view of the track operates on the second floor. Call for reservations. Improvements continue here, including track work and a redesigned homestretch.

OTHER SPECTATOR SPORTS

The False Creek waters near Science World host competing dragon boat teams in the latter half of June. The sport, similar to canoe racing, was imported from Hong Kong and remains a legacy of the 1986 world exposition, Expo 86. The Dragon Boat Festival is a weekend-long celebration of the city's ethnic diversity with teams representing a number of nationalities and causes.

In July, the streets at the east end of False Creek roar with the sound of ChampCar engines when the Championship Auto Racing Teams tour comes to town for the Molson Indy Vancouver. It's the biggest annual outdoor sporting event in Western Canada and was first run in 1990.

From May to September, the Whitecaps (both men's and women's teams) play soccer in the A-League with teams from around North America. The venue is Swangard Stadium in Burnaby's picturesque Central Park. The challenges are great in the A-League circuit, which is graded just below Major League Soccer, the US first division. Unlike Vancouver's other major sports teams, this one is stocked almost entirely with locals who rose through the ranks of amateur soccer. Tickets are $12 to $22.

RECREATIONAL SPORTS

There's no shortage of water in Vancouver for canoeing, kayaking or windsurfing. Deep Cove and Howe Sound are ideal for these activities, but nearby False Creek, Kitsilano and

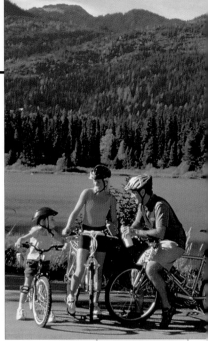

Ambleside are also viable options. Watch out for commercial vessels. Windsurfing's best local venue is English Bay, where rental equipment and lessons are available. Experts head to the blustery north end of Howe Sound in Squamish for some of North America's finest conditions.

Cycling around Vancouver is the best and fastest way of seeing the natural and man-made sights. Not all of Vancouver's streets and bridges are bicycle-friendly, though officials in the city and its suburbs have slowly moved to construct special routes dedicated to cyclists.

Favourite bicycle routes include the Richmond dike system on Lulu Island, passing through the fishing village of Steveston. Another popular route is the False Creek to Point Grey waterfront path. The Pacific Spirit Regional Park has a wealth of trails for all abilities. Whistler is also a cycling magnet. But the undisputed champ for popularity and accessibility is the Stanley Park seawall. Don't forget your helmet: it's the law to wear it while cycling.

Some people wouldn't take a walk in the park without a club, balls and a tee. Luckily, there are many places to do that in Vancouver. The area boasts a variety of public, private and semiprivate golf courses. For the novice, there are pitch-and-putt courses at Stanley Park and Queen Elizabeth Park. The University Golf Club, Langara and Fraserview are among the nearest to downtown. Richmond's Mayfair Lakes offers plenty of water hazards on what was once a farm. En route to Whistler, the Furry Creek course spills down a mountainside, providing unique challenges and an unbeatable view of Howe Sound. Continuing onward, the Whistler area now has five courses, designed by the likes of Jack Nicklaus, Arnold Palmer and Robert Trent Jones Junior.

CYCLING AT WHISTLER

GOLFING AT WHISTLER

Vancouver is known for its abundance of rain. But in the mountains on the North Shore, where it's higher and colder, winter sports enthusiasts will find a variety of recreation options. Grouse Mountain, Cypress Bowl and Mount Seymour all offer top-quality downhill and cross-country skiing and snowboarding. Grouse adds sleigh rides and outdoor ice skating. Cypress and Seymour are similarly popular with those who use toboggans and inner tubes. Grouse is the most accessible, with direct public transit service and a breathtaking aerial tram ride from its parking lot.

Hiking is another popular activity on the West Coast. You don't have to go far, either, to get away from the hustle and bustle of city life. In Vancouver, visit UBC's Pacific Spirit Regional Park and Stanley Park. In nearby Richmond, the dike system is flat and close to the Gulf of Georgia and the Fraser River. On the North Shore, Seymour and Cypress provincial parks offer a multitude of trails. Lighthouse Park in West Vancouver is another option, but the most challenging is the Grouse Grind, a 2.7-kilometre (1.6 mile) hike up Grouse Mountain. Depending on the avalanche risk, it's open from April through October. Summer hiking at Whistler offers spectacular views. When climbing or hiking in any of B.C.'s mountains, always be prepared with the proper equipment and clothing. Even on the sunniest days, the weather can be unpredictable.

If you'd rather have wheels on your two feet than two wheels and a seat, try in-line skating. Helmets, gloves, knee and elbow pads are highly recommended. The Stanley Park seawall isn't just for bikes. In fact, in-line skaters outnumber cyclists some summer days. For a more serene skate, try the wooded wonders of North Vancouver's Lower Seymour Conservation Reserve, until recently known as the Seymour Demonstration Forest.

There's no better place to relax or work up a sweat during the summertime than one of Vancouver's many

sandy beaches. Kitsilano and English Bay are the most popular, which means space is at a premium on the best days. You might want to try Second or Third Beach at Stanley Park, or venture westward toward the University of British Columbia to Jericho or Spanish Banks. If you can do without clothes, the clothing-optional Wreck Beach at the end of Point Grey is always an alternative. Another good bet is Ambleside, over the Lions Gate Bridge in West Vancouver. All are good for swimming, but the best outdoor swimming is at the 137-metre-long (450-foot) Kitsilano Pool, open mid-May to September. Indoors, it's the Vancouver Aquatic Centre on the north side of English Bay under the Burrard Street Bridge.

KIDS' STUFF

MARIAN GILMOUR

Children of every age, and those who are simply young at heart, can choose from a variety of interactive cultural activities or sample second-to-none outdoor experiences. Many of the best things in Vancouver are free. Almost every green space offers opportunities for play and the city's multicultural makeup lends excitement to just about every aspect of the city.

If it should happen to be raining, head for indoor venues such as Science World, the H.R. MacMillan Space Centre or the Vancouver Aquarium Marine Science Centre. The films shown at the CN IMAX Theatre at Canada Place and the Alcan OMNIMAX Theatre at Science World offer big-screen opportunities to experience adrenalin-inducing excitement from climbing mountains to underseas explorations. The size and intensity of these productions may be a bit overwhelming for younger children. Check with venue staff before taking the whole family.

Some of the attractions mentioned throughout this guide are seasonal, others are once-a-year special events. It is always wise to call ahead to find out what is going on the day you want to visit. Phone for hours, admission prices and travel directions.

OUTDOOR ATTRACTIONS

Hold on to your kids for a spectacular walk across the swaying wood and cable footbridge of the Capilano Suspension Bridge and Park. This popular North Shore attraction spans the Capilano River Canyon and hangs 69

CAPILANO SUSPENSION BRIDGE

metres over the raging river's waters. Towering evergreens, tall totem poles and Living Forest and Story Centre exhibits make this a quintessential West Coast experience. Also on the North Shore, Lynn Canyon Park hosts an Ecology Centre, great hiking and another swinging footbridge, which is 73 metres above the rapids of Lynn Creek.

The Van Dusen Botanical Garden is home to an Elizabethan hedge maze that kids will love to get lost in. The hedge is about five feet high and you'll enjoy going in with your younger children. There are wooden steps throughout so short people can climb up and discover they are not really lost. More than 6,500 diverse plants flourish in this 22-hectare garden. Young folks and old will find many living things to admire.

LYNN CANYON ECOLOGY CENTRE

The best urban walk in the forest can be found at Pacific Spirit Regional Park, which surrounds the University of British Columbia. It's a good place to experience a typical coastal forest with cedar and fir trees. Expect to share the 50 kilometres of trails with joggers, dog walkers, cyclists and horseback riders. Trail maps are available at the Park Centre on West 16th Avenue just west of Blanca Street.

Stanley Park offers numerous attractions spread throughout its 404 hectares (1,000 acres). Kids of all ages will want to ride the miniature train that travels almost a mile through a Pacific Northwest rainforest. The Children's Farmyard features barnyard animals and is always a hit with the younger set. Lower Brockton Oval features a display of totem poles that represent cultures of various BC First Nations.

Another great place for children to experience birds and animals is the Greater Vancouver Zoo in Aldergrove. Its park-like 48 hectares are home to 194 species of animals, including tigers, wolves, zebras, rhinoceroses, hippos and camels. The zoo is 48 kilometres east of Vancouver and is open year round. The Reifel Migratory Bird Sanctuary, located on Westham Island at the south arm of the Fraser

PLAYLAND AT THE PACIFIC NATIONAL EXHIBITION GROUNDS

River, provides an outing that goes well with a bag of seeds. Feed the birds or climb the four-storey wooden observation tower to get the big picture. Most paths are wheelchair accessible and there are picnic tables. North Vancouver's Maplewood Farm is a two-hectare petting farm of barnyard animals including rabbits, goats, cows, horses, donkeys, sheep and lots of ducks, geese and chickens. Little kids will love the big, white bunnies and the residents of the goat pen. The farm features seasonal special events and weekend pony rides in summer months.

Playland, open from April to the end of September, offers 35 outdoor rides ranging from the traditional wooden roller coaster and ferris wheel to the Ring of Fire and the Rainbow. There are also games and attractions and, of course, cotton candy and foot-long hot dogs. Playland is located on the Pacific National Exhibition grounds on East Hastings Street. Call for times and days.

VANCOUVER MARINE ANIMAL SCIENCE CENTRE

WATER PLAY

MAPLEWOOD FARM

Depending on the time of the year, Vancouver's eleven sandy ocean beaches offer fine swimming. The water temperature rises to approximately 65°F/18°C, perfect for a hot summer day. Lying in tidal pools, digging holes or building sandcastles and driftwood structures can be a lot of fun. Lifeguards are on duty from Victoria Day through Labour Day at Second Beach and Third Beach in Stanley Park, English Bay, Sunset Beach, Kitsilano Beach, Jericho Beach, Locarno Beach and Spanish Banks.

Kitsilano Pool is a huge outdoor heated pool and its

THIRD BEACH

graduated slope makes it excellent for small children. It's open from Victoria Day to mid-September. Second Beach Pool, in the heart of Stanley Park, is another favourite outdoor destination. After exhausting the pleasures of the pool's three small water slides, take a stroll to the nearby sandy beach or check out the ever-popular children's playground that boasts a real fire engine.

Truly fabulous indoor pools include the Vancouver Aquatic Centre, Burnaby's Eileen Dailly pool, New Westminster's Canada Games Pool and Surrey's Newton Wave Pool.

A swim in a clean, relatively warm mountain lake can be yours after a short trip to Sasamat Lake north of Ioco. There is no lifeguard at Sasamat, but it's the kind of place where older kids can spend the whole afternoon floating on inner tubes or air mattresses. Weekdays are definitely the preferred time to go to this popular local spot.

AT SECOND BEACH PLAYGROUND

The Granville Island Water Park and Adventure Playground offers water cannons (ground-level spouts that gush water), a safe waterslide and shallow wading areas. The park is supervised in season and parents can sit on the grass and enjoy the excitement. The Stanley Park Water Park, just north of Lumberman's Arch, offers much of the same action but also has equipment suitable for children with physical disabilities. Splashdown Park is located just before the Tsawwassen ferry terminal and offers a mile of twisting waterslides. There are also hot tubs, patios to picnic on, small slides for little kids, a toddlers' pool, video arcade and mini-golf.

CHILDREN'S CULTURE

Vancouver's premiere event for kids is the Vancouver International Children's Festival. Oceanfront Vanier Park becomes a festival village for this one-week event, which begins in late May. Outstanding international and top-notch local talent present fine-quality performing arts. After more than a quarter of a century, the festival still aims to create lifelong lovers of arts and culture. The purchase of show tickets includes admission to the festival site. Check out the box office at the festival gates for often-available rush tickets. Otherwise, a small fee allows you on-site to enjoy the roving entertainers, face painters and the multicultural community stage.

Spring break (mid-March) brings the Theatre Festival for Young Audiences to life. Five different companies offer performances at the Waterfront Theatre on Granville Island and Burnaby's Shadbolt Centre for the Arts. Year-round, the Vancouver East Cultural Centre (VECC), a delightful heritage performance space in the heart of the East Side, presents a Saturday afternoon Kids Series. Exciting musical or dramatic performances are offered about once a month.

The VECC's Youth Program offers those between the ages of fourteen and nineteen the chance to see almost any performance for a $2 admission fee. This is a true bargain since nearly all performances at the centre are outstanding. For a good laugh, take in the Vancouver International Comedy Festival, which runs the last 10 days of July on Granville Island. Outrageous and hilarious free street entertainment is presented every hour from noon to 5 p.m. Some ticketed events are suitable for families.

For longer stays with children, Arts Umbrella on Granville Island offers a wide range of exciting classes for young folk. Several classes hold year-end public performances in late May and early June. Dancers (modern, tap and ballet) as well as actors, animators and filmmakers showcase their work at public venues.

On the third Sunday of each month, the Vancouver Art Gallery offers SuperSunday, an opportunity for families with school-aged children to experience art in a new way. An annual visual arts show by budding artists is also mounted at the Buschlen Mowatt Gallery at the end of May.

Young readers take a place of honour at the Vancouver International Writers (& Readers) Festival. Held in October at various Granville Island locations, the festival dedicates three days to children's events. Twelve months of the year, head for the lower level of the Vancouver Public Library at Library Square. The area is devoted to children. Kids can spend hours cruising the picture books, but there are also computers available and a great selection of children's reference works, foreign language books and videos. Displays of children's art are often featured. If you're buying books, Vancouver's Kidsbooks on West 4th Avenue treats kids as serious readers. From time to time, they offer readings, book launches and

FUN AT THIRD BEACH

WRITERS FESTIVAL

book signings with favourite authors. The knowledgeable staff and the outstanding collection of books make this a delightful place to shop and browse.

HISTORY AND LIVING CULTURE

The Cedar Cottage/Trout Lake Pow Wow held at Trout Lake Community Centre on Mother's Day weekend offers a glimpse into the rich cultural traditions of Canada's First Nations people. This event features intertribal dancing and drumming, hoop dancing, a princess pageant, and arts and crafts displays.

B.C. SPORTS HALL OF FAME

FIRST NATIONS DANCING

Take a walk into the past at the Burnaby Village Museum and Carousel. More than thirty authentically restored buildings and a costumed staff recreate a 1920s village. There are hands-on activities for children and seasonal special events at Christmas and throughout the year. There is also a beautifully restored C.W. Parker Carousel, circa 1912. Open seven days a week from late April to September and in December. The Fort Langley National Historic Park marks the site of a reconstructed Hudson's Bay Company post. Open year-round, children can see and sample life as it was in the last century.

The BC Sports Hall of Fame, located at Gate A in BC Place Stadium, is more than a collection of medals, trophies, personal mementoes and photographs. High-energy kids can get a workout in the Participation Gallery, climbing a rock wall, testing their pitching arm or sprinting against the clock.

FORT LANGLEY

ANNUAL EVENTS

GAIL BUENTE

PAINTED DRAGON PROWS

SNOWSHOEING AT WHISTLER RESORT

Vancouver is known as a city of hale-and-hearty outdoor types who spend their leisure time communing with nature. What isn't so well-known is that these rugged individualists are also fiercely loyal to their festivals and cultural events. Whether it be Canadianized versions of age-old celebrations of its many ethnic groups, or brand-new locally created traditions, Vancouverites treasure their annual festivals.

WINTER

During the holiday season, two Vancouver traditions really stand out: the Christmas Carol Ships, a musical sail around Burrard Inlet and False Creek, and New Year's Day's notorious Polar Bear Swim at English Bay, proving that Vancouver is indeed the tropics of Canada. A third outdoor winter tradition, the Annual Winter Eagle Festival in the Squamish-Brackendale area 74 km (46 miles) north of Vancouver, has become immensely popular. An eagle count is taken just after the New Year. During the past twenty-plus years, tallies have ranged from 1,500 to a world-record high of 3,766. Throughout the month of January, guided walks, concerts, a photo contest and an eagle art show round out the main event.

Instead of celebrating winter, many Vancouverites spend the cold months looking ahead to summer. In the dead of February they hide out at BC Place Stadium,

DRAGON BOAT RACE

daydreaming at the Annual Boat Show, and soon after at the Home and Garden Show.

SPRING

Springtime starts in March with a gathering of wine enthusiasts at the Annual International Wine Festival. Held at the Vancouver Convention and Exhibition Centre as a fundraiser for the Vancouver Playhouse, it's a lavish week-long wine and culinary event.

By May, the festivals have begun to bud, a hint of the blossoming that takes place in the summer months. One bright May morning, thousands of runners from across North America and around the world arrive to participate in the Adidas Vancouver International Marathon, Canada's largest marathon.

Kids have a festival all their own in late May, though it's just as much fun for older folk. Featuring dance, theatre, music, puppets and clowns, the Vancouver International Children's Festival is unquestionably one of the high points of the spring season.

In June, False Creek fills up with dragon-prowed boats for the annual Alcan Dragon Boat Festival. As legend has it, dragon boats began 2,000 years ago in Chou Dynasty China. These days, dragon boat races are a spectacle of rare beauty. Each brightly painted twelve-metre boat is powered by a team of twenty, all paddling in unison to the beat of a drum. The Vancouver race is the largest dragon boat festival in North America, and one of the best in the world.

JAZZ FESTIVAL IN DAVID LAM PARK

SUMMER

Summer in Vancouver is a non-stop festival. Leading off the season from the end of June into July is the du Maurier International Jazz Festival. It promises something for every jazz lover, and it's not false advertising. With nearly 400 performances in 40 clubs and halls, plus dozens of free outdoor concerts, the offerings range from hot to cool, from familiar standards to wild innovations. Truly international in scope, the Jazz Festival embraces Brazilian samba, African soukous, European free jazz, Asian fusion and North American blues, to name a few.

BARD ON THE BEACH

Throughout the summer months, a professional Shakespeare festival known as Bard on the Beach takes over Vanier Park in Kitsilano. Productions are staged in a backless tent, so the audience can enjoy the play, the sailboats gliding past the cityscape and the glow of sunset on the distant mountains. It's a truly magical backdrop to the performances.

CELEBRATION OF LIGHT FESTIVAL

Tickets often sell out for this popular series, so make a reservation to ensure a seat.

Mid-July is the "folkal" point of the summer for about 25,000 diehard fans at the Vancouver International Folk Music Festival. Crowds have gathered at Jericho Beach Park annually for more than twenty years to listen to hundreds of artists sing and play. The following weekend, folkies who want something smaller and more intimate head out to the Mission Folk Festival in the Fraser Valley.

July also brings the Vancouver International Comedy Festival, the Symphony of Fire Fireworks Festival and the Illuminares Lantern Festival, a community-based paper lantern festival that now attracts a crowd of thousands while retaining its magical neighbourhood feel. Out of town, the Harrison Festival of the Arts focuses on international Afro-Latin cultures in the spa town of Harrison Hot Springs.

The fun continues in late July, when those who love speed and fanfare line the banks of False Creek for the annual Molson Indy race.

In just a few years since its inception in 2000, Festival Vancouver has become one of the must-see events on the festival calendar. During the first two weeks in August, a remarkable array of themed classical, jazz and world music concerts feature top-notch local and touring artists from around the world at venues throughout the city.

In mid-August, all eyes are on the sky at the Abbotsford International Airshow, held in Abbotsford, B.C., about an hour's drive from Vancouver.

The final fling of summer is the Pacific National Exhibition (PNE), held during the final two weeks of August. Take the kids to visit the petting farm, ride the roller coaster and chow down on corn dogs and candy floss. Be sure not to miss the Demolition Derby. It's good, old-fashioned familyfun.

HARRISON FESTIVAL OF THE ARTS

FALL

Summer officially ends with the close of the PNE on Labour Day weekend, but there's no need to slow down quite yet. Visitors can still look forward to a weekend of camping out at the Chilliwack Bluegrass Festival. Or come inside and immerse yourself in one of the fall performance festivals. The Vancouver Fringe Festival, for two weeks in September, is a theatre event for those who enjoy a gamble. Combining established and emerging performing companies, the productions are wildly varied. You're always sure to find at least one unexpected gem in the lineup.

Next comes the Vancouver International Film Festival, one of the finest film festivals on the continent. It has a reputation for innovative yet accessible programming, with an emphasis on films from Canada and Pacific Rim countries.

Taking place on Granville Island in October, the Vancouver International Writers & Readers Festival is a week of readings, roundtable discussions and talks by the most exciting writers from around the world and around the corner. There's nothing dry about this festival of books; the atmosphere is always relaxed and festive. Some of the most popular events are The Sunday Brunch with visiting authors; the Poetry Bash; and the Literary Cabaret, each a feast of words, music, food and drink. Some of the readings are planned with young people in mind. French-language writers are also featured.

WRITERS FESTIVAL

VANCOUVER
NEIGHBOURHOODS

DOWNTOWN

BARBARA TOWELL

Vancouver is a relatively new city. In 1884, William Van Horne, the influential general manager of the Canadian Pacific Railway, visited what was then the logging village of Granville. He made two recommendations: that the tiny village of approximately 100 buildings become the terminus of the first cross-Canada railway, and that it be renamed Vancouver. In spite of the Great Fire of June 13, 1886, which totally destroyed the new city, a boom was on. By 1889, more than 10,000 people lived here. The Greater Vancouver area today numbers more than 2 million people.

Throughout its brief history, Vancouverites have fought hard to preserve the city's heritage buildings. Downtown Vancouver is proof of some success. A walk in the area reveals a satisfying mix of old and new. Old here means buildings from the late nineteenth century and early twentieth century. New is as recent as the Vancouver Public Library's central branch, which opened in 1995.

Vancouver's history can be traced through the architecture of its downtown core, which encompasses West Georgia Street to the south, Burrard Street to the west, Cordova Street on the waterfront to the north (look for the mountains) and Cambie Street to the east. It's fair to say that politics, business and faith shaped the city. The result is an eclectic mix of buildings, starting from the château-like

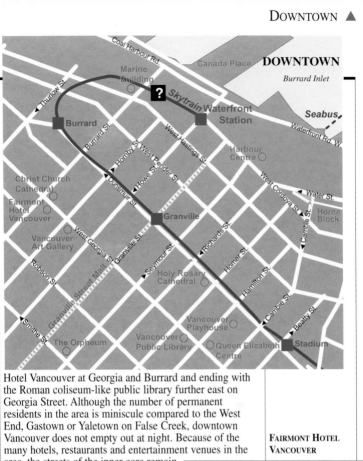

DOWNTOWN

Burrard Inlet

Hotel Vancouver at Georgia and Burrard and ending with the Roman coliseum-like public library further east on Georgia Street. Although the number of permanent residents in the area is miniscule compared to the West End, Gastown or Yaletown on False Creek, downtown Vancouver does not empty out at night. Because of the many hotels, restaurants and entertainment venues in the area, the streets of the inner core remain fairly busy until midnight.

FAIRMONT HOTEL VANCOUVER

FAIRMONT HOTEL VANCOUVER

First came the Canadian Pacific Railway (CPR), then came progress. Our walk begins at the corner of Georgia and Burrard where, in 1928, construction began on the Hotel Vancouver. This grand hotel, designed by the CPR in the impressive style of its Château Lake Louise and Banff Springs Hotel, would convince travellers that Vancouver was not a damp parochial backwater but a glistening modern metropolis. The next year, the stock market crashed and construction came to a standstill. For nearly a decade, the hotel's unfinished steel skeleton stood as a reminder of grim economic times. Only the impending

87

CHRIST CHURCH CATHEDRAL

royal visit of King George VI in 1939 brought about its hasty completion.

In the intervening period between start and completion, tastes changed. Ideas of tradition gave way to faith in the modern. As a result, the lower arcade, lobby and VIP suites were finished in an Art Deco style rather than the original classical approach. When Hilton took over management in the 1960s, much of the interior was redecorated yet again. Modernization now meant returning the lobby to a more classical form. The most impressive features of the Fairmont Hotel Vancouver today remain its steep green copper roof and its sly, slightly impish gargoyles.

CHRIST CHURCH CATHEDRAL

Across the street from the Fairmont Hotel Vancouver is the lovely and vibrant Christ Church Cathedral (690 Burrard Street), seat of the New Westminster Anglican Diocese. Designed by C.O. Wickenden, churches in this Gothic-revival style thrived in Canada in the nineteenth century, with each denomination mounting its own modifications (compare the Catholic Holy Rosary Cathedral noted later). The austere lines and interior atmosphere of Christ Church speak of its ties to Britain. Christ Church was built to serve the growing population of the city's West End, but initial funds were sparse. The inaugural service on October 6, 1889, was held in a granite basement, the only finished part of the building. In the aptly named "Root House," fifty-two parishioners were warmed by a coal-fire boiler. To raise money, parishioners purchased stock in the church's

DOWNTOWN SHOPPERS

construction company. Within six years, the sandstone structure was complete, with additions in 1909 and 1940. The interior boasts an impressive ceiling with beams of Douglas fir. Of the church's twenty-nine stained-glass windows, three are by William Morris. They were acquired in 1984 on permanent loan from the Vancouver Museum and can be seen on the north-facing wall on the west side. The first organ was installed in 1895, employing an organ blower at the rate of five dollars a month. The pipes of the second organ can be seen in the church, though they are no longer functional. Be sure to check out the regular musical events taking place here. Information is available at the church or on their website at www.cathedral.vancouver.bc.ca.

As with many of Vancouver's older buildings, the cathedral was threatened with demolition in more modern times. In 1976, after five years of lobbying, the building was named a "Class A" heritage site by the municipality.

MARINE BUILDING

A five-minute walk north along Burrard Street towards the mountains brings you to the spectacular Marine Building (355 Burrard). Erected in the Art Deco style, its construction cost its Toronto-based developers $2.5 million in 1929. By 1930, the developers were broke and offered the building to the city for $1 million. When legislators refused to pay, Britain's Guinness family spotted a bargain and stepped in, purchasing it for much less. The same fiscally astute family built the Lions Gate Bridge in 1938, and ran it as a toll bridge until it was sold to the B.C. government in 1963.

The Marine Building's architects, McCarter and Nairne, suggested a design reminiscent of a "great crag rising from the sea, clinging with sea flora and fauna, tinted in sea-green, touched with gold." Indeed, no other Vancouver building is more finely finished. No visit to the Marine Building would be complete without a venture inside, through its extraordinary front door with its bronze grills and Art Deco zigzags. The lobby's walls include terra cotta friezes depicting the history of transportation and the colonial discovery of the Pacific Coast. The building was restored in 1989.

MARINE BUILDING

**MARINE BUILDING
EXTERIOR DETAILING
AND INTERIOR
(BELOW)**

WATERFRONT STATION

Crossing over to West Cordova, proceed past Canada Place with its five white "sails" to Waterfront Station, built by the Canadian Pacific Railway (601 West Cordova) in 1914. The present edifice was preceded by two earlier ones, a timber structure in 1887 (where the first passenger train arrived on May 23, 1887) and a château-style station in 1898-99. Waterfront Station was the only building in Vancouver designed by the firm of Barott, Blackader and Webster. In the words of architectural historian Harold Kalman, their creation is the most "self-consciously pompous building type [made] in the early part of the century." It is indeed a grand terminus with its expansive column façade and pilastered waiting room. It now serves as an entrance to both SkyTrain and SeaBus public transit systems.

Shops fill the former waiting room, but the public aspect of the site has eroded, as there are no longer public washrooms and seating is scant. Paintings on the upper walls depict Canadian landscapes set in the West. The building was restored in 1976-77.

SINCLAIR CENTRE

SINCLAIR CENTRE

Crossing Cordova, you can enter the Sinclair Centre from its rear entrance or head a block up the hill to its main entrance at 757 West Hastings Street. The building was completed by the department of public works in 1910 to house the post office and other federal offices. In 1939, an extension was added at 325 Granville Street. The two "faces" of the Sinclair Centre reflect very distinct economic periods.

The original building was executed in an Edwardian Baroque style that married architectural influences from both the French and English. Built for $600,000, its rusticated granite basement continues up to smooth columns reaching past the second and third floors. The fourth floor includes dormer windows. The entire structure is finished off with an impressive clock tower. The granite exterior hides an early example of a fireproof steel frame.

King George VI was kept busy on his royal visit to Vancouver in 1939. He not only opened the Hotel Vancouver but also the extension to the post office. The addition could not be more contrary to the design and intent of the original building. The first building was erected during Vancouver's construction and land speculation boom. As a result, it is highly ornate, expressing optimism in the future wealth of the country. The extension, on the other hand, was finished at the tail end of the Depression. Its exterior walls are bereft of decoration except a minimal application of pilasters used to harmonize with its predecessor. Interestingly, it was the original building, not the extension, that was occupied in 1935 by 750 unemployed men, as it more aptly captured the spirit of federal power. Their demands for relief led to a violent backlash from police and a number of the protesters were hospitalized.

HARBOUR CENTRE TOWER

The Sinclair Centre is now a shopping mall, retaining many of its original architectural and decorative highlights.

HARBOUR CENTRE AREA

Exit the Sinclair Centre on Hastings Street and walk east to Simon Fraser University's Harbour Centre at 515 West Hastings Street. There is usually a small but interesting art show in its impressive modern lobby. Downstairs is a good bookstore and a food fair. The Harbour Centre Tower is home to the Lookout!, a visitor attraction. Not notable architecturally, the tower does offer one of the finest views in the city.

A block away, at 342 Richards Street, the Century House is worth a peek. Designed by J.S.D. Taylor and completed in 1912, it is noteworthy not because of its classical style (there are other, finer examples to be found), but for a particular detail which is best described as magic realism: the building is crowned with a pair of winged beavers. One can only wonder how contemporaries viewed these particularly whimsical little creatures which are part beaver and part bird. The best view is from across the street.

WINGED BEAVERS ON CENTURY HOUSE

Continuing south along Richards to Pender Street, note the neon waterfall of the former Niagara Hotel, now Ramada Inn (435 West Pender). Fifty years ago, Vancouver was ablaze with neon, winning it the title of the neon capital of North America. It's hard to imagine a landscape where the Ramada Inn's sign could be considered modest, but in neon's heyday there was one neon sign for every eighteen residents. Suburban expansion in the 1960s linked neon with urban decay. Modernization of the downtown core proved to be the demise of neon in Vancouver. The Vancouver Museum now houses a sampling of Vancouver's neon history.

HOLY ROSARY CATHEDRAL

Back on Richards Street, you can't miss the Holy Rosary Cathedral (646 Richards). In 1900, when most of Vancouver's buildings were no higher than three stories, the cathedral's twenty-one-storey peak must have cast an impressive shadow. Built during a period of considerable church debt, some parishioners questioned the sense of the monumental Gothic-revival structure. The building was dubbed McGuckin's Folly after the priest whose efforts made construction possible.

Built of Gabriola Island sandstone with granite foundations, the church's asymmetrical towers are its most prominent visual feature. The cathedral bells are of particular auditory interest. In the east tower, eight bells are tuned to a full octave, producing up to 5,000 different sequences. Inside the cathedral, granite-encased marble columns support an arched ceiling. Among the many stained-glass windows are eight depicting biblical scenes. Visitors are welcome.

TAKING IN THE SIGHTS

HOLY ROSARY CATHEDRAL

LIBRARY SQUARE

Continue south a few more blocks to Georgia Street, then head east to Library Square, the home of the Vancouver Public Library's central branch (350 West Georgia). Described as a rectangle within an ellipse, the controversial design by Moshe Safdie & Associates with Downs/Archambault and Partners resembles a Roman coliseum. Opened in 1995, the nine-storey-high structure houses the library, an adjoining office tower and retail shops on the lower level concourse. Library Square includes two outdoor plazas, which often host special events. The concourse, with its six-storey-high view of the internal workings of the library, is a great place to catch your breath over an excellent cup of coffee, a slice of pizza or an ice cream cone. Sit, sip and do some serious people watching.

WEST END

JAMES OAKES

DAVIE STREET

The West End is Vancouver's original residential neighbourhood, occupying the western half of the city's downtown peninsula. Once home to blue bloods living in stately mansions surrounded by gardens and quiet streets, the area has evolved into a remarkably diverse community — home to single parents, upwardly mobile singles, gays and lesbians, foreign students, recent immigrants, senior citizens, low-income transients, condo owners and wealthy retirees. The West End, in short, is a success story of urban livability that is the envy of cities across North America.

BOUNDARIES

The West End is the most densely populated square kilometre in Canada. Zoning maps show Georgia and

MANHATTAN BUILDING

Burrard Streets as the northern and eastern boundaries, while Stanley Park and English Bay create the western and

southern extremes. Laid out on a simple grid pattern, the main streets of the West End running east/west are Beach, Davie, Robson and Georgia. The main north/south streets are Denman, Thurlow and Burrard. Included within the West End's boundaries are three distinct commercial zones, running along Robson, Davie and Denman streets. Public transit

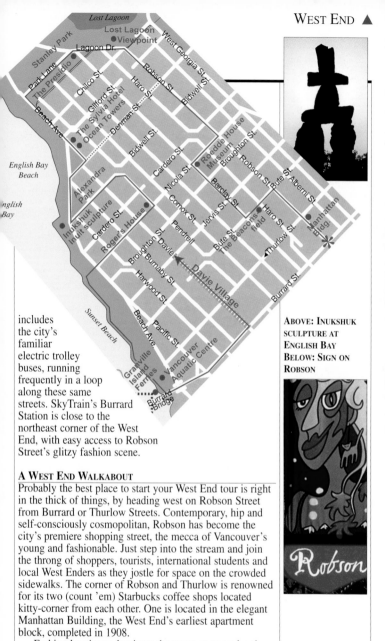

The following map labels appear:

Lost Lagoon
Lost Lagoon Viewpoint
Lagoon Dr.
West Georgia St.
Stanley Park
Park Lane
The Presidio
Chilco St.
Gifford St.
Haro St.
Robson St.
Bidwell St.
Beach Ave.
The Sylvia Hotel
Ocean Towers
Denman St.
English Bay Beach
Bidwell St.
Cardero St.
Roedde House Museum
Broughton St.
English Bay
Alexandra Park
Nicola St.
Robson St.
Bute St.
Alberni St.
Inukshuk Inuit sculpture
Cardero St.
Rogers House
Comox St.
Barclay St.
Jervis St.
Haro St.
The Beaconsfield
Thurlow St.
Manhattan Bldg.
Broughton St.
Davie
Pendrell
Bute St.
Burnaby St.
Davie Village
Harwood St.
Burrard St.
Sunset Beach
Beach Ave.
Pacific St.
Granville Island Ferries
Vancouver Aquatic Centre
Burrard Bridge

ABOVE: INUKSHUK
SCULPTURE AT
ENGLISH BAY
BELOW: SIGN ON
ROBSON

includes the city's familiar electric trolley buses, running frequently in a loop along these same streets. SkyTrain's Burrard Station is close to the northeast corner of the West End, with easy access to Robson Street's glitzy fashion scene.

A WEST END WALKABOUT

Probably the best place to start your West End tour is right in the thick of things, by heading west on Robson Street from Burrard or Thurlow Streets. Contemporary, hip and self-consciously cosmopolitan, Robson has become the city's premiere shopping street, the mecca of Vancouver's young and fashionable. Just step into the stream and join the throng of shoppers, tourists, international students and local West Enders as they jostle for space on the crowded sidewalks. The corner of Robson and Thurlow is renowned for its two (count 'em) Starbucks coffee shops located kitty-corner from each other. One is located in the elegant Manhattan Building, the West End's earliest apartment block, completed in 1908.

Fashion boutiques dominate the scene at street level along the next block of Robson, overlooked by an excellent selection of upstairs restaurants, including Tsunami Sushi, Moxies, CinCin and Zefferelli's. You can continue along the high-energy Robson stroll for several more blocks, but try venturing into the heart of the residential West End by taking a left at Bute Street. You'll soon come to a leafy little park complete with benches and flower beds. Overlooking it is The Beaconsfield, a stately, if somewhat run-down, stone and brick structure. This is one of the West End's oldest remaining apartment buildings.

Three blocks further on (take a right at Barclay Street

ROEDDE HOUSE MUSEUM

and proceed down the hill to Broughton Street), you'll come to the Roedde House Museum (1415 Barclay), another architectural treasure of the West End. Roedde House stands among a collection of restored, late nineteenth century wood-frame houses in Barclay Heritage Square. Carefully restored with period furnishings and décor, the museum is a journey back in time to the height of Victorian and Edwardian elegance.

After soaking in the atmosphere, head back out to Robson Street and continue west down the hill towards Stanley Park. Although the lower end of Robson is being gentrified with upscale shops and condominiums, it has the friendly atmosphere of an urban village with green grocers, pizza shops, video rental outlets and a 1960s-style Safeway.

On the far side of Denman Street, in the exclusive area known to locals and realtors as "West of Denman," Robson becomes strictly residential for its final two blocks until it merges with Lagoon Drive. Here, on a slope overlooking Lost Lagoon, visitors are greeted with one of the best city views, a 180° panorama of Stanley Park, Coal Harbour and the North Shore mountains.

Admire the view while walking south along Lagoon Drive, but when you reach Nelson Street take a moment and look upwards at the row of high-rises bordering the park. Standing among the conventional 1960s and 1970s towers, is the post-modernist Presidio, designed by Vancouver architect Richard Henriques, who in turn was inspired by Austrian architect Adolf Loos' Villa Karma near Montreaux, Switzerland. Many of the Presidio's multimillion dollar suites were purchased in the early 1990s by offshore buyers who reportedly enjoy their residences for only a few weeks every year. Once you've come back to earth, follow the pedestrian path running along the edge of the park until you come to Beach Avenue and the shores of English Bay.

THE SEASIDE

ENGLISH BAY JOGGER

Swimmers began flocking to English Bay when the West End was first developed in the 1890s. By the turn of the twentieth century, summertime crowds travelled to the popular bathing beach on the newly opened Robson and Denman streetcar line. Today, the Brighton-style pier has long since disappeared, but the holiday-resort atmosphere along the beach is as strong as ever. At the first sign of a sunny day, the area is invaded by sunbathers, beach lovers, dog walkers and windsurfers.

The ivy-clad Sylvia Hotel on Beach Avenue, overlooking English Bay, still offers visitors perhaps the best accommodation location-wise for the money. It was built in 1911 as the Sylvia Court Apartments before the Depression forced the owner to rent it out as a seamen's hostel. After the war, it moved upscale and branched out into the liquor business, opening the city's first cocktail bar in July 1954, thus allowing Vancouverites to enjoy a civilized cocktail at long last. You can still admire the view of the bay over a cocktail in what remains one of Vancouver's best bars.

THE SYLVIA HOTEL

Next door to the Sylvia, at 1835 Morton Avenue, stands the Ocean Towers, a jazzily shaped apartment building dating from 1957. Across the street, at the intersection of Denman and Davie, a cluster of imported palm trees completes the exotic "British California" ambiance. Take a brief side trip along Denman Street, which offers beachwear, bicycle rentals, cappuccinos, a fresh juice bar and an amazing variety of international cuisine. Pedestrians like to think they rule the street and traffic moves by at a crawl.

Don't forget that English Bay is also an evening destination. Locals and visitors come out to walk along the seawall promenade, listen to musicians and watch the sunset beyond the anchored freighters and the mountains of Vancouver Island. During the annual Celebration of Light fireworks festival in July and August, upwards of 300,000 people gather around the bay to watch the spectacular international displays.

ALEXANDRA PARK BANDSTAND

At the eastern most end of the English Bay beach, you'll find an Inuit sculpture by Alvin Kanak. Commissioned by the Northwest Territories for Expo 86, the large granite blocks represent a human figure with welcoming, outstretched arms and is based on the signposts that guide hunters in the North.

From here, cross Beach Avenue at the pedestrian light to the lovely Alexandra Park, named after the consort of King Edward VII. It boasts a pretty wooden bandstand constructed in 1914 for outdoor concerts, as well as a marble fountain adorned with a brass plaque honouring the city's beloved Seraphim "Joe" Fortes. Generations of

GRANVILLE ISLAND FERRIES

children learned to swim from this Barbadian immigrant, who acted as lifeguard and special constable at English Bay until his death in 1922.

From the northeast corner of the park, walk north on Bidwell to Davie Street, turn left, and head up the hill until you come to the impressive Roger's House at 1531 Davie. One of the last survivors of the West End's age of opulence, this elegant mansion-turned-restaurant was designed by Samuel Maclure, one of the most prolific architects of well-heeled Vancouver society, for local sugar magnate Benjamin Tingley Rogers.

To continue exploring the West End's southern flank, return to the seashore via Nicola Street and then stroll toward the Burrard Street Bridge until you arrive at Sunset Beach. This marks the end of the English Bay Seawall and the entrance to False Creek. At the foot of Thurlow Street stands the Vancouver Aquatic Centre, which houses a fifty-metre pool, a children's pool and a diving tank, among other indoor recreation facilities. Behind the Aquatic Centre you'll find the West End landing of the Granville Island ferries. The little passenger ferries run regularly from dawn until dusk, serving English Bay, Vanier Park in Kitsilano Point and Granville Island.

ROGER'S HOUSE

THE TWENTY-FOUR-HOUR VILLAGE

Our final destination, what's becoming known as Davie Village, is bit of a hike back up on the West End's central plateau. Just follow the pedestrian path across from the entrance to the Aquatic Centre, which leads to the north end of the Burrard Street Bridge. From there, walk north along Burrard Street for three blocks then hang a left when you come to a pair of gas stations at the corner of Davie Street.

Here's where you'll find the locals going about their daily routines: picking up the dry-cleaning, checking their e-mail at the Internet cafe, buying groceries at the 24-hour

DAVIE VILLAGE

supermarket, getting a prescription filled at the mega-drugstore or having a meal at one of the many reasonably priced ethnic restaurants along the street.

And just in case you hadn't noticed the profusion of rainbow freedom flags along the street, Davie Village is also the traditional core of Vancouver's gay community, with clubs, bookstores, and cafes located close by. The busy Gay and Lesbian Centre on Bute Street houses a drop-in centre, lounge and library. By night, Davie supports a lively social scene. Gay bars like Numbers, The Fountainhead and Pumpjacks are usually packed. Several all-night eateries are open to all. For midnight snacks, try the Fresco Inn, Hamburger Mary's, or the Oasis, a relaxed piano bar where unrepentant smokers can still enjoy a puff on the outdoor patio. It's all part of life on the wild side in Vancouver's swingin' West End.

GASTOWN

LEANORE SALI

Stand in Maple Tree Square looking west along Water Street. The red-brick streets of Gastown are bustling with people. Local residents stop to chat with their neighbours, international students rush to their classes, business people dodge the throngs to make their luncheon appointments and visitors from around the world wander through the shops and restaurants, stopping en route to pose for photographs by Gastown's world-famous steam clock. In Gastown, residents and tourists have learned to enjoy life in the streets in much the same way Europeans do.

The handsome façades of the brick buildings reveal a mix of antique stores, boutiques and street-level galleries that contain a broad selection of Canadian First Nations art. In restaurants housed in former warehouses, diners are offered a variety of cuisine and price ranges. The nightlife is lively with a selection

GASTOWN

STEAM CLOCK

of nightclubs, cabarets and pubs that cater to every age group.

Although Gastown still remains a favourite location for architectural firms, design companies, music promoters and advertising agencies, it is also beginning to attract other young urban professionals.

GASTOWN'S HISTORIC PAST

The original name of the small settlement around which Vancouver grew was unofficially known as Gastown. The first settler was Captain John "Gassy Jack" Deighton, a Yorkshire man who'd been a sailor, prospector, steamboat pilot and saloon keeper. Gassy Jack arrived at Burrard Inlet in the fall of 1867, opened his Globe saloon and prospered. Almost immediately others came to join him.

By the 1870s, Gastown was a multicultural community of saloons, hotels and grocery stores catering to mill workers, lumbermen, ships' crews and whalers. During the next decade, the community underwent a growth spurt following the announcement that it would be the site of the Canadian Pacific Railway terminus. By 1886, it had 1,000 buildings and 3,000 residents. On April 6 of that year, it was officially renamed Vancouver.

Shortly after, on June 13, 1886, a brush-clearing fire blazed out of control and burned the town to the ground. While destroying the old town, the Great Fire spurred the biggest building boom in West Coast history. The area prospered until Vancouver's economic boom collapsed in 1914. From the 1930s to the 1950s, Gastown, once the heart of Vancouver, became a virtual backwater.

Gastown remained in decline until the early 1960s when a few enterprising merchants and property owners, recognizing the architectural heritage underneath the grime of the old buildings, began to put some money into

EUROPE HOTEL

restoring them. City Hall joined in the cause. New street lamps were installed, streets and sidewalks were bricked, and the meandering courtyards and mews were left intact. In 1971, the Province of British Columbia designated Gastown a historic district.

GASTOWN TOUR

Start your tour at Gassy Jack's statue in Maple Tree Square. Facing east, you'll see the Europe Hotel, built in 1908 by Angelo Calori. A flatiron-shaped building, built to fit the triangular-shaped lot, the Europe was the earliest reinforced concrete structure in Canada and the first fireproof hotel in Western Canada.

The building directly behind Gassy Jack's statue is the Byrnes Block (2-8 Water Street). Built in 1886 by George Byrnes, a former sheriff of the Cariboo during the gold rush days, this was one of the first brick buildings in Vancouver. It once housed the Alhambra Hotel, one of the city's fancier establishments at the time.

Take the entrance off Carrall Street to the central courtyard known as Gaolers Mews. This is where the town's first jail and the home of Gastown's first constable were located. Vancouver's first city council meeting was held here. The site later housed the city's first post office and later the city's first fire hall. The building was renovated in 1974 to create the interior courtyard and office and retail complex.

THE OLD SPAGHETTI FACTORY

Exit onto Water Street. As you stroll west along Water, take the time to browse through the many galleries and shops along the way. Many galleries specialize in West Coast and Inuit art, offering the largest selection in Western Canada and representing internationally renowned First Nations artists.

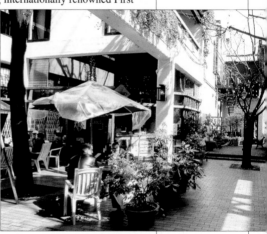

On the north side of the street you'll see a large building housing the Old Spaghetti Factory Restaurant (55 Water). It was built in 1907 as the warehouse and headquarters for Malkins, one of BC's main food wholesalers. The upper floors were renovated in 2002 to accommodate live-work studios.

Continue along Water Street crossing to the north side at the corner of Water and Abbott Streets. As you continue your stroll west along Water, notice the courtyard, built in 1974 and designed to blend in with its older neighbours. Just west of the courtyard is 139 Water Street, built in 1898 as the first warehouse for Malkin's wholesale grocery business. Renovated in 1996 into apartments, this building is an excellent example of Gastown living today.

GAOLERS MEWS

Across the street, under the Gastown Parkade, a new and innovative educational and cultural experience opens in 2004. Called Storyeum, the 9,290-sq. metre (100,000-sq. ft) indoor venue will showcase the colourful history of Canada's West Coast. Storyeum's creativity is bound to add yet more pizazz to the area.

At the corner of Water and Cambie Streets is Gastown's famous steam clock. Although built in 1977, the movements of the steam clock are based on an 1875

WATER STREET

design. A continuous supply of steam feeds the clockworks from the steam vent beneath the street. Cross over to the south side of the street. The red-brick building on the southeast corner of Water and Cambie is known as the Leckie Building. It was built in 1910 by the Leckie family as a shoe and boot factory. Renovated in 1990 for office and retail use, the Leckie Building is an excellent example of the timber construction used in early Gastown buildings.

Stroll south on Cambie to Cordova Street. Turn right at the corner and meander west along Cordova. The buildings along this strip of Cordova Street once housed merchants outfitting gold seekers headed for the Klondike. Today, the area specializes in antique stores and boutiques offering clothes by Vancouver fashion designers. The building on the northwest corner of Cambie and Cordova was built in 1888. It was known as the Masonic Temple as it housed the Masonic Grand Lodge. Next door is the Horne Block, built by land investor and city politician J.W. Horne. Designed by Nathaniel Stonestreet Hoffar, the city's first important architect, the Horne Block was the mid-1880s most exquisite venture into the Victorian Italianate style of architecture.

At the entrance to the alley off Cordova is the Le Magasin building. Check out the face ornaments on the fibreglass frieze. These face ornaments are life masks of notable entrepreneurs from Gastown's 1960s revival and the individuals responsible for the revitalization of the area during the 1970s. Take the back entrance of Le Magasin and walk through the building to exit onto Water Street. On both sides of street you will see the best examples of 1890s architecture still standing in the city.

Cross over and continue west along Water Street until you get to The Landing (375 Water). This converted warehouse, built by the Kelly Douglas grocery company in 1905 from profits made from outfitting Klondike gold seekers, reflects the general history of wholesaling in Gastown. The building was renovated in 1988 as a retail and office complex. Enter the building and walk over to the large window overlooking the harbour. From here you get a spectacular view of Vancouver's port and railway system.

THE HORNE BLOCK

CHINATOWN

JOANNE POON

Vancouver's Chinatown is the third-largest in North America, a bustling community encompassing Chinatown proper as well as neighbouring Strathcona. Back in the early 1880s, the then-swampy Chinatown land was on the edge of False Creek. Geographically, Chinatown stretches from Gore Avenue east to Carrall Street, and west on Pender and Keefer streets. This historic area began to grow in the late nineteenth century after the completion of the Canadian Pacific Railway. Many Chinese railway workers stayed in Canada, moving to the "Saltwater City" for jobs. The majority lived in Chinatown. A predominantly male society, the workers contracted for seasonal jobs in canneries and lumber mills. They lived alone, far from their families in China, unable to bring them to Canada because of the repressive head tax and a closed-door immigration policy introduced

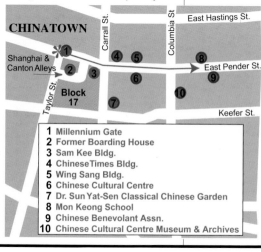

CHINATOWN

East Hastings St.

Carrall St.

Columbia St.

Main St.

Shanghai & Canton Alleys

Taylor St.

East Pender St.

Block 17

Keefer St.

1 Millennium Gate
2 Former Boarding House
3 Sam Kee Bldg.
4 ChineseTimes Bldg.
5 Wing Sang Bldg.
6 Chinese Cultural Centre
7 Dr. Sun Yat-Sen Classical Chinese Garden
8 Mon Keong School
9 Chinese Benevolant Assn.
10 Chinese Cultural Centre Museum & Archives

in 1885. Chinese entrepreneurs like merchant Chang Toy and Canadian Pacific Railway Chinese agent Yip Sang were precursors of Chinatown's commercial development.

CHINATOWN TOUR

The epicentre of historical Chinatown is the intersection of Carrall and East Pender streets. Stand on the corner and look around. The southwestern block of the intersection was known as Block 17. It was here, at 87 East Pender, that a seven-storey boarding house complex once stood. Built by a group of Chinese merchants, the complex included stores on the ground floor and residential quarters on the upper floors. The majority of the residents were the Chinese "married bachelors" who came to Canada alone. After the anti-Asian riot in 1907, when 2,000 members of Vancouver's Asiatic Exclusion League stormed Chinatown and Japantown, an iron gate was erected at the building's main entrance to protect its residents from attack. At night, the gate was locked for security purposes. More recently, the building housed SUCCESS, a major community and immigrant services agency (now relocated to new headquarters at 28 West Pender Street). Shanghai and Canton alleys also ran off Block 17. They were once busy with stores, restaurants, barbershops and Chinese opera theatres. When Dr. Sun Yat-Sen visited Vancouver in 1910, he drew an audience of 1,000 to one of the theatres. Both alleys were demolished in the 1940s when non-Chinese industries began to move into the area. Look for the street plaques commemorating their history.

The Guinness Book of Records calls Block 17's Sam Kee Building (8 West Pender) the narrowest building in the world. The Sam Kee Building belonged to a wealthy Chinese merchant, Chang Toy. When he bought the land in 1903, it was a standard-sized lot. In 1912, the government decided to widen Pender Street and expropriated twenty-four feet from the front of the lot, leaving only six feet on which to construct a building. Which is what Chang Toy did to spite the officials. Although narrow, the 1913 building included a bathhouse in the basement for the use of the married bachelors living upstairs. As there were no bathroom facilities in the building, the

TOP: SHOPPING ON PENDER NEAR GORE
MIDDLE: CHINATOWN BANNER

SAM KEE BUILDING

residents had to pay to use the bathhouse. The building is now owned by Jack Chow Insurance.

Across the street (116 East Pender) stands a building that belonged to the Chinese Freemasons (Cheekongtaong). It was the office of the *Chinese Times*, one of the first locally printed Chinese newspapers. When Dr. Sun Yat-Sen visited Vancouver to raise funds for the 1911 Revolution in China, he stayed here. To support the revolution, the Freemasons mortgaged the building.

The location of the Chinese Cultural Centre (50 East Pender) and Dr. Sun Yat-Sen Classical Chinese Garden (578 Carrall) was the site for Vancouver's Jubilee Celebration in 1936. For the festivities, the entire area was lit up and decorated with a Chinese arch and pagoda. In 1980, the Chinese Cultural Centre was built. The colourful China Gate, marking the entrance of the centre, was originally displayed at Expo 86. Near the China Gate are two bronze inscriptions. One commemorates the industry and sacrifices of Chinese railroad workers. The other honours the efforts of Chinese-Canadian Second World War veterans to gain voting rights for Chinese people living in Canada, a goal accomplished in B.C. in 1947.

Stop in at the Chinese Cultural Centre Museum and Archives (555 Columbia) to view exhibitions on Chinese arts and the history of Chinese-Canadians.

Across from the Chinese Cultural Centre stands the Wing Sang Building. Constructed in 1889, it is both the oldest building and the first brick building in Chinatown. It was built by Yip Sang, a successful Chinese merchant with four wives and twenty-three children. The entire family lived here and Yip ran his import-export business, the Wing Sang Company, on the ground floor. If you look up, you'll note the inscription "1889" on the original building. As the family and the business grew, Yip Sang expanded with a bay-windowed addition and a six-storey building on the back. He linked the front and back buildings with a staircase on the third floor. One of the interesting architectural features is the door on the second floor facing Pender Street. Since the swamps of False Creek still extended to the area, the door was used for loading and unloading goods.

TOP: CHINESE CULTURAL CENTRE MUSEUM AND ARCHIVES
MIDDLE: SCULPTURE AT DR. SUN YAT-SEN CLASSICAL GARDEN
ABOVE: BUST OF DR. SUN YAT-SEN

CHINA GATE

STORES AND ASSOCIATIONS

Walking towards Gore on Pender, you enter another section of Chinatown. Here, you might be attracted at first by the different storefronts, including herbal outlets, jewellers, restaurants and arts and crafts companies. When you look up, you'll be amazed to see the historic buildings around you. All share similar features: a slender shape, decorated with Western-style pillars and Chinese-style recessed balconies. Balconies like these were common to the buildings in South China. The pillars and the pediments supporting them were heavily influenced by Western architecture. This combination of Chinese and Western styles is a characteristic of Chinatown architecture.

TOP: HISTORIC BUILDING ON PENDER STREET
MIDDLE: AT THE MARKET
BOTTOM: MON KEONG SCHOOL

Many of these buildings are now the offices of Chinese associations. They are surname associations, for example the Lee, Wong and Chin associations. Others were formed with people from the same village in China. All played a significant role in the life of early Chinese immigrants. Associations offered help and financial aid to members in need, and places to gather socially and share news from home. Today, members still visit their associations to play mah-jong, meet friends, practice Cantonese opera and celebrate Chinese festivals.

The Chinese Benevolent Association (108 East Pender Street) was formed at the turn of the century and the building erected in 1901. After the Second World War, the Chinese Benevolent Association, together with other associations and individuals in the community, successfully lobbied for the vote and the repeal of the Chinese Exclusion Act of July 1, 1923, which had effectively suspended Chinese immigration to Canada.

The Wong Association, one of the largest surname associations in the area, founded the Mon Keong School (123A East Pender) in 1925, mainly for children of the

Wong clan. Children attended Chinese-language classes after school, which was one of the ways Chinese parents ensured language proficiency for their children. The school is still in operation.

One newcomer to Chinatown is the summertime night market held Thursdays through Sundays. Several streets are closed to traffic, attracting throngs browsing for bargains on everything from delicate glass figurines to clothing and antiques. Another newcomer is the purple, red and gold Millennium Gate arching over Pender Street near Taylor. It symbolizes the area's rich history and enduring presence.

There are many other historic buildings to visit in Chinatown. Why not take one of the popular walking tours offered by the Chinese Cultural Centre to learn about them?

COMMERCIAL DRIVE

GARY MCFARLANE

"The Drive" isn't the only drive in Vancouver, but everyone knows it means Commercial Drive, a remarkably diverse assemblage of shops, cafés, parks and community and cultural centres. Like much of Vancouver, the area was densely wooded late into the nineteenth century. The Salish Indians once hunted elk here and its long-gone forests fed the historic Hastings lumber mill. The first homes were built in the working-class suburb of Grandview in the early years of the twentieth century. If you wander through the streets east of The Drive you can easily imagine Vancouver as it was in 1910. Grant Street, Lakewood Drive, Rose Street, Salsbury Drive and Napier Street, among others, retain many of these grand and eccentric buildings, some decaying rustically, others lovingly restored.

ITALIAN NEIGHBOURHOOD

Following the First and Second World Wars, waves of Italian immigrants settled in the area. The Drive is still the place to shop for prosciutto, sausages, great rounds of cheese and biscotti at the numerous bakeries, delis and produce markets. During soccer season, sitting in Caffé Roma Sports Bar (1510 Commercial) is a sensation not unlike Milan at rush hour. Sip an espresso under a reproduction of the Sistine Chapel at Calabria Bar (1815 Commercial), rub elbows with Roman sculptures and peruse portraits of Italian stars.

The Drive has great restaurants, all very gentle on the

wallet. Go with the special of the day, as you would in Italy. Lombardo's, in the Il Mercato shopping mall (1641 Commercial) and Marcello's (1404 Commercial) seem to be in competition to make Vancouver's best pizza. La Rocca (1565 Commercial) is another long-time favourite. Check out The First Ravioli Store (1900 Commercial) for the best fresh pasta in the city. Then stand in line for fresh gelato at Gelateria Dolce Amore (1598 Commercial).

COFFEE AND CULTURE

Social life on The Drive centres on tiny cafés. Coffee is taken very seriously here, and not only by Italians. Local Ethiopian eateries feature a ritual that includes coffee beans roasted at the table; Harambe Café (2149 Commercial) is said to be the best. Reincarnated beatniks lounge at Bukowski's (1447 Commercial). Belgian Fries (1885 Commercial) reputedly has the best poutine in Western Canada. Vegetarians throng Sweet Cherubim for their ingenious vegan desserts. Check out the exquisite homemade truffles at Dutch Girl Chocolates (1002 Commercial). Havana Restaurant (1212 Commercial) features an art gallery, dance lessons and Cuban cigars on the menu — but this being Vancouver and not Havana, they can't be smoked on site.

Quirky specialty shops abound on the Drive. Worth browsing are the Magpie Magazine Gallery (1319 Commercial) and Beckwoman's (1314 Commercial), a curiosity shop complete with beads and incense. Vancouver artisans fill Dr. Vigari Gallery (1312 Commercial).

Local cultural meccas include the Vancouver East Cultural Centre, also known as The Cultch (1895 Venables), located in a former Methodist church. One street north, the WISE Hall (1882 Adanac) headlines folk and world music. Catch jazz-with-your-tapas at the Latin Quarter (1305 Commercial). The funky Waazubee Cafe (1622 Commercial) has turntabling DJs on many evenings, and Café Deux Soleils (2096 Commercial) has rock and alternative acts as well as on-tap selections from the acclaimed Storm microbrewery located nearby.

GRANVILLE ISLAND AND FALSE CREEK

ALMA LEE

Before Granville Island was built, there were two sandbars at this location used as a fish enclosure by First Nations people before European contact. As Vancouver grew, the sandbars' proximity to False Creek made them the ideal site for industry. After many failed attempts to reclaim the sandbars, the newly formed Vancouver Harbour Commission gave the go-ahead in 1915 for them to be turned into an island. Until just after the Second World War, the area was choked with sawmills and factories manufacturing everything from barrels to boilers and from chains to cement. By the 1950s, the area was a toxic wasteland. Something had to be done. In 1972, a group of young architects and urban planners known as "The Barefoot Gang"

GRANVILLE ISLAND FERRY

107

BURRARD BRIDGE FROM GRANVILLE ISLAND

brainstormed the redevelopment of Granville Island. Their vision, scoffed at by many, created the unique environment it is today.

A UNIQUE URBAN TRANSFORMATION

Although the grimy industries are gone, Granville Island remains a place where people work. These are merchants from all walks of life and cultural backgrounds. The butcher, the baker, the candlestick maker would be an apt rhyme to describe the island. In the Granville Island Public Market, it's fun to get to know the folks who are so incredibly knowledgeable about their products, whether it's fresh fruit from the Okanagan, exotic fish from the

Southern Hemisphere or fine cheeses from around the world. One of my favourite places is the bakery and French specialty foods store La Baguette et L'Echalote, which appeals to my thinking that I must have

PUBLIC MARKET MERCHANT

been French in another life.

You can get to the island by Aquabus ferry or False Creek Ferry, TransLink bus (the #50 bus, False Creek. South on Granville to the entrance), on foot, by bike or in-line skates. Getting your car onto the island and parking it can be a chore, although paid covered parking is fairly copious. If you prefer a little exercise, park off-island in the day lot at Lamey's Mill Road and The Castings and walk west along the False Creek seawall for the flavour of the terraced residences and their lovely gardens. The view of the city and the mountains from here is spectacular. The walkway takes you north onto the island at the False Creek Community Centre, close to the children's water park. This free water park is a good choice if you have younger children. Sit and rest while you watch them play in safety. Check out the Kids Only Market next door to the Crystal Arc. In the adjacent pond, look for turtles basking on stones in the summer. Across the street is the Granville Island Brewing Company, where you can stop and sample their product.

Pick up a map at the Information Centre (1398 Cartwright Street), to help you circumnavigate the island.

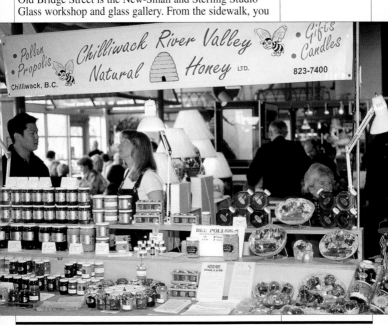

If you get lost, don't worry — you just might stumble onto a little-known treasure. After I'd worked on the island for six or seven years, I walked into Dig This, a gardening shop, and exited by the back door to find two or three hitherto unknown great little shops and a tiny café. One special off-the-beaten-track spot is the mound at the far east end of the island, a great place to take in the tranquil view of boats moored on False Creek, to say nothing of the view of Mount Baker on a clear day.

A TOUR OF THE ISLAND

To make a circle of Granville Island, head east on Cartwright Street. You'll pass Arts Umbrella, a facility for young aspiring artists, dancers and musicians. At the end of Cartwright is the Granville Island Hotel, a boutique hotel with an excellent patio restaurant, brew pub and many charter boats moored close by. Walking west on Johnston Street, Sea Village on the north side is an eclectic mix of float homes with impressive container gardens on the decks. Continue along to the Emily Carr Institute of Art & Design. Drop in and see what's on at The Charles Scott Gallery. As you stroll on, you can't miss Ocean Cement, one of the last industrial tenants located here. You'll remember that the industrial nature of Granville Island still exists when you dodge cement trucks or pass a shop that makes nails. Notice that many of the islands' buildings are constructed from corrugated metal, retaining the industrial look. Next to Ocean Cement, the Creekhouse Gallery is home to a mix of shops, galleries and offices. Nearby on Old Bridge Street is the New-Small and Sterling Studio Glass workshop and glass gallery. From the sidewalk, you

BLACK STONE PRESS

BLACK STONE HAND PRESS

can watch glass-blowing in progress.

As you walk past the Arts Club Theatre, you'll come to the star of the Island, the Granville Island Public Market. From the vivid bouquets of flowers outside to the locally grown fresh fruit and vegetables inside, it's a feast for the eyes and taste buds. Best advice: nibble your way through the market; there are often free samples.

Leaving temptation behind, check out The Net Loft across from the Public Market. In the past, fishers repaired their nets here; today, it's yet another surprise of little shops. On the water nearby, you'll find Vancouver's love affair with the water continues with boat builders, boat repairers, chandlers, boat charter rentals, kayak rentals, fishing boats and live-on moorages. You'll pass Granville Island Museums, a fascinating three-in-one spot with excellent collections for anglers, rail enthusiasts and ship-lovers.

Every day, visitors to Granville Island travel around the world with the music of the buskers, whether they're flute players from the Andes or a piper from Scotland. Stand-up comics and magicians entice you to stop, take a break and laugh at their antics. The arts come to life as you watch artisans at work at Black Stone, David Clifford's hand press (1249 Cartwright); at Paper Ya, purveyor of handmade paper, in the Net Loft; and in the Diane Sanderson weaving studio (#15-1551 Johnston). Festivals are an ongoing attraction, including a new play festival in May, comedy and jazz festivals in June, a folk music festival in July, a wooden boat festival in August and the Vancouver International Writers & Readers Festival in

ART IN THE PUBLIC MARKET

October. In December, the Christmas Carol Ships form a convoy to dazzle onlookers along False Creek with a myriad of sparkling lights. As a visitor, you might even plan a special holiday to enjoy one of these annual events.

Granville Island is justifiably famous. And famous people come here to visit. You never know whom you'll see, from superstar Canadian author Margaret Atwood to superstar actors busy filming in Hollywood North (please, no autographs!). You can do practically anything on Granville Island — exchange money, buy books, learn how to scuba dive or kayak, even live there. Anything to do with the outdoor West Coast style is pretty much available here. Granville Island is the kind of place that invites you to explore again and again.

KITSILANO

KELSEY MCLEOD

To reach Kitsilano from downtown Vancouver, head south over the Burrard Street Bridge. Turn right at Cornwall Avenue and you are in Kitsilano, often simply called Kits, one of Vancouver's oldest neighbourhoods. It fronts the waterfront from the Burrard Street Bridge to Alma Road, its tree-lined streets reaching south to West 16th Avenue. There is amazing diversity in every aspect of Kits, including housing, shopping and people.

Kitsilano lays claim to Canada's highest number of well-off young singles, and stands apart as a neighbourhood whose citizens are better educated than average. From research based on Statistics Canada came the infamous quote, "You've got a degree of intellectual arrogance here."

KITSILANO NEIGHBOURHOOD

HENRY HUDSON ELEMENTARY SCHOOL

WATERFRONT PANORAMA
If going by the MacDonald #22 bus, alight at Cypress Street, the first stop past the Burrard Street Bridge. The Henry Hudson Elementary School (1551 Cypress), one of Vancouver's

Burrard Inlet

KITSILANO

Old Hastings Mill Store

Point Grey Rd.

West 1st Ave.

Tatlow Park

West 4th Ave.

Alma St.

Blenheim St.

Macdonald St.

Broadway West

VANIER PARK CYCLISTS

oldest, stands four-square across the street, its brick-hued walls and white-trimmed windows drawing the eye. Early in the last century, a favoured pastime for its pupils was catching frogs in the then-swampy surrounding area.

Starting a waterfront promenade, head down Cypress Street toward the mountains. Ahead of you towers a 30.5-metre-high (100 foot) totem pole, a replica of one given to Queen Elizabeth II in 1958 to commemorate B.C.'s Centennial. Carved by famed Kwakiutl carvers Mungo Martin, Henry Hunt and David Martin, the totem is a fitting reminder that this area was originally a Squamish Indian village called Sun'ahk. The name Kitsilano itself is derived from that of Chief Khahtsalanough of Sun'ahk and his descendants.

Turn right at Whyte Street, cross Chestnut Street, and head past the Vancouver Museum on your left. Pause a moment to view its Haida hat-shaped roof and the huge crab-shaped fountain out front. As you continue toward English Bay, the Music Conservatory is on your right, the Vancouver City Archives and H.R. MacMillan Space Centre and Planetarium are on your left. The Vancouver City Archives look like an underground bunker.

TOTEM POLE IN HADDON PARK

At the foot of the street is the Coast Guard Station and a marina where countless pleasure boats are moored. As you walk along the shore of Vanier Park, look across to the city's outer harbour toward Vancouver Island, the peaks of which could be visible. Pleasure boats, perhaps a tug with a scow and likely a Coast Guard vessel may be seen heading in or out on patrol. Above, you just might see a bald eagle in the air or sitting in the tall trees.

Heading further west along English Bay, you'll come to the Vancouver Maritime Museum, where its A-frame building houses the famed Royal Canadian Mounted Police vessel *St. Roch*. The *St. Roch* was the first ship to sail the Northwest Passage from both west to west and west to east, and to circumnavigate North America.

You are now in Haddon Park, named after

English Bay

Vancouver
Maritime
Museum

H.R. Macmillan Space
Centre and Planetarium

Vancouver Museum

Kitsilano Point

Hadden
Park

Kitsilano
Pool

Kitsilano
Beach

Whyte St.

Vanier Park

Burrard
Bridge

nt Grey Rd.
Cornwall Ave.

Cornwall Ave.
West 1st Ave.

Chestnut St.

Burrard St.

West 4th Ave

Arbutus St.

Cypress St.

Broadway West

millionaire property developer and philanthropist Harvey Haddon, who bequeathed half a million dollars to Vancouver parks before his death in 1931.

Ahead is Kitsilano Beach. The bathhouse is where the belligerent pioneer Samuel "Gritty" Greer built Kitsilano Point's first dwelling. Unfortunately, his arrival clashed with the provincial government's grant of 6,000 acres to the Canadian Pacific Railway. Greer went so far as to fire buckshot at both the sheriff and his deputy. After he was convicted of common assault, the CPR, gained possession and extended their tracks to the foot of Balsam Street.

Nearby is the 137 metre-long (45-feet) Kitsilano Pool, an outdoor summer classic nestled next to the beach. The Kitsilano Showboat, an institution since 1936, is located above the pool. The Showboat amphitheatre showcases amateur performers free of charge during the summer months, giving tiny dancers in tutus a chance to strut their stuff. Leaving Kitsilano Park, it's a pleasant winding stroll to the foot of MacDonald Street. Cornwall Street becomes Point Grey Road at one of the curves.

OCEAN VIEW

Tatlow Park is on your left, with its rounded bridge and the remnants of what was once a salmon-spawning stream. Beside it is an apartment complex built on the former

KITSILANO SHOWBOAT

TATLOW PARK

BRIDGE IN TATLOW PARK

ALMA STREET SHOPPING

palatial estate of Killarney, once the gathering place for the city's elite. Mrs. Jessie Hall, its hostess, was the daughter of Gritty Greer. She was the first child of European descent born in the Cariboo and spent her youth netting smelt along the beach. She married James Z. Hall, Vancouver's first notary public and first volunteer soldier. They built Killarney in 1908, complete with a fireplace with inlaid shamrocks. Rest here awhile or in one of the nearby mini parks overlooking the outer harbour where international ships lay at anchor, bows to the wind.

This area was once home to summer cottages. People rowed across English Bay before the bridges provided access. Most of the cottages have been torn down, but one at the foot of Alma Street across from the Hastings Mill Store Museum is little changed. The Hastings Mill Store Museum was originally built around 1865 at the Hastings Mill sawmill on Burrard Inlet. It was moved here in 1930 to be maintained by the Native Daughters of British Columbia. Inside, a collection of First Nations artifacts and items from pioneer days are well worth a visit.

INLAND

Kitsilano has an amazing variety of housing, with very few high-rises in the Kits Beach area — a by-law prevents more. If you're interested in real architecture, wander the neighbourhood streets and avenues. Streets run north and south, avenues run east and west. Many of the original stately homes survive, complete with their peaked roofs and front verandahs where pioneers sat on summer evenings. MacDonald, between Cornwall Street and West 7th Avenue, is a good area for these.

Shopping? In the 1960s, West 4th Avenue was infamous as a haven for youthful hippies. Today, the avenue is all about shopping, from Burrard to Balsam Streets. A few blocks up, there's more shopping along Broadway to Alma Street. Browse the jewellery stores, ethnic importers, clothing boutiques, thrift stores, bookstores (including Kidsbooks, the city's best children's bookstore). When you need a break, choose from dozens of Kitsilano fine dining and casual restaurants, cafés and coffee shops, many with outdoor seating.

The foot of Alma Street, Kitsilano's western boundary, is a fitting end to your walk. Sink your tired bones into one of the benches facing the salt chuck overlooking the Jericho Yacht Club anchorage. Gaze towards West Vancouver. The white pinnacle of the Point Atkinson lighthouse catches the eye, its light flashing rhythmically. Just off Point Atkinson is Manson's Deep, the traditional place for sea burials for Vancouver's mariners.

UBC

CHRIS PETTY

On any given day in the academic year, upwards of 45,000 students, faculty, staff and visitors arrive on the campus of the University of British Columbia to work, study and enjoy the ambiance of Canada's third-largest university. Perched out on the end of Point Grey, some 20 minutes from the city centre, UBC boasts one of the prettiest campuses in the country. With its forest setting, landscaped gardens and spectacular views across the Strait of Georgia and Howe Sound, visitors can often be heard to mutter, "How the heck do they get any work done around here?"

The new 'University Town,' an eight-neighbourhood housing development for students, faculty, staff and off-campus purchasers, is under construction and set to attract

TOP LEFT: CHAN CENTRE
TOP RIGHT: THE IONA BUILDING AT THE VANCOUVER SCHOOL OF THEOLOGY, UBC

an additional 20,000 people to the university's core. As a small city, UBC has all the amenities: concert halls, restaurants (from greasy spoons to fine dining), theatres, sports facilities, bars and shops. As a university, it has the vitality that goes along with a population skewed towards the younger end of the scale. UBC is a walker's paradise. Gardens, wide boulevards, outside eateries, stunning architecture, gorgeous viewpoints and quiet, off-the-beaten-path spots for rest and reflection draw visitors throughout the year.

MAIN LIBRARY

HISTORY

UBC became a degree-granting institution in 1915. Originally housed in old warehouses and church basements near Vancouver's City Hall, the plan was to move UBC to Point Grey, but the First World War stopped construction. "The Great Trek" in 1922, in which students, faculty and alumni marched in demonstration from downtown to Point Grey, was the culmination of a noisy campaign to get the government of the day to resume building the campus. It worked. The Great Trek, and the sense of intrepid adventure shown by the marchers, has become a working metaphor at UBC, and is celebrated at every opportunity. The Point Grey campus opened in 1925.

BELKIN ART GALLERY

Those first buildings remain some of the most remarkable on campus and are quite wonderful examples of neo-Gothic architecture. Main Library, just off Main Mall, features superb stone masonry, stained-glass windows and brass fittings. Look for the two little stone monkeys on the front wall. Each holds a book, one saying "Funda," and the other "Evolut," reflecting the Scopes Monkey Trial controversy that raged at the time. Main Library has one of the most spectacular study rooms in the country, called the Learning Commons. Have a seat in a comfortable leather chair, bask in the sunlight shining in through 30-foot-high stained glass windows, and wish you could enrol. Main Library, like most other buildings on campus, is open during daytime hours and is fun to wander through.

A TOUR OF UBC

The university offers free walking tours daily from May to August, starting at the Student Union Building (SUB), which include orientation to the main campus amenities and academic facilities. You can also pre-book group tours. But the best place to start your own tour is at the Rose Garden. Drive onto the campus via Chancellor Boulevard (an extension of Fourth Avenue), until you get to the Rose Garden parkade. You can park here all day for a few dollars. Take the elevator up from the parkade and look north towards the mountains. You're on the Flagpole Plaza above the actual Rose Garden. The view from the Rose Garden — Howe Sound and the North Shore's Coast mountains fading off into the distance — stretches before you like a travel poster. The garden itself is spectacular and in bloom from early spring until well into fall.

As you contemplate the great view, remember that the world-class UBC Museum of Anthropology is just across the road and to the left. The museum, along with the Nitobe Memorial Garden and UBC Botanical Garden, should not be missed. The museum has one of the top First Nations art collections in the world, and the Arthur Erickson–designed building is a wonder on its own.

MAIN MALL

Main Mall stretches the length of the university from the Flagpole Plaza to Thunderbird Stadium. Short side trips from the Mall bring you to virtually all the university's features. The Chan Centre is nearby (that big, round building that looks like a giant industrial widget), as is the Belkin Art Gallery, Frederic Wood Theatre and the UBC School of Music. The Chan Centre auditorium, which seats 1,400, is said to have the best acoustics in town. In addition to ticketed performances, free recitals by local and international performers, as well as practices by the UBC School of Music, are often held here.

C.K. CHOI BUILDING

For tickets, free tours and free events, check with the box office. The Belkin Gallery just across the way shows travelling art exhibits as well as the university collection. It is open daily. Check, too, the program at the Fredric Wood Theatre, home to UBC's theatre program.

Continue along Main Mall to the huge library plaza and the Koerner Library. Brand new and state-of-the-art, it is called the "green jewel" of the campus by the architect. Locals think it's either beautiful or horrifying, but all agree the Koerner stands out. Take the elevator up to the top and look east to the Main Library and the Coast Mountains in the distance.

KOERNER LIBRARY

SITES OF INTEREST

UBC has many great buildings. One of the most interesting is the C.K. Choi building west of the Koerner Library on West Mall. It's the most environmentally tuned building on campus and is built out of recycled materials from the Old Armouries (demolished a few years ago). It's also probably the only new building in Vancouver that has chemical toilets.

South on West Mall is another UBC wonder, the First Nations Longhouse. Built to house First Nations programs, it also serves as a gathering place for First Nations students. Enter and note the huge sculpted log poles and other pieces of First Nations art. Outside, follow the cool sounds of a waterfall to one of the most relaxing (and little-known) hideaways on campus.

From the Longhouse walk east on Agricultural Road, past Main Library to East Mall and the Student Union Building. That building and the nearby Aquatic Centre (indoor and outdoor pools), War Memorial Gym and Student Recreation Centre, make up the most active non-academic area of the campus. UBC has the largest intramural sports program in Canada. A visit to any of the latter three buildings shows why. The facilities are first rate.

The UBC Bookstore, the largest university bookstore in Canada, is located across the bus loop from SUB. It has a huge selection of academic books, a well-stocked fiction and magazine section, as well as gifts, clothing, computers, art supplies and electronics.

Back on Main Mall heading south is the dome of the Astronomical Observatory, just beside the UBC Geophysical Observatory (which monitors earthquake activity) and the Geological Museum. All these facilities are open to the public.

UBC BOOKSTORE

Perhaps the most interesting building at UBC appears just before Main Mall descends into parking lots and athletic fields. The lobby and study areas of the Forest Sciences building are nothing short of a post-modern forest glen. Huge beams made of Parallam (which looks like popsicle sticks glued together) spread up to the roof three storeys above. Everything in the building shows off the quality and beauty of wood construction, and the whole thing has the delightful odour of a cedar chest.

NORTH SHORE

ROCHELLE VAN HALM

It's the Coast Mountains that anchor Vancouver's majestic setting: the North Shore comprises a wilderness just thirty minutes from downtown Vancouver. Residents enjoy a beautiful community well-endowed with recreation opportunities, excellent shopping and the beauty of nature best explored from the hiking trail. While some residents still see black bears and deer in their backyards, there are plenty of big-city attractions in the communities of West and North Vancouver.

WEST VANCOUVER

After crossing the Lions Gate Bridge, the first exit takes you into West Vancouver, one of Canada's richest communities, evidenced by the visible presence of luxury import cars on the roads. Like its residents, the municipality takes pride in its appearance. Every year, it plants 30,000 spring flowering bulbs, tends 180 hanging flower baskets and creates major floral displays. Follow Marine Drive between the two sides of Park Royal Shopping Centre, a home for fashion mavens. Next comes Ambleside Park, boasting beaches, a playground, skateboard park, duck pond, Ambleside Par 3 Golf Course and an off-leash dog park. The West Vancouver Sea Walk begins along the shoreline, one of the community's best-used facilities. Dogs are relegated to their own path on the other side of the fence, between 18th and 24th streets. Seals bob in the distance, salmon leap, summer cruise ships pass nightly and savage winter storms toss logs high onto the shore.

AMBLESIDE PARK

LIGHTHOUSE PARK

Ferry Terminal · To Whistler · Cypress Prov. Park · Grouse Mountain Resort ▲ · Lynn Headwaters Regl. Park · Mt. Seymour Prov. Park · Capilano Lake · Whytecliff Park · Capilano River Regl. Park · Capilano Rd. · ▲ Mt. Seymour · Fisherman's Cove · 99 · Marine Dr. · Capilano River · Trans Canada Hwy · Deep Cove Rd. · Indian Arm · Lighthouse Park · Burrard Inlet · Ambleside Park · **NORTH SHORE** · Lions Gate Bridge · 1A 99 · Seabus · Mt. Seymour Pkwy. · 2nd Narrows Bridge · Burrard Inlet · Belcarra Regl. Park

At the foot of 14th Street, the fishing pier at Ambleside Landing is used day and night. Ferry service began here in 1909 and ended in 1947.

The terminal, built in 1913, was renovated into the well-visited Ferry Building Gallery for community art exhibits. History lives nearby at the West Vancouver Museum and Archives, housed in an old ballast-stone house built in 1940 by Gertrude Lawson, daughter of John Lawson, who is known as the father of West Vancouver. The floral clock at the foot of 15th Street — considered ill conceived by some residents — occasionally tells the correct time!

FERRY BUILDING GALLERY

After strolling Bellevue Avenue, lined with fashionable shops, follow Marine Drive to West Vancouver's Memorial Library, which has the highest per capita circulation of any library in Canada. Across Marine Drive is Memorial Park, where large rhododendrons bloom each spring. Follow the path over the bridge to the playground by the stream, where the historic Village Walk begins. Nearby is the new geothermal-heated Aquatic Centre with an ozone-treated leisure pool, waterslides and hydrotherapy.

In the 2400-block of Marine Drive, the village of Dundarave blooms with hanging baskets and a summer flower boulevard. The shops include an old-style hardware store with whatever you might need; plus antiques, art and gelato. Capers is the choice for an organic lunch on the deck overlooking the ocean. In late summer, the annual

WEST VANCOUVER MUSEUM

country-and-western hoedown fills the street with square dancing and kids' pony rides.

Another pier at the foot of 25th Street marks the end of the Sea Walk, along with playgrounds, an interesting sculpture of a girl on a turtle, a sandy beach for swimming and lunch from a concession stand with architectural merit and a stunning English Bay view. The Beach House at Dundarave Pier offers more upscale dining in a building finely restored from its 1912 beginnings. The restaurant offers a heater-warmed patio to allow diners to enjoy their meals long after the sun sets into the Pacific. Marine Drive meanders westward, past grand estates with multimillion-dollar cliff-hanging homes and a few original seaside cottages from the 1920s and 1930s. In the 3700-block of Marine Drive, the once-treacherous Suicide Bend allows room to pull over for a photo of the ocean, Point Grey beyond, and a closeup look at freighters anchored in the bay. Explore local beaches with their own natural attractions at West Bay (public access off Radcliffe Avenue), Sandy Cove (at Rose Crescent) and Stearman (off Ross Crescent).

The government's Fisheries and Oceans laboratory (4100-block of Marine Drive) now studies salmon on the site where the Great Northern Cannery packed fish from 1891 until 1967. Outside the Cypress Park Market (4360 Marine Drive) historic photos show the neighbourhood of years ago. Watch for Piccadilly Road South, and take a left turn into lower Caulfeild, the English-style village designed by Francis Caulfeild in the 1920s. The neighbourhood celebrates on the village green in front of St. Francis-in-the-Wood Anglican Church, a favourite for weddings.

Returning to Marine Drive, turn left at Eagle Harbour Road to visit a small neighbourhood beach, watch local children learn to sail and Eagle Island residents use a cable ferry to haul themselves and their groceries home, a stone's throw from the mainland.

From Marine Drive, turn north onto Cranley Drive for Seaview Walk, part of the TransCanada Trail. The path leads from Nelson Creek to the old rail bed, overlooking hundreds of boats moored in Fisherman's Cove and leading to the Gleneagles Golf Course. The municipally-owned eighteen-hole course provides ocean views from the greens. Retrace your steps and continue west on Marine Drive, snaking up the rocky hillside.

NORTH VANCOUVER

Follow the signs to Highway 1 East/Highway 99 South, known locally as the Upper Levels Highway, for a quick trip east with views of English Bay, Burrard Inlet and Vancouver. When the skies are clear, you can see as far as Vancouver Island and Mount Baker. Take Exit 22 and follow Mount Seymour Parkway to the Parkgate Village Shopping Centre, then turn left at Mount Seymour Road.

Halfway up Seymour Mountain, you'll find a lookout point from which to view Simon Fraser University, Indian Arm and the wilderness beyond. Hiking trails begin farther up where the road ends in the top parking lot.

Returning downhill, turn left at Mount Seymour

Parkway and watch for the close-up view of Indian Arm, nestled in mountains shrouded in mist. Turn left onto Deep Cove Road for the short drive into the forested cove. This franchise-free town offers unique cafés for lunch or coffee, where you'll meet the locals when you take a break from your sidewalk stroll. At the Deep Cove Cultural Centre, residents are invited to participate onstage or backstage. The Seymour Art Gallery features local artists, and the Shaw Theatre, the Deep Cove Heritage Association and Arts in the Cove provide opportunities for artists of all ages and aspirations. From Deep Cove Lookout at the foot of Gallant Avenue, see weekenders stocking up for a cruise up Indian Arm. Join them on a rental paddle from Deep Cove Canoe and Kayak Centre and view waterfront homes on Panorama Drive. A public footpath follows the shore to Panorama Park where live music fills summer evenings. The Baden Powell hiking trail begins just north of the park. This forty-eight-kilometre trail links Deep Cove to Horseshoe Bay across the North Shore mountains.

North Vancouver is well-equipped for local culture. Live theatre is offered at Presentation House. Upstairs, the Presentation House Gallery is renowned for its photography exhibitions. North Vancouver Museum and Archives focuses on the local history of logging, shipbuilding and early community development and features a walking tour of historic houses. Just down the hill is Lonsdale Quay Market where you can buy live crabs, whole salmon or just a sandwich, fresh pasta, vegetables, flowers and Italian deli specialties. Children can blow off steam in the upstairs ballroom. The Lonsdale Quay Hotel overlooks the Cates tugboat operation and the SeaBus, a commuter ferry, links Lonsdale Quay with downtown Vancouver. The Lower Lonsdale area is undergoing redevelopment from its shipyard past. At the foot of Lonsdale Avenue, visit the Pacific Great Eastern railway station, built in 1913. It retains elements of the past, as well as information about walking tours and a proposed walk-through of the underbelly of a giant ship.

TOP: **LONSDALE QUAY MARKET SIGN**
MIDDLE: **LYNN CANYON PARK SUSPENSION BRIDGE**

SEABUS

OUTDOOR FUN

Lighthouse Park (off Beacon Lane at Marine Drive, West Vancouver) offers trails through an old-growth forest of giant Douglas firs, pines, hemlocks and arbutus trees that look as if they're peeling rust-red bark. Stroll to Point Atkinson lighthouse, built in 1912 and still operating. When fog rolls in, the foghorn is very loud. The rocks are a great vantage point to view the freighters and sailboats in English Bay.

Whytecliff Park offers rocky

POINT ATKINSON LIGHTHOUSE

views to Bowen Island and the passing ferries, plus picnic sites and a climb up Whyte Islet, accessible at low tide. The stony beach is popular for divers as marine life is protected in an underwater reserve.

Porteau Cove, 25 kilometres (15 miles) north of Horseshoe Bay off Highway 99, is one of the few places you can camp alongside Howe Sound. An artificial reef of shipwrecks at the cove provides interest for divers. Walking trails lead through the picnic area to a small hill with a lookout.

During winter, skiing and boarding are no more than 30 minutes away from downtown Vancouver at three different mountains. From Highway 1, take Exit 8 and follow Cypress Bowl Road to Cypress Provincial Park for downhill and cross-country skiing, snowboarding and snowshoeing day and night. The 75-year-old rustic Hollyburn Lodge serves homemade chili, bakes its own bread and during ski season, packs the house with Saturday night bluegrass or folk music. Whatever the season, the Highview Lookout provides a tremendous view of the City of Vancouver, the Fraser Valley, Richmond, the Strait of Georgia and the Gulf Islands beyond. Summer hiking on Cypress Mountain ranges from Yew Lake Trail, an easy interpretive loop that is wheelchair and stroller accessible, to the rugged 30-kilometre (18 mile) Howe Sound Crest Trail.

Grouse Mountain offers excellent downhill skiing and snowboarding on 22 runs. Sleigh rides through alpine meadows, outdoor skating, snowshoeing and the latest, showshoe running, are also offered. Hiking in the summer includes the Grouse Grind, a steep climb up beneath the Skyride. At the top, Grouse offers guided walking tours and paragliding for the ultimate view.

Mount Seymour provides natural terrain that's ideal for learning to ski or snowboard. There are snowshoe trails and snow tubing as well.

In North Vancouver, Lynn Canyon Park is a wilderness not far from civilization. The Lynn Canyon Suspension Bridge, less well-known than its well-promoted cousin, the Capilano Suspension Bridge, is just as spectacular in a more natural setting. The Ecology Centre reveals how civilization affects the natural environment. There's also good fun for the kids with puppets and animal displays.

WHYTECLIFF PARK

VICTORIA

Restaurants

1. Blue Crab Bar and Grill
2. Brasserie L'Ecole
3. Bravo Restaurant
4. Café Brio
5. Canoe Club
6. Empress Room
7. Foster's Eatery
8. Hugo's Grill and Brewhouse
9. J & J Won Ton Noodle House
10. Paradiso di Stelle
11. Point Ellice House
13. Rebar Modern Foods
14. Suze Restaurant and Lounge
15. Swans Brewpub
16. The Temple
17. Victorian Restaurant
18. Zambri's

Hotels

1. Admiral Inn
2. Bedford Regency Hotel
3. Best Western Carlton Plaza
4. Best Western Inner Harbour
5. Chateau Victoria Hotel
6. Hotel Grand Pacific
7. Coast Victoria Harbourside Hotel and Marina
8. Days Inn on the Harbour
9. Fairmont Empress Hotel
10. Executive House Hotel
11. Quality Inn Green Gables
13. Harbour Towers Hotel
14. Laurel Point Inn
15. The Magnolia Hotel and Spa
16. Delta Victoria Ocean Pointe Resort Hotel and Spa
17. Queen Victoria Hotel & Suites
18. Ramada Huntingdon Manor
19. Strathcona Hotel
20. Swans Suite Hotel
22. Travellers Inn Downtown
22. Victoria Plaza Hotel
23. Victoria Regent Hotel

EXPLORING VICTORIA

D. C. REID

More British than the British, Victoria lines its streets with 3,000 hanging baskets every summer. Even in February, residents count the flowers for the benefit of snowbound Canada, recording well over one billion blooms some balmy winters.

KABUKI CAB

Compact and pretty, Victoria lies at the southern end of Vancouver Island. Vehicle traffic arrives at Swartz Bay's ferry terminal 30 minutes north of the city as well as at the Inner Harbour terminal, with scheduled ferry arrivals from Seattle and Port Angeles. Air travellers land at Victoria International Airport and take the scenic Pat Bay Highway. Others arrive on one of several daily helicopter flights from downtown Vancouver or the Vancouver International Airport, landing at the Helijet terminal within minutes of Victoria's city centre.

Once settled into your downtown hotel, Victoria is a walker's delight, with many of the main attractions mere minutes from one another. For variety, hitch a ride in a human-powered Kabuki cab, or lounge back in a horse-drawn carriage. Double-decker English buses whisk patrons to the world-famous Butchart Gardens. Historical interest trips leave from the Inner Harbour bound for Beacon Hill Park and surrounding neighbourhoods. For something completely different, head to the Oak Bay Marina, where you can feed wild seals by the docks.

The centrepiece of the city lies at the corner of Belleville and Government streets. The ivy-covered Empress Hotel opens onto the causeway, Carillon Tower and Royal British Columbia Museum. Famed for its exhibits of natural history, aboriginal lore and gold-rush paraphernalia, the museum ranks high with visitors. Completing the corner are the grey granite Parliament Buildings with green-weathered copper domes. At night, the Parliament Buildings are spectacularly lit with 3,300 tiny lights.

A few blocks away, Fort Street houses antique shops and book dealers. Bastion Square marks the site of the original Fort Victoria, and the McPherson Playhouse offers performances all year. There are small ferries in the Inner Harbour, and you can take a pleasant walk along the Songhees boardwalk and by the Dungeness crab displayed at Fisherman's Wharf.

If you don't know where to begin, phone Tourism Victoria at (250) 953-2033 or visit their office at 812 Wharf Street, across the street from the Fairmont Empress Hotel. Alternatively, there are several sightseeing companies in the city to take you on guided bus, carriage or walking tours.

A BRIEF HISTORY

D. C. REID

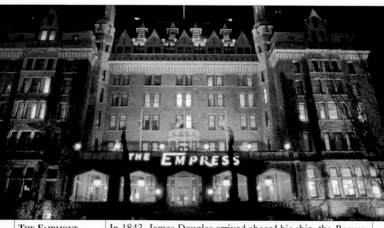

In 1843, James Douglas arrived aboard his ship, the *Beaver* to become chief factor for the Hudson's Bay Company. His new Fort Victoria owed its origin to American territorial ambitions. At the time, Great Britain and the United States disputed control of the Pacific Northwest. Shrewdly judging that the 49th parallel ultimately would become the border between the two nations, the Hudson's Bay Company sent Douglas from its Columbia River depot to set up operations on Vancouver Island's southernmost tip, thereby solidifying trade in beaver and sea otter pelts.

Douglas wrote, "The place itself appears a perfect Eden in the midst of the dreary wilderness." Through the Hudson's Bay Company, he leased the entire area of Vancouver Island for a mere seven shillings a year. This move forestalled American expansionism.

THE GOLD RUSH

The 1858 Fraser River gold rush transformed Victoria from a sleepy village of 500 inhabitants to a bustling, brawling settlement of 25,000 gold seekers. Seeking to keep Victoria ahead of Vancouver in development, Douglas declared the town a free port and taxed all traffic in goods.

When British Columbia joined Canada in 1871, Confederation Day marked a glorious binge in taverns and streets with speeches and naval guns saluting. In the same year the quintessential B.C. artist, Emily Carr, was born. At the time, her stark, savage style earned nothing but hostility.

Victoria's growing prosperity proved short-lived. The gold rush crash resulted in plummeting land values and the population shrank to 1,500 souls. Amor de Cosmos, the

First Peoples mask

West's first radical newspaper baron, railed against the government, criticizing the law-and-order-prone James Douglas as a species of cockroach. When Arthur Kennedy succeeded Douglas as governor, de Cosmos won election to the House of Assembly.

Economic Change

Matching the theatricality of its new Legislature, Victoria's free port status conferred control over all B.C. trade in mining, lumbering, fishing, land sales, brewing and shipbuilding. By 1900, Victoria's population had tripled to 20,000 and business boomed. Francis Mawson Rattenbury, soon to become the province's most famous architect, designed the Provincial Legislature (commonly, but erroneously, called the Parliament Buildings) in 1898 and The Empress Hotel soon after.

But again the good times were short-lived. A fire during the First World War devastated the city core. The collapse of the seal hunt resulted in financial ruin for 80 per cent of Victorians. Salmon canneries and shipbuilding factories were moved to Vancouver. The Canadian government outlawed the opium trade. Victoria's economics changed from business and finance to government and tourism.

Tourism

Fortunately Victoria's lingering financial demise received a restorative tonic: prohibition was declared in the United States. In the 1930s, whiskey from downtown factories moved through Smugglers Cove at night and sped to nearby American ports.

Royal BC Museum

After the Second World War, retirees discovered Victoria, bringing with them over $50,000,000 per year. Construction of new Legislature wings, banks, law courts, power authorities, retail space and a refurbished City Hall altered the skyline for good. Along with the arrival of old money came the stability of the government payroll and the expanding tourist trade.

Capitalizing on Victoria's tourist potential, The Royal British Columbia Museum was completed in 1970 along with the Carillon Tower, producing an atmosphere of quiet opulence. Since 1971, the sixty-two-bell tower, largest of its type in Canada, has tolled the arrival of visitors every fifteen minutes during its summer and fall season. And visit they do: *Conde Nast Traveler* magazine voted Victoria the best city in the Americas and Vancouver Island as best North American island in 2003.

TOP ATTRACTIONS

LESLEY KENNY

**THE PARLIAMENT
BUILDINGS**

**GOVERNOR JAMES
DOUGLAS**

THE PARLIAMENT BUILDINGS

The name of this key Victoria landmark is a misnomer. The only Canadian House of Parliament is in Ottawa. In Victoria, the Parliament Buildings (named after a bill was passed in the 1890s) actually house the Provincial Legislature, where the members of the legislative assembly sit. Tours run every day in the summer and when the house is in session, you can sit in the galleries and watch the ad-libbed performances. The Parliament Buildings are on Belleville Street, adjacent to The Fairmont Empress Hotel, overlooking the Inner Harbour.

In 1856, Governor James Douglas, the first governor of the colony of Vancouver Island, issued a proclamation to elect a House of Assembly. Seven members were elected from four districts. Governor Douglas didn't believe that the common folk had much to say about how they were governed so he added a catch: all voters had to own at least twenty acres of land. This meant that in the first so-called democratic election, forty people were allowed to vote for the seven representatives. All of the elected reps had ties to the Hudson's Bay Company. Three just happened to be enemies of Governor James Douglas.

The first legislative assembly had little power. The only source of money it had was through the sale of liquor licenses. The Hudson's Bay Company was the legislative assembly's rival for authority, with vast amounts of money at its disposal from trading profits and land sales. In the beginning, the assembly was basically a place for public criticism of the Douglas administration. The assembly didn't have money for much-needed roads, nor did it have the authority to levy taxes or give grants. Meanwhile, the downtown core of Victoria was expanding, largely because of the gold rush, which was attracting immigrants from all over the world.

The first government buildings were built by a German immigrant, Herman Otto Tiedmann. These were built between 1859 and 1864 and called the Bird Cages for their design. The Bird Cages replaced the old colonial offices inside Fort Victoria. After Confederation with Canada, in 1871, the first parliament of British Columbia met in the Bird Cages. Most of these structures were demolished in 1898 to make way for the stone and marble buildings you see today.

The Parliament Buildings were designed by Francis Mawson Rattenbury, a twenty-five-year-old architect from Leeds, England. The buildings were under construction from 1893 until their completion in 1898, all for less than $1 million. The stones were cut locally. The slate for the roofs was brought in from Jervis Inlet, off Vancouver Island. Inside the four-level buildings, the marble in the assembly hall was brought in from Italy, while the marble in the rotunda was imported from Tennessee.

The diamond jubilee celebration of Queen Victoria was scheduled before the completion of the Parliament Buildings. To show its appreciation, the government decided to honour the anniversary by hooking up thousands of tiny lights to the outside of the buildings. The buildings were like this for special occasions until 1956. From then onward, the lights have been turned on every day at dusk and turned off at midnight. There are more than 3,300 bulbs outlining the buildings, giving them a faintly Disney-esque look.

But there's more behind this manicured façade than meets the eye. Soon after he designed the Parliament Buildings, Francis Rattenbury became the Canadian Pacific Railway's western architect. He designed The Fairmont Empress Hotel, Victoria Crystal Gardens (on Douglas Street, behind the hotel) and numerous banks and mansions

THE PARLIAMENT BUILDINGS AT NIGHT

in Victoria and Vancouver. His affair with Alma Pakenham, thirty years his junior, resulted in his being snubbed by polite Victoria society. He left his wife and moved to England with Alma. This move proved fatal.

After their move, the new Mrs. Rattenbury took a new lover, George Stoner, the family's eighteen-year-old chauffeur. In 1935, Stoner was charged with the bludgeoning murder of the famous architect. He was sentenced to death, though after public outcry he was given life in jail. Alma, thinking that her lover was going to be executed and realizing that her life in society was over, committed suicide by stabbing herself and then falling into a river where she drowned.

THE INNER HARBOUR AND FISHERMAN'S WHARF

Victoria's truly picturesque Inner Harbour is just a few steps from the Parliament Buildings. Walk down the steps either from Government or Belleville streets, and you'll find an eclectic group of buskers and artisans offering their talents and wares. If you've spent the day shopping, you could sit on one of the benches or stone steps and

watch the boats come into dock or small aircraft taxi along the water for a mid-harbour launch. If you sit by the window at Milestone's restaurant on Wharf Street, you can enjoy a harbour view.

You're welcome to walk around the dock and look at the privately owned boats. On occasion you will see a meticulously restored sailboat or a reproduction of a historic explorer's ship. If the urge to get on the water overtakes you, there's always the ten-minute Harbour Ferry ride over to the West Bay Marina in Esquimalt. From there you could walk back along a boardwalk beside the ocean. You'll also pass by Spinnakers, one of Victoria's fine micro-breweries and also a pub, with patio seating looking out at the Inner Harbour.

All around the Inner Harbour, on Government and Belleville streets, horse-carriage rides are available, as well as double-decker bus tours. On the other side of the Inner Harbour is Fisherman's Wharf, where the commercial fishing boats dock. From both harbours, you can see the *Coho* ferry on its way to and from Port Angeles, or the speedier catamaran, destined for Seattle. No matter which way you face, the Inner Harbour is within a five-minute walk from major tourist attractions as the boutiques along Government Street.

THE FAIRMONT EMPRESS HOTEL

Probably one of the most photographed Victoria landmarks, The Fairmont Empress Hotel overlooks the Inner Harbour, adjacent to the Royal British Columbia Museum and the Parliament Buildings. The Fairmont Empress is one of a series of château-style luxury hotels in major cities across Canada. Designed by Francis Rattenbury (architect of the Parliament Buildings), it was built in 1908 for $1 million. The Fairmont Empress was restored to the tune of $45 million in the late 1980s when it was closed for six months and completely gutted on the inside. The grand-style hotel, its towering brick walls semi-covered in ivy, has 460 rooms and thirty-three suites on seven floors, with an eighth floor to be added soon. There are eighty different room configurations, some with vaulted ceilings, some with interesting nooks and all with down-filled duvet covers. In 1999, *Travel & Leisure Magazine* rated The Fairmont Empress Hotel number three in North America, and number thirty-five in the world.

There's no shortage of luxury extras here. The Crystal Ballroom shows off its eighteen crystal chandeliers and mirrored ceiling. The two restaurants offer regional cuisine and the Bengal Lounge (one of two lounges) is known for its curry buffet. There are sauna rooms, a swimming pool and a whirlpool, as well as a modern fully-equipped health

THE CRYSTAL BALLROOM

133

GATE OF HARMONIOUS INTEREST

club, complete with massage therapy. The hotel expects to add a $5.5-million health spa in the near future.

On a typical summer day, The Fairmont Empress Hotel registers 1,200 visitors. The Queen of England doesn't stay here, but she does come for tea when she's in town. In fact, afternoon tea is open to everyone. There are four seatings a day in the summer. For $49.95 (summer rate), you can have tea and sandwiches with 400 other diners in the elegant main lobby.

Some of the employees of the hotel have worked at the Empress for more than thirty-five years, some for almost fifty years. The strangest thing that appeared in the lost and found, reported one, was jewellery worth a quarter of a million dollars. It eventually found its way back to an amazed owner.

Double-decker bus tours leave frequently in front of the hotel on Government Street. Boutique shops in the downtown core are just a block away. The concierges at the front desk are well-versed in tours and travel plans.

FAN TAN ALLEY

CHINATOWN

The two blocks that make up Victoria's Chinatown may seem small, but once you pass through the arched Gate of Harmonious Interest, at Fisgard and Government streets, you could easily spend an entire afternoon browsing, shopping and eating. At one time, this "forbidden city" covered several city blocks and bustled with more than 100 businesses, three schools, a hospital, two churches, five temples and two theatres. It is Canada's oldest Chinatown. Until the late 1800s, it was the largest Chinese settlement north of San Francisco.

The elaborate red-and-gold-tiled archway was the first permanent Chinese arch in Canada. In 1981, it was dedicated to symbolize the spirit of cooperation between the two cultures. Two hand-carved stone lions stand guard over the entrance, a gift from Victoria's twin city, Suzhou, China.

Modern Chinatown may be smaller than it was at the turn of the century, but the variety of food and shopping still holds its appeal. The merchants are out early each morning, setting up their outdoor vegetable markets. That hard-to-explain craving you have for wonton soup can be satisfied at almost any hour of the day. Walk along this street carefully so you don't miss Fan Tan Alley. This narrow passage — some say the narrowest street in Canada — is home to several artist studios and boutiques. Its more exotic history is that this was home to opium dens at the end of the nineteenth century.

FAN TAN ALLEY

An enjoyable way to spend a Sunday morning is at dim sum. This traditional Chinese brunch feast is served to you one delicious course at a time. Polish this down with a pot of Chinese tea and you're ready for your walk back downtown.

THE ART GALLERY OF GREATER VICTORIA

The only Shinto shrine outside Japan sits in the Asian Garden of the Art Gallery of Greater Victoria. If you walk up Fort Street from downtown for one and a half kilometres, you'll come to Moss Street. The art gallery is tucked in just around the corner.

SHRINE AT THE ART GALLERY OF GREATER VICTORIA

Although some of the art gallery is housed in a historic mansion built in 1889, from the outside the main building looks more like a high school. The gallery's main base is Gyppeswick mansion, built by the Spencer family and donated in 1951. Although the gallery has grown in size, the mansion is a significant part of the tour, from the tile painting of the Arthurian legend, Knights of the Round Table, to the large dollhouse in the wooden hallway. The dollhouse is complete with tiny perfect furnishings. This house is perfect in more ways than one: it's under glass, so there are no dusting chores for its tiny occupants. Step outside the mansion into the Asian garden. This is a peaceful spot, more subtle than colourful. A wooden Shinto shrine lends a reflective quality. The shrine was found abandoned in Japan and was rescued in 1987 and brought to the gallery.

There are six gallery spaces devoted to the works of B.C. artist Emily Carr. Her passionate nature paintings are compared to those of Georgia O'Keeffe and Vincent van Gogh. Some seniors in Victoria remember that Emily Carr herself was a visitor of the Spencer family, in the very mansion that is now the home of much of her original paintings. Also in these galleries are the works of contemporary Canadian artists, North American and European historical artists and traditional and contemporary Asian artists. There are more than thirty-five exhibits per year. Inside, the permanent collection of more than 15,000 pieces (the largest in B.C.) includes some of the finest examples of Japanese art in Canada. Most of these items are not on display every day, but one of the permanent exhibitions is a fourteenth-century Buddha head. The City of Victoria's Ming dynasty bell was moved here from Beacon Hill Park in 1990, perhaps because local kids of all ages figured out that if you curled your body up just right, and placed your hands and feet just so, you could hide inside the dangling bell.

Once a year, in the summer, the art gallery turns itself inside out for The Moss Street Paint-In. From the art gallery on Moss Street, all the way down to the beach at Dallas Road, artists line the sidewalks with their palettes and easels and thousands of people turn out to watch them at work. The gallery also offers several community programs on a regular basis including drop-in discussion groups twice a month. Tours run every day and there are lecture series throughout the year as well as art appreciation programs for children and a popular children's festival in September.

The gallery offers selected paintings for rent, private or business use, and some of these paintings are for sale. There's also a gift shop. From the art gallery you are only a short walk away from Craigdarroch Castle or the gardens at Government House (open to the public year round).

THE ROYAL BRITISH COLUMBIA MUSEUM

Adjacent to the Parliament Buildings, one of the most renowned museums in North America is open 363 days a year. The Royal British Columbia Museum, founded in 1886, sits on the corner of Belleville and Government streets. More than

HMS DISCOVERY

100 full-time staff and 335 volunteers run the dozens of exhibits and three large galleries. In the 26,000-square-foot-building, more than 10 million items document the human and natural history of British Columbia (though only a fraction of these are on display at any one time).

The Royal B.C. Museum is designed to allow you to experience British Columbia history through your senses. Of course, you can read the printed materials, or take the time to study all the accompanying display legends and documentation, but even if you just strolled through each room and hall, looking and listening, you would pick it up by osmosis. Perhaps a good gauge of the museum's success and popularity is the evidence at the entrance gate: thousands of Victoria locals return each year, alone, with guests or with their kids, to see the latest exhibit or spend an afternoon examining the items on all three floors.

Although each of the exhibits are in themselves worth seeing, it is the three galleries that have drawn the acclamation of curators and visitors from all over the world.

In the Gallery of Natural History, lifelike dioramas of forest and beach scenes complete with taxidermied animals and audiotaped sounds of the outdoors are strangely real. The trees, rocks and sand look inviting, except for the large grizzly hunting for fish and the stuffed mountain cat looking

GRIZZLY BEAR; LIVING LAND, LIVING SEA EXHIBIT

hungry himself. The history of settlement and development are documented with artifacts, pictures and scenes behind glass which, using a series of timed spotlights, literally illuminate the progress and struggle over the centuries. Many of the halls, all softly lit, pipe in a running dialogue discussing the items behind the glass. But beware the child who keeps pressing the "repeat" button.

The First Peoples' Gallery, founded in 1970 with the support of the local First Nations community, documents their triumphs and tragedies. Enlarged reproductions of early photographs, along with artifacts, video and audio, lead you through aboriginal history. Spend a contemplative moment in the Big House, still used for ceremonial purposes on occasion. In fact, the Big House is owned by the local First Nations community. That gives it the unusual distinction of being the only space in the museum that

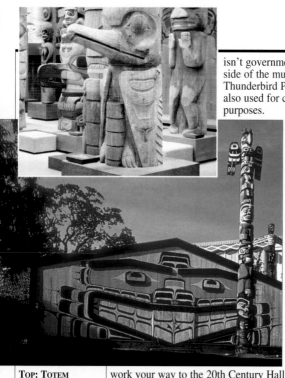

isn't government property. At the side of the museum building in Thunderbird Park is a longhouse, also used for ceremonial purposes.

In the Modern History Gallery you can walk along a nineteenth-century cobble-stoned road and look in the windows of old-time businesses: the saloon, the Chinese herbalist, the dressmaker. There's a 1913 Model T car named Elizabeth in the garage. You can see a miniature mill at work in the logging section as you eventually work your way to the 20th Century Hall. In this exhibit, a living-room scene has been replicated for each decade of the twentieth century, incorporating technological and design developments. Compare the history of the telephone, from a big wooden box on the wall to a cordless phone.

TOP: TOTEM GALLERY, FIRST PEOPLES' EXHIBIT
BOTTOM: GIANT WOOLLY MAMMOTH, LIVING LAND, LIVING SEA EXHIBIT

From the tiny to the gigantic, the museum has

something interesting or weird for everyone. For the bug collector, there are insect larvae and strange little critters that once roamed the territory where megastores now stand. Contrast these with the giant woolly mammoth, the museum's unofficial symbol and mascot, but don't embarrass yourself by asking who shot him. The woolly mammoth died in B.C. some 9,000 years ago.

Quite fascinating is the tiny, intricately decorated Chinese slipper-shoe, once worn by a woman who had her feet bound. You can't help but wonder if she embroidered it herself. And of course history includes things that some of us actually remember, such as John Lennon's 1965 psychedelic Rolls Royce. It's owned by the museum though it's often travelling (on loan for a mere $20,000).

In 1998, National Geographic opened an IMAX theatre in the

museum. This is a movie theatre with a six-storey screen and steeply pitched seats for 400. All movies are about countries or wildlife and they run several times a day. You can buy a combined pass for the museum and the IMAX theatre.

Museum staff suggest you take three or four hours to experience all the galleries and exhibits available. After your trek through history, relax in the cafe next door to the three gift shops.

THE MARITIME MUSEUM OF BRITISH COLUMBIA (ABOVE AND BELOW)

THE MARITIME MUSEUM OF BRITISH COLUMBIA

The Maritime Museum of British Columbia is in the middle of downtown Victoria, between Government and Wharf streets in Bastion Square. Located in Victoria's original 1889 provincial courthouse, the museum is home to a collection of more than 5,000 artifacts that tell the story of B.C.'s oceangoing history. Through its many precision-built models and antique nautical equipment, the galleries at this museum pay tribute to the Royal Canadian Navy from its early days. As well, they document the era of the elegant *Empress* steamships, vessels of the same vintage as the *Titanic*. The economy-class version is also represented in the paddle wheelers that once steamed through the province's inland waterways.

Although most items are under glass, there are a few things you are actually encouraged to touch and operate. There's an 1864 torpedo and some other nasty hardware you can play with (under supervision, of course). The old cage lift elevator, still there since the building was the provincial courthouse, was installed for one of the rather portly judges. It seems that there was some doubt as to whether he could continue to walk up the three flights of stairs to his courtroom without risking a heart attack. Today, you can climb into the elevator and get a ride to the third floor where you can watch a movie of a trip around Cape Horn, from the perspective of a four-masted sailing vessel in a storm. When you return to either the second or first floor, depending on the skill of the lift operator, you may have to take a small step up, or down, into the room.

The courthouse on the third floor is occasionally used for hearing cases today when the new court on Broughton Street gets jammed. But be warned: ghosts of cases past may be haunting these rooms. The original gallows were just a short distance from the courthouse and the executed were buried in paupers' graves in the courtyard. The remains of nine such unlucky citizens have been found during upgrading, but it is believed that there are still three graves somewhere under what is now the museum.

Museum staff have invented a treasure hunt for kids. There are written clues scattered throughout the building and the winners are rewarded with a treat. This is nice for kids, and great for parents.

If you'd like to take home a book for your nautical library, the museum's bookstore offers a comprehensive selection of maritime books on Vancouver Island, as well as the other items you find in most museum gift shops. After your trip through the museum, you can walk across the square for a pint to talk about your own seafaring days and then wander down towards the water where you may just look at the Inner Harbour in a new light. The museum is open seven days a week with extended daytime hours in the summer.

EMILY CARR HOUSE

A few short blocks behind the Parliament Buildings, at 207 Government Street, you'll find Emily Carr House, built in 1864. Emily Carr, Canada's first independent artist and writer, was born here in 1871, just a few months after British Columbia became the newest province in Canada. At the time, the house was located in a rural setting. The architecture of the artist's family home is described as both San Francisco Victorian and English Gingerbread. You can tour the restored rooms and see some of Carr's own pottery and sculpture as well as some of the family's original possessions.

Later in life, Emily Carr was an ingenious housekeeper. She rigged up a rope-and-pulley system and tied it to her sitting room chairs. When she didn't want visitors, she'd haul the chairs to the ceiling. Imagine as well her household menagerie, including her beloved pet monkey, Woo, and her griffon dogs.

In contrast to the Victorian artifacts, a modern

convenience has been added. A computer terminal is available in the house for guests to look up information about the life and work of Emily Carr. One of the other rooms is called The People's Gallery and is used to present the works of Canadian artists. These changing exhibits can be viewed from May to September. Parking in this area is cramped at best, so the ten-minute walk from downtown is your best bet.

EMILY CARR HOUSE

HELMCKEN HOUSE

Helmcken House is the oldest house in British Columbia on its original site. It was built in 1852 for Dr. John Sebastian Helmcken, after he married the daughter of Governor Sir James Douglas. Dr. Helmcken was a surgeon with the Hudson's Bay Company who went on to become a statesman and helped negotiate B.C.'s entry into Canada.

Originally, Helmcken House was a three-room log house. As the family grew, so did the house. Today there are guided tours through the restored rooms, which are set up with many of the original Victoriana knicknacks and furniture pieces in an attempt to make the house feel lived in. Although there are velvet ropes keeping you out of most of the rooms, you can sit on the reproduction sofa in the parlour, formerly the room where ladies entertained. Upstairs in the attic, there are old trunks and books and wooden toys you can examine. Dr. Helmcken's original nineteenth-century medical kit is on display on the top floor in the newest part of the house added in 1883.

Helmcken House is right beside the Royal British Columbia Museum and adjacent to Thunderbird Park, where you can sometimes watch totem poles being carved.

HELMCKEN HOUSE

POINT ELLICE HOUSE

In the middle of an industrial area, in what seems like the heart of a wrecking lot, there is a little oasis called Point Ellice House. Caroline and Peter O'Reilly owned Point Ellice House in the late 1800s. Both emigrated from England in the 1850s,

POINT ELLICE HOUSE DINING ROOM

Caroline after having spent some time in India looking for a British officer to marry. Instead, she married Peter O'Reilly in 1863 and they spent the next few years in Victoria and on the mainland. After the birth of her second child, Caroline wanted to settle in Victoria to be near her own family. When they established their home at Point Ellice House, she was the quintessential lady of the house, organizing dinner parties and social events. Point Ellice House quickly became the place to be for local schmoozers.

Peter O'Reilly, after emigrating to Canada at the age of 31, was employed as a justice of the peace, a magistrate, a gold commissioner, a collector of revenue, an assistant commissioner of lands, an Indian agent and a coroner. From 1864 to 1881 he served on the British Columbia Legislative Council as a magisterial appointee. In 1881, he retired as a judge.

The gardens at Point Ellice House have been restored according to the meticulous notes kept by daughter Kathleen O'Reilly. Some of the heritage varieties of plants here are not often found in modern gardens. Today, the English-garden atmosphere is often used for private functions such as weddings, company parties and special anniversaries.

Inside the house, more than 10,000 original O'Reilly items have been catalogued by conservators and are on display, touted as the largest collection of Victoriana in its original setting. There is an audio tour of the house narrated by the "house boy," which no doubt makes Caroline O'Reilly turn in her grave.

Point Ellice House is located at 2616 Pleasant Street. If you travel west over the Bay Street Bridge and turn north on Pleasant Street, you'll see the large Point Ellice House sign. You can also get there from the Inner Harbour by taking a small Harbour Ferry across the water.

POINT ELLICE HOUSE

CRAIGDARROCH CASTLE

Though magnificent, it isn't really a castle. The Gaelic translation of Craigdarroch is "rocky oak place." Certainly the Dunsmuir family, who built Craigdarroch, couldn't have imagined how apt this name would be.

Craigdarroch was built in the late 1880s. Robert Dunsmuir and his wife, Joan, had emigrated from Scotland and before moving to Victoria, lived in Nanaimo (a 90-minute drive north of Victoria today). In Nanaimo, Robert Dunsmuir began to make what became his fortune in mining. As mine superintendent for the Hudson's Bay Company, Robert discovered his own coal seam and started his own company, exporting the coal to San Francisco. In 1882 the family moved to Victoria, where Robert served as the representative for Nanaimo in the provincial legislative assembly.

The stone mansion built for the Dunsmuir family was built on the highest point in Victoria. Originally, there was a lake, a bridge, streams, an orchard, tennis courts, a coach house, stables and a gazebo on the estate. All that's left today is the mansion, the south lawn and its original stone wall. Robert Dunsmuir died shortly before completion of Craigdarroch, but his wife moved in with some of her daughters (she had eleven children) and grandchildren. Presumably they lived comfortably in the thirty-nine rooms on four floors with seventeen fireplaces. The mansion was designed, even then, with gas lighting, electricity, plumbing and the new telephones.

The interior panelling and woodwork of Craigdarroch was prefabricated and sent from Chicago. Inside the mansion you will be treated to the best collection of residential stained and leaded glass on the West Coast. In

DINING ROOM AT CRAIGDARROCH CASTLE

the grand entrance hall, the white oak staircase and sandstone fireplace greeted visitors to Craigdarroch, after they parked their coaches under the porte-cochère. On the second floor, two of the bedrooms are restored to their original Victorian state. In the Billiard Room, on the third level, you can stand on the Douglas fir floor and get a good view of the Juan de Fuca Strait and the Olympic Mountain range in Washington State. But the best view is from the tower, with its blue dome ceiling and curved doors and windows with circular stained-glass windows fitted above the doors. From here you can have an unobstructed vista of the ocean and mountains.

Some years after Robert Dunsmuir died, his two sons began legal proceedings against their mother for control of their generous trust funds. When one son died, he left his estate to his brother, who continued to engage Mrs. Dunsmuir in a legal battle that made newspaper headlines across Canada. Some reports say that Joan Dunsmuir was a recluse during the last eighteen years of her life, spending most of her time on the second floor of "rocky oak place."

BUTCHART GARDENS

Butchart Gardens is not a botanical gardens; it's just for show. But what a show it is. Butchart Gardens is 21 km (thirteen miles) north of Victoria, halfway between the Swartz Bay ferry terminal and Victoria. In the early 1900s, this 130-acre estate was the site of a rock quarry, where Robert Pim Butchart built his successful cement factory. Today, there are fifty acres of garden in the meticulously well-kept estate. The five main areas are the Sunken Garden, the Japanese Garden, the Rose Garden, the Concert Lawn and Ross Fountain.

Robert Butchart was born in 1856, the oldest of eleven children in a Scottish family living in Owen Sound, Ontario. In his early twenties he formed a partnership with some friends and began to manufacture Portland cement. The successful twist to his entrepreneurial idea was that Robert packaged and transported his cement in sacks, rather than the cumbersome barrels used at the time. As urban Canadian centres sprang up, the demand for cement increased, as did Robert Butchart's business. The young man went west.

In 1902, Robert moved to Victoria, where a nearby limestone deposit at Tod Inlet provided him with the materials needed for his business: limestone, clay, fresh water and the possibility of transportation by sea. Shortly thereafter he established the Tod Inlet Cement Plant, on the grounds of what is now Butchart Gardens. His Toronto-born wife, Jennie Foster Butchart, and their two daughters, moved to the site and set up their home. Mrs. Butchart was a certified chemist and sometimes worked in the cement factory — presumably for love, and not money. To hide the unsightly factory from view, Jennie Butchart planted some trees and shrubs. When their formal residence was complete, she turned her hand to the construction of a Japanese garden, with the help of Japanese landscape artist Isaboru Kishida.

In 1908, the limestone supply from the quarry was exhausted and it was abandoned. The story goes that an offhand comment made to Jennie Butchart by a friend — "Even you would be unable to get anything to grow in there" — was the inspiration of what is now the famous Sunken Gardens. Jennie had tons of topsoil brought in by horse and cart from nearby farms, and she used a bosun's chair to lower herself down the sides of the quarry, where she tucked ivy into the crevices, knowing it would one day cover the bleak walls. Rock gardens were made with the unearthed stones. A deep part of the three-and-a-half-acre quarry was lined and filled with water from a natural spring, forming a lake forty feet deep in places. The Sunken Garden took nine years to make, and was completed in 1921.

BUTCHART ROSE GARDEN

JAPANESE GARDEN

The Italian Garden, the most formal of all the gardens, was completed in 1926. The bronze girl-and-dolphin statue in this garden was purchased by the Butcharts in Italy. The Rose Garden was completed in 1930, and here too the centrepiece wrought-iron wishing well was imported from Florence, Italy. As her gardens grew, Mrs. Butchart hosted hundreds and then thousands of curious guests, offering them tea and showing them around the gardens for free. In the 1930s, she and her husband were honoured with citizenship awards from the City of Victoria.

In 1939, thirty-five years after starting their garden work, the Butcharts presented the gardens to their grandson, Ian Ross, who continued to devote the same care until his death in 1997. It was Ian Ross who oversaw the illumination project in the 1950s. At the time, it was one of the largest underground wiring projects in North America. Hundreds of miles of electrical cords were laid in the ground so that specially hidden lights would show off the gardens at night. Ross Fountain, at the far end of the gardens, was named for Mr. Ross, and the patterns made here by the lights and the 21-metre-high spray continue for many hours before they are repeated.

Every year 400,000 new bulbs are planted by the fifty full-time gardeners. On summer nights, there are fireworks

MING DYNASTY BELL

choreographed to music and concerts featuring local actors, singers and dancers. Throughout the gardens teak benches are strategically placed for viewing. (Some of these benches were made from the decking of British sailing ships.) You can have afternoon or high tea (more substantial) in what was the original Butchart residence, but it's not free anymore.

If you're driving, follow Blanshard Street as it becomes Highway 17, and turn left on Keating Cross Road (about 21 km north of Victoria). From there, follow the signs to the gardens. Public transit and private tour buses will also get you there. Everybody knows where the Butchart Gardens are.

BEACON HILL PARK

Centrally located Beacon Hill Park is across from the greatest soft ice cream drive-through in town (The Beacon Drive-In on Douglas Street). The combination of soft ice cream and the oldest and largest park in Victoria is difficult to resist. When the city was granted Beacon Hill Park in trust in 1882, the council introduced by-laws regulating the use of the park. To this day, you may not graze your cattle here or discharge firearms. Nor should you use the grass to clean your carpets.

You get the strange sense that Beacon Hill Park is made up of different rooms, each one with an ambiance of its own. You can roll up your pant legs and paddle in the wading pool on a hot day, or you can stroll through one of the more shady "rooms" and watch the ducks and swans from one of the wooden bridges, arched over a stream. The swans have a royal pedigree, from the first ones shipped from The Royal Swannery on the Thames in the 1940s. There is an English-style rose garden as well as exotic eucalyptus and palm trees and the gnarled native Garry Oak.

Starting as early as February, the daffodils and crocuses spring up everywhere. Their bright yellows and purples complement the blue-green plumage of the peacocks you encounter on your walk. Bird watchers have recorded more than 150 species of birds in the park. If you are accompanied by a child, you can wander around the petting zoo with the goats and sheep, piglets, chickens and a pony (open in summer only). If you come on the right day, you may catch an outdoor concert, a Shakespeare-in-the-park performance or the harmonies of a tenor and his diva in the bandshell. Or, on a Saturday morning, you might take in some cricket on the outskirts of the park. Beacon Hill Park is a no-commercial zone, so bring your own picnic lunch.

If you walk up the hill, past the 350-year-old Chinese Bell, you can rest in the Checker House where you'll get a great view of the Olympic Mountain range south of the

FOUNTAIN IN BEACON HILL PARK

WATERFOWL AT BEACON HILL PARK

FORT STREET ANTIQUES (ABOVE) AND SHOP (BELOW)

border. It was on this hill that two beacons were set up in the mid-1800s to guide ships and it was for these beacons that officers of the Hudson's Bay Company named the park. On the other side of the hill, towards Dallas Road and the ocean, is the official "Mile 0" of the Trans-Canada highway. If you cross the street here, you can follow the path along the cliffs or climb down the steps to one of the beaches. If you're driving, or biking, the route along Dallas Road is probably the most spectacular in Victoria. You'll pass several scenic lookout points along the ocean and some prize-winning neighbourhood gardens.

OAK BAY

About three kilometres east of downtown Victoria lies the village of Oak Bay. If you drive up Fort Street and veer right onto Oak Bay Avenue, follow the road into this British-style shopping district. It has a bookstore, gift stores, women's clothing stores as well as a mews with various eccentric items on both sides of the street (from lingerie to children's toys).

At the corner of Oak Bay Avenue and Hampshire, the Blethering Place is a cozy English-style teahouse in which to rest your feet. Amidst lace-covered tables and English memorabilia, you can treat yourself to a platter of crustless sandwiches and enjoy scones with cream and raspberry jam and your favourite black (or herbal) tea. It's a better value for your dollar than afternoon tea at The Empress, though the atmosphere is a tad more modest.

If you follow Oak Bay Avenue past the shops, curve to the right, take a left on Windsor Street and you will come to the Oak Bay Marina on Beach Drive. (If you take a right, you can have tea or a big dinner at the charming Windsor House Tearoom, 2540 Windsor Street). There's a decent cafeteria at the marina as well as the more posh restaurant. Either one gives you a view of the boats in the harbour through the large windows. If you walk along the path beneath the restaurants, you have a good chance of getting up close and personal with one of the many seals that hang around waiting for scraps of fish from the daily catch.

Willows Beach is just a short drive east along Beach Drive from the marina (turn right when you leave the parking lot). This sandy beach and play area for kids is lively in the summer, especially if you're young and have the latest in fashion swimwear. Admire the great view of Mount Baker, a mountain and extinct volcano in the State of Washington.

If you turn left as you leave the marina, you'll find the Oak Bay Beach Hotel on Beach Drive. Inside this Tudor-style hotel is The Snug, an English-style pub where you can relax with a beer and a decent meal. If there's room, you can sit on the patio overlooking the gardens and the ocean.

SHOPPING

MELANEY BLACK

Downtown Victoria, or Old Town Victoria, can be covered on foot in about an hour — a little longer if you stop at one of the many world-famous attractions nestled among fine examples of turn-of-the-century architecture. Lucky for you, one of these buildings, The Fairmont Empress Hotel, is also a good place to start your shopping tour.

FAIRMONT EMPRESS HOTEL/VICTORIA CONVENTION CENTRE

For most shoppers, Victoria begins here. The Fairmont Empress, a historic Canadian Pacific hotel, holds centre stage in Victoria's signature Inner Harbour. This elegant setting tempts travellers with objets d'art, designer clothes and exotic chocolates in shopping areas throughout the upper and lower hotel reception areas. Pewter and porcelain collectibles, sculpture and English woollens are all part of The Fairmont Empress shopping experience. Aboriginal art and masks can be found in the Art of Man Gallery at the back of the hotel where it joins the Victoria Convention Centre. Among the convention centre stores on adjacent Douglas Street, you will find Collections of Madison Avenue, a fine clothes retailer, and the renowned Stephen Lowe Art Gallery.

149

GOVERNMENT STREET

Moving up Government Street from The Fairmont Empress front entrance, you'll find Harbour Trading Company at the corner of Government and Wharf streets. This holds a compendium of Canadian and international gifts: art prints, blown glass, fleece sports apparel and collectibles.

Government Street abounds with treasures for the discriminating shopper. For those with a penchant for chocolate, try Rogers Chocolates or Purdy's Chocolates. Irish Linen Stores boasts a wide assortment of table linens and home goods, as well as some women's clothing. For lovers of fine British tweeds, British Importers has a complete selection of men's clothing and accessories. Similarly, W&J Wilson offers Aran and Payne sweaters and several lines of men's apparel.

ROGER'S CHOCOLATES

If you love fine china, head for Sydney Reynolds for Spode, St. George, Royal Victorian and Brown Dorset. From here, you can stroll to Copithorne and Row, which features Waterford crystal and Wedgwood and Dresden figures. You'll also appreciate its Belleek and Swarovski china and quality giftware.

**MIDDLE: CHINA AT SYDNEY REYNOLDS
BOTTOM: GOVERNMENT STREET**

No less than three Victoria stores are devoted exclusively to Christmas decorations and novelties, and two of these can be found on Government: The Spirit of Christmas and the Original Christmas Village. One block west towards the water is Christmas House. If you're looking for beautifully made decorations, ornate Christmas gift items and a variety of Christmas icons, these elves' workshops are open year-round.

A major landmark in Old Town Victoria is the very contemporary Hudson's Bay (now called The Bay) Centre Mall, a four-tiered shopping area built around a central courtyard, fountain and clock, spanning an entire block of Government Street from Fort Street to View Street. Those searching for the familiar will find it in Bryan's Fashions,

La Senza Lingerie, Mariposa, Bentley, Aldo Shoes, Tabi International, Boutique of Leathers and the Body Shop.

Across the street from The Bay is historic Munro's Books, nestled in a 1909 building. You'll find books for every interest. Next door is a B.C. icon, world-famous Murchie's Tea and Coffee, where you can buy Olde English and exotic teas, local coffee blends and gifts for caffeine connoisseurs. To complete the European flavour of the area, consider Crabtree & Evelyn for English toffee, soaps and scents and the finer things in life.

Wharf Street, one block west, primarily features restaurants that appeal to a variety of palates. If, however, you'd like to buy an interactive gift for those at home, you could have your pseudo-historical picture taken at Grandpa's Antique Photo on Wharf and Yates streets, choosing from a selection of costumes to suit your personality.

YATES STREET

If you appreciate and/or collect blown glass, shoppers can walk east up Yates to Broad Street and drop in on a live glass-blowing demonstration at Starfish Glassworks. Many of the artists sell their wares in the studio, where you will find everything from traditional forms to avant-garde expressions of the art in a myriad of colours.

Yates Street is also the place for those with a sweet tooth for British confections. The British Candy Shoppe teases taste buds with British toffee, biscuits and grocery items. A block farther up you'll find the English Sweet Shop, offering a similarly tempting array of English chocolates and sweets.

TOP: SHOP ON FORT STREET
ABOVE AND BELOW: ART AT SA-NUU-KWA GALLERY
BOTTOM: SWEATERS AT COWICHAN TRADING POST

First Nations art is very popular in Victoria. While the Art of Man Gallery deals in large-scale art works on canvas or soapstone sculptures, the Cowichan Trading Company features locally designed and knit Cowichan sweaters, small carvings and a wide assortment of less formal crafts. Hill's Indian Crafts also sells gold and silver jewellery, as well as moccasins, carvings and Inuit art.

MARKET SQUARE

Market Square, a collection of specialty stores built around a central courtyard, has something for all ages.

MARKET SQUARE

Out of Hand features the work of local artists, ranging from intriguing fountains to elegant objets d'art and framed acrylics, while Marigold Galleria is bursting with ceramic sculpture, glass and contemporary collectibles. For the young or the young at heart, try Foxglove Toys or sample the latest bestsellers at Griffin Books. There's even a store — Waffles, A Doggie Diner — for your favourite canine friend.

You'll find exotic gifts at Hoi Polloi and La Cache, and cafes to suit every taste. You can also sample the decadent pleasures of Fat Phege's Fudge Factory. Bricks of your favourite fudge flavours are created while you watch.

CHINATOWN

The Gates of Harmonious Interest at the corner of Government and Fisgard streets mark the entrance to the smallest Chinatown in Canada. Here you'll find an eclectic mix of east and west. Quonley's combines groceries and gifts in bamboo, wicker and brass. Nestled among the open-air markets, restaurants and exotic aromas on Fisgard is the Chinatown Trading Company, offering hand-painted ceramics, mats, bamboo, affordable gift items and housewares. Next to the Chinatown Trading Company is the entrance to Fan Tan Alley, a hodgepodge of storefronts that cater to more global interests. From musical instruments to artists' studios to African clothing and jewellery, these close quarters provide a unique shopping experience. Back on Fisgard beyond the alley is Fan Tan Gallery, a sensual array of textures and colours, batik, woods, glass and folk art from around the world.

ANTIQUE ROW

ANTIQUE ROW

Packed into two city blocks on Fort Street, Antique Row draws those who appreciate the beauty of history. Each vendor has a particular specialty. Period furniture is found at Charles Baird and Faith Grant. Look for china, depression glass or pottery at The Glass Menagerie and the Old Vogue Shop. You'll find silver and jewellery at Maggie Dove and a little bit of everything at Recollections. Whatever you're looking for, Antique Row offers a rich assortment of pre-millennium artifacts.

DINING

Gary Hynes

Although the Victoria dining scene is generally more laid-back and sedate than its trendy Vancouver cousin, an influx of younger chefs over the last few years is proving it has more to offer than the places on the Inner Harbour tourist beat. The city now offers many good restaurants, bistros and cafes. Neighbourhoods such as Cook St. Village and Antique Row are catering to an increasingly sophisticated crowd who are demanding quality and good service at affordable prices.

Compared to other major Canadian cities, high-quality dining is generally less expensive. Start your culinary tour in the city first and take in the charms of the heritage buildings and colourful gardens of Victoria. Then, if you're willing to take a short drive into the country, you will find many top tables set amidst spectacular West Coast surroundings. Dine at the Aerie Resort, high atop a mountain overlooking the long fiord-like Finalyson Arm, or make a pilgrimage to Sooke Harbour House, one of Canada's gastronomic treasures.

BENGAL LOUNGE AT THE FAIRMONT EMPRESS HOTEL

FINE DINING

Fine dining in Victoria in most cases means an emphasis on what is local and in season. The valleys and coastal areas of Vancouver Island are a haven for small farmers, many of them escapees from the big cities on the mainland. Many chefs scour the farm gates of the Cowichan Valley, Metchosin Valley or Saanich Peninsula trying to outdo

153

CAFE BRIO

their rivals in sourcing out the most flavourful blackberries or the rarest heirloom tomatoes. Throw in the catch from the sea, such as local spot prawns, Dungeness crab, sablefish and a variety of wild salmon, and why would they want to cook with faraway global ingredients anyway?

In town, for four-star dining and impeccable service, there's The Victorian Restaurant in the Ocean Pointe Resort and Spa. This sleek, contemporary room has the best seats for viewing the city's skyline across the waters of the Inner Harbour, including the Parliament Buildings. Executive Chef Craig Stoneman excels at creating menus that feature local elk, venison and other game. Slightly uptown, along the trendy Antique Row, Cafe Brio serves up some of the

THE VIEW FROM OCEAN POINTE

best food in town. The art-filled room may be loud for some but the kitchen sources its crispy salad greens from a local farm. The staff is warm and knowledgeable and Greg Hayes' wine list always features a rare find or two. The cooking is contemporary Pacific Northwest and chef Chris Dignan creates wonderful multi-textured food combinations. A new addition to the dining scene is The Temple, located in a historic bank building close to the waterfront. Chef Sam Benedetto creates etherial dishes that are deceptively simple in their presentation but delightfully complex on the palate. Try the seafood — it's second to none.

The most sumptuous restaurants, however, are to be found just outside of town. No one visiting Victoria should miss one of Canada's top restaurants, the Sooke Harbour House. Fredrica and Sinclair Philip started this country inn nineteen years ago and have been receiving accolades ever since. Dazzlingly innovative and delightfully eccentric, the kitchen remains a crucible for modern Canadian regional cuisine. A close second is The Aerie Resort perched high up on the Malahat. Here, diners feast on the regionally-inspired creations of Chef Letarde, whose French techniques give a refined twist to the local ingredients he adores.

At the far tip of the Saanich Peninsula, near the ferries to Vancouver, chef Pierre Koffel of The Deep Cove Chalet has been turning out some of the most sophisticated dishes to be found in the province. There's fresh foie gras flown in from Quebec, truffle soup, scrambled eggs with caviar and a cellar full of vintage Bordeaux and Sauternes.

BISTROS, CAFÉS

Victorians are an outdoorsy lot and prefer not to dress up if they can help it. Therefore, the most popular destinations are the bistros and cafes springing up all over the city. A

THE HERALD ST. CAFE

husband-and-wife team look after Paprika Bistro in the city's tony Oak Bay area. Here, George Szasz's Hungarian background combines with his ability to present light, yet vividly flavoured dishes to make a night out in this intimate room a pleasure. At Brasserie L'Ecole, chef Sean Brennan and wine sommelier Marc Morrison team up to present classic French bistro dishes using Vancouver Island ingredients. Devotees swear by the steak and frites, which are tossed with parmigiano and doused with truffle oil. The daily cheese board offerings are not to be missed.

Casual modern restaurants are a hot category in Victoria. And no wonder. The prices are affordable, the food is well-prepared and contemporary and the people-watching, the entertainment. Suze Restaurant and Lounge has the downtown buzz of the martini set and is the place to go for people-watching and international, casual fare. Bravo, on Store Street, is relaxed elegance. At Rebar, a funky, quirky downtown café, you will discover that you never knew health food could be so good. You'll find inventive, delicious and guilt-free food.

TEAROOM ON FORT STREET

Victoria is also a city on the go and cafés where quick lunches and the best coffees keep its denizens well-fuelled never lack patrons. Zambri's, located downtown in a tiny strip mall behind a London Drugs, holds the title as the best Italian café. Order from Peter Zambri himself as he stands cooking at the stove in his small, open kitchen. He'll size you up and tell you what you should have. You can't go wrong with the Illy espresso. There's suave Foster's Eatery by the Bay Centre for designer sandwiches and Paradiso di Stelle on Bastion Square for gelato. Bond Bond's, the city's top bakery, serves simple, fresh lunches. A new trend are gourmet delicatessens that offer small meals. Great ambience can be found at the newly expanded Ottavio in Oak Bay and at La Collina on Cedar Hill Road. As well, both offer large selections of

155

fine cheeses, pastries and other gourmet products. Of course, Barb's Fish & Chips at Fisherman's Wharf is the spot for reliable fish and chips, hauling in both Victorians and visitors to this funky dockside take-out.

SEAFOOD

Good seafood is harder to find than you would think for this coastal city, but three restaurants come to mind when the urge for fresh fish hits. The Blue Crab Bar & Grill in the Coast Harbourside Hotel is Pacific Northwest casual and has a great water view. Check out the blackboard for the specials of the day and don't skip the desserts here — they're delicious. The Marina Restaurant at the Oak Bay Marina is just the nautical setting to sample fine naturally-smoked Black Cod braised in local Merridale cider. Twenty minutes outside the city, in Sidney, at another marina, Dock 503 keeps the focus finely tuned on the freshest seafood. After dinner take the time to explore Sidney's many used bookstores.

WITH TEA AT THE FAIRMONT EMPRESS

BREW PUBS

Since owner Paul Hadfield got an act of parliament to allow pubs to brew their own beer, Victoria has been a leader in craft brewing in Canada. Popular brews at his Spinnaker's Brew Pub include his light and lemony Hefeweizen wheat beer and a smoky Dunkleweizen. Do try their hot and sour soup, which is made from their own India Pale Ale malt vinegar. Other brew pubs worth a visit are Hugo's, Canoe, the Penny Farthing and Swans.

A SPOT OF TEA

For many, Victoria and English High Tea are synonymous. The Fairmont Empress Hotel holds court as the queen of teas. It isn't cheap, but the chance to sit amid such splendour while sipping on properly steeped and poured tea and munching on dainty sandwiches and flaky scones is worth the price of admission. Another fine spot for tea is Butchart Gardens outside town on picturesque Brentwood Bay. It is especially refreshing after a tramp around the spectacular gardens of Victoria's number-one attraction, the Butchart Gardens.

CHINATOWN

ETHNIC EATERIES

Victoria is a melting pot where different culinary cultures come together to add spice and nuance to the eating scene. Victoria's Chinatown, with its colourful history and other Asian influences, is shoulder-to-shoulder with grocery stores overflowing with the exotic and restaurants often serving the freshest fish in town. The always busy J & J Won Ton Noodle House, a simple noodle shop featuring tasty Chinese fare, is worth a visit.

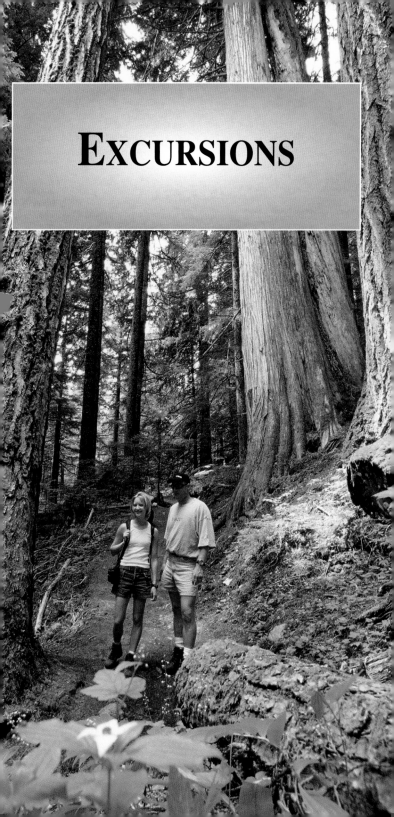

EXCURSIONS

WHISTLER

CONSTANCE BRISSENDEN

WHISTLER AND BLACKCOMB MOUNTAINS

Just when the world thought that Whistler, consistently voted North America's top ski and snowboard resort, couldn't get bigger or better, it was awarded the 2010 Olympic and Paralympic Winter Games. Sure, it shares the honour with Vancouver, but in the eyes of the locals, Whistler is the focus.

Forty years ago, Whistler was serviced by one ski lift. Travelling from Vancouver, 120 kilometres (75 miles) away, took seven hours on a rugged dirt road. By 1975, responding to tremendous growth, the Resort Municipality of Whistler, British Columbia's first and only resort designation, was created. This enlightened decision paid off.

SNOWBOARDER IN WHISTLER

Today Whistler is an international mega-star as well as a four-season destination. More than two million people visit annually. For eight months of the year, there's action on the slopes: skiing and snowboarding on the side-by-side Whistler and Blackcomb mountains from late November to mid-June (on Blackcomb to April 30), and again on Blackcomb from mid-June to mid-August on Horstman Glacier. The resort's extensive lift system is capable of carrying more than 59,000 skiers and riders per hour. With fifteen high-speed lifts (out of a 33-lift system), Whistler and Blackcomb boast the most high-speed lifts at a single resort in North America. You can also try cross-country skiing, snowmobiling, heli-skiing, heli-snowboarding, snowshoeing and sleigh rides. Ski and snowboarding lessons for adults and children are offered on both mountains.

In addition to accolades for its two mountains, Whistler Resort has been praised for best overall resort design, combining ski-in, ski-out convenience with distinctive nouveau European architecture. The original Whistler Village is now joined by Upper Village (also known as Blackcomb Benchlands) at the foot of Blackcomb Mountain and Village North off Lorimer Road. All three are within easy walking distance of one another. Creekside, the original Whistler site four kilometres south of Whistler Village, has experienced a recent building boom. The result is a more family-oriented alternative, with condominium-style lodging, kid-friendly restaurants and quick access to Whistler kids and family zones on the mountain.

SNOWMOBILING

As befits a town of more than 12,000 year-round residents, Whistler offers a complete range of services, including the Whistler Medical Centre, Whistler Public Library and the Whistler Museum and Archives. A new First Nations Cultural Centre is in the planning stages.

Nearly a dozen art galleries tempt visitors who may want to take home a First Nations carving or finely designed jewellery as a keepsake. Luxurious winter wear is also a shopping highlight. As befits an international resort, Whistler dining is exceptional. There are more than ninety restaurants, cafés and pubs. Visitors can also enjoy a variety of live entertainment in clubs and lounges.

In 1914, Alex and Myrtle Philip opened the Rainbow Lodge and soon had visitors backpacking in to canoe and fish the five local lakes. In 1966, when the first ski lift opened on Whistler Mountain, summer took a back seat, but it's now returned as a major draw. In late spring and fall, expect to find a quieter Whistler, with a number of attractions closed.

WHISTLER VILLAGE IN SUMMER

You get to Whistler by scheduled bus and air service as well as charter buses, taxis, limousines and charter air service. If you drive, take Highway 99 from Vancouver. Expect construction delays prior to the 2010 Olympic and Paralympic Winter Games. Free short-term parking is available in the Day Lodge outdoor parking area (off Lorimer Road). Free indoor parking is below the Royal Bank building (turn right off Village Gate Boulevard onto Whistler Way).

With the help of the Whistler Activity and Information Centre, it's easy to plan your holiday. For contact information, see Listings under Excursions/Whistler.

WHISTLER MOUNTAIN

Consider for a moment the thrill of Whistler Mountain's longest run, a satisfying eleven kilometres (6.8 miles). The mountain offers 1,480 hectares (3,657 acres) of skiable terrain, with twenty per cent designed for beginners, fifty-five per cent for intermediate skiers and twenty-five per cent for advanced to expert skiers.

Choice is the name of the game. Ski from the Whistler Gondola or Whistler Creekside. A third Whistler Mountain access point was added in 1999 with the Fitzsimmons Quad, installed between the Blackcomb Excalibur Gondola and Whistler Gondola. It connects with the new Garbanzo Express that goes up, up, up with the greatest vertical rise of any chair on either mountain. On your way to the top, don't forget to count the more than 100 marked runs below.

Whistler Mountain also attracts enthusiastic snowboarders, with options for all. The Terrain Park is now ten and a half hectares (25 acres) of snowboarding freedom, ideal for newer riders. Expert boarders can start at the top at the Peak and Harmony Express and work their way down to intermediate and beginner levels. The Chipmunk Terrain Park debuted in 2002, an area more than 335 metres (1,100 feet) long with a vertical drop of 182 metres (600 feet). Park riders can take hits on rollers, hip jumps and spines, with a mini-snow cross track within the park. The Whistler Pipe, 91 metres (300 feet) long with walls up to four metres (thirteen feet), is for experienced park riders.

To satisfy culinary cravings, check out Whistler Mountain's restaurants. The newest is the Chic Pea at the top of Garbanzo Express, a rustic 230-seater serving pizzas, soups and humongous cinnamon buns. Old favourites include the renovated 1,740-seat Roundhouse Lodge with its full fast-food menu, and Pika's with its cafeteria-style offerings. Both eateries are at the top of the Whistler Express Gondola. Steep's, located in the Round House Lodge, offers casual seated dining. The Raven's Nest, at the top of the Creekside Gondola, boasts spectacular views and outdoor seating as well as hearty soups, stews and salads. Located at the Whistler Creek Base (at the bottom of the Creekside Gondola), Dusty's Bar & Barbeque, home to the Canadian BBQ Championships, takes you from breakfast to après-ski fun with an authentic BBQ taste.

BLACKCOMB MOUNTAIN

Blackcomb's nickname is the Mile-High Mountain. Launched in 1980 as a brand-new facility, Blackcomb rivalled Whistler until the merger of both mountains in 1996 under the Intrawest name. The merger has been spectacularly successful in terms of mountain improvements and Whistler's growth.

Blackcomb is serviced by three base areas: Excalibur Village Station, Upper Village Blackcomb Base (known as the Daylodge) and Excalibur Base II Station. There are more than 100 marked runs. Fifteen per cent are designed for beginners, fifty-five per cent for intermediate skiers and thirty per cent for the advanced and expert group. A few seasons back, the mountain unveiled its superb Excalibur gondola system, featuring ninety-seven eight-passenger sit-down cabins capable of carrying 2,600 skiers an hour. Combined with the Excelerator high-speed quad chair and the Glacier Express, skiers can climb from village to glaciers in nineteen minutes.

Snowboarding has an impressive niche in Blackcomb's challenging six and a half hectare (16-acre) snowboard Terrain Park, accessible by its own lift, the Catskinner Triple Chair. Like Whistler Mountain, Blackcomb has different parks aimed at different abilities. The Big Easy Terrain Garden is the place to start as an introduction to freestyle features. Work up to Highest Level, 525 metres (1,720 feet) long with a 148 metre (485 foot) vertical drop. Park features include big table tops, hips, spines, rails and jibs.

Dining on the mountain is a must. For a warm-up, grab a freshly-brewed coffee or have lunch at the Mountain Grill, located in the Rendezvous at the top of Solar Coaster. Horstman Hut, at the top of 7th Heaven, serves a variety of hot food including soups, stews and jambalaya. Crystal Hut, with its rustic theme, offers wood-oven prepared steak and salmon, Belgian waffles and an evening fondue program. Glacier Creek, at the base of the Jersey Cream and Glacier Express quad chairs, is Blackcomb's largest dining facility. Upstairs is River Rock Grill, with ten food market areas ranging from made-to-order deli sandwiches to Asian stir fry. Downstairs is the B.C. Eatery featuring fresh West

DOWNHILL SKIER

KIDS AT WHISTLER RESORT

Coast cuisine in a bistro-style atmosphere. For casual seated dining, head to Christine's in the Rendezvous with its view of Wedge Mountain and Armchair Glacier.

Blackcomb Benchlands is a mix of hotels, shops, restaurants and condominiums centered in and around Château Whistler Resort. The Château, built in the grand Canadian Pacific Railway style, features stone-clad fireplaces and domed ceilings painted with gold leaf. Just walking through is a vicarious pleasure. In 2004, the adjacent Four Seasons Hotel opens to rival the Château in luxury and glamour.

SUMMER ACTIVITIES

You can still canoe down the River of Golden Dreams in Whistler, a favourite of Alex Philip in the early 1900s. The mountains, and the resort's five lakes (Alpha, Nita, Alta, Lost and Green), are still there. What has changed, however, is the way you experience them. Mountain biking on Whistler Mountain is hugely popular. Or try summer skiing and snowboarding on Blackcomb, helicopter and float plane flights, glider rides, paraglides, valley bus and four-wheel drive tours, in-line skating, horseback riding, hayrides, white-water rafting, jet boating, kayaking and good old, unadorned hiking. Try the Ancient Cedars Trail for an easy, four-kilometre hike to old-growth forest. A unique experience is a four-by-four jeep ride to active bear dens with bear researcher Michael Allen. Ride the lifts to sightsee on the glaciers on Blackcomb Mountain, but take a very warm jacket. Golfing is also a favourite, with four local designer courses in awe-inspiring settings.

When you need a break from all that healthy physical stuff, take in some culture. Street entertainers, band concerts, art shows, jazz, blues and even symphony concerts will entertain you and your family. Throughout the summer and fall, annual festivals add energy to the scene, from the Whistler Arts Festival in June to Cornucopia, a food and wine festival in November.

Children get plenty of attention at Whistler and Blackcomb Mountains. The Adventure Zone Activity Centre at the base of Blackcomb includes activities such as rock-climbing at The Great Wall Underground. Swim with the family at the Meadow Park Aquatic Centre or ice skate at the Meadow Park Arena. At the five local lakes, swimming, picnicking, fishing and canoeing are options. Château Whistler runs the Tennis Tigers camp daily in July and August. First-run movies are shown at the Rainbow Theatre and Village 8 Cinemas. As well as nature walks, families can challenge the easygoing Valley Trail on rented bikes, skateboards or in-line skates. Children's mountain-bike camps are a big draw on Whistler Mountain. For more information on children's activities, contact the Whistler Activity and Information Centre.

TOP: KAYAKING ON THE RIVER OF GOLDEN DREAMS MIDDLE: HORSEBACK RIDING IN WHISTLER

BLACK BEAR IN WHISTLER

GULF ISLANDS

ANNE SMART

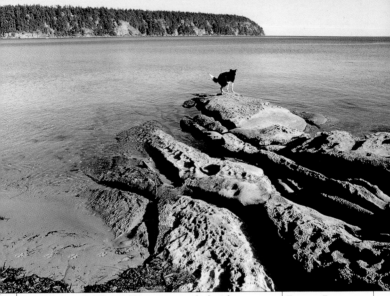

In 1792, Captain George Vancouver, exploring the waters between the mainland and what is now Vancouver Island, believed himself to be in a gulf rather than a continuous body of water. The numerous islands and islets in the Strait of Georgia therefore became — erroneously — the Gulf Islands. Nestled in the lee of Vancouver Island, they exert an irresistible charm, luring both visitors and immigrants from around the world.

In the 1850s, some of the earliest settlers were slaves from south of the border. Others, naturally, were European. Altogether, the settlers formed an eclectic mix: the Hudson's Bay Company, which had previously controlled the area, developed trading outposts and some of their Hawaiian employees also settled here. Japanese families, often originally engaged in small fishing operations, came later. Several developed market gardens. Chinese settlers were not uncommon. These early families worked hard to clear the forest and establish farms on the 160 acres they could claim in the new British colony. Logging, farming, fishing and attempts to mine were the earliest occupations. With a mild year-round climate on their side, some of the islands soon supplied a major part of the Canadian fruit market, until the province's Okanagan Valley on the mainland took over the role. Old orchards are still very evident throughout the islands.

TRIBUNE BAY ON HORNBY ISLAND

HELLIWELL PARK ON HORNBY ISLAND

Early settlers faced many challenges. Some were confronted by First Nations bands, who came seasonally to the shores to fish and gather shellfish. Local transportation in canoes and rowboats resulted in drowning deaths. Cougars were rampant and children frequently had to be protected from these hungry predators. Living in the islands today, by contrast, is idyllic. Good paved roads abound and ferries run to many of the islands — some even have scheduled air transportation. Residents of the closer islands, with good ferry service, actually commute to work on Vancouver Island. More frequently, except for those who retire to the kind climate, islanders tend to work at home. Jobs are scarce though, and many people choose to live simply and pursue their talents, selling the varied artistic results in local stores and markets. Many acclaimed artists live here, some even selling from their own home-studios.

STOPOVERS

B.C. Ferries' circle route offers scenic daytrips to several of the islands. For those who want to stay and visit a while, accommodations are varied on most of the larger islands, and include bed and breakfasts, hotels, lodging rooms and cabins. There are also several places to camp in provincial parks or on private campgrounds. Although the islands are lovely in wintertime quietness, gorgeous during blossom-bedecked spring months and magnificent in fall colours, most visitors come in summertime. It's a good idea to arrange your summer accommodations in advance with the help of local tourism agencies, accessible now by mail, telephone or on-line.

Most people arrive by ferry, perhaps watching for sea life, such as seals raising their heads in curiosity, or otters running the rocks of the shores in search of shellfish. Bald eagles and herons swooping over the water are a frequent sight. Some vacationers seek the tranquility of isolation. They come simply to enjoy quiet walks in the woods with only the songs of the birds for background noise. Others will want a strenuous hike first, earning the peaceful contemplation of a Gulf Island panorama from a fragrant mountain meadow.

If you like mingling with other visitors and locals, the islands offer craft shops, markets and local pubs and restaurants. Those who like to fish can spend their leisure time at a freshwater lake well-stocked with trout, or in an oceangoing boat, taking a chance at hooking a mighty salmon. Hikers, bikers, paddlers, sailors, golfers, shoppers and the downright lazy all have their ideal image of the perfect holiday. The Gulf Islands can please them all.

SALT SPRING ISLAND

The largest of the thirteen major Gulf Islands, with several freshwater lakes, Salt Spring is named for its salty north-end mineral springs. It is the most heavily populated of the Gulf Islands. Irregularly shaped and about 27 kilometres (16 miles) long, it has a population of approximately 10,000. Salt Spring boasts the only hospital facilities and the only high school in the Gulf Islands. It also has three ferry terminals. Accommodations here are plentiful and range widely in cost and type.

SALT SPRING ISLAND'S ECOLOGICAL RESERVE

You'll find three distinct villages on the island, each with stores, restaurants and a pub. Fulford Harbour in the south, and Vesuvius in the north, are quite residential. Ganges, in the narrowed mid-section, is the commercial centre. Each village has its own distinct personality and all can be explored on foot. Some residences date back to the early settlers. Some are barely more than cabins, and some of recent vintage are far more elaborate. Note the sturdy and sometimes eccentric fencing around the vegetable gardens, designed in various formats to discourage deer, those prolific and voracious vegetarians.

Allow plenty of time to explore the treasures to be found in Salt Spring's numerous craft shops, galleries and studios. Before leaving, stroll the Ganges sea walk to enjoy the views of the chain of islands in the long harbour and the yachts at moorage and anchor.

GALIANO ISLAND

GALIANO ISLAND

Some people consider Galiano the most scenic of the Gulf Islands, with its shoreline ranging from high bluffs to sandy beaches. Nearly as long as Salt Spring Island, Galiano is less than nine kilometres (5 miles) at its widest, but boasts seven parks. The nature of the land and the lack of water have made farming on Galiano a challenge, making fishing, historically, a more important industry.

The population here grows very slowly compared to most Gulf Islands. For some time, it has stood at little more than 1,000 residents. This small group is fiercely independent, exerting recent political action to preserve their island from clear-cutting.

Several accommodation options are available on Galiano, including camping. Montague Harbour

DIONISIO POINT PARK ON GALIANO

Park, in the south end, has white-shell beaches and a lagoon that can be explored by a trail system. Dionisio Point Park, in the north end, features natural sandstone sculptures along its shoreline.

GABRIOLA ISLAND

This island can be circumnavigated by bike in several hours. Many of its several thousand residents commute daily to Nanaimo on Vancouver Island to work, since it's only a twenty-minute ferry run between Descanso Bay and downtown Nanaimo. Gabriola is an easy place to visit for a day if you're exploring Vancouver Island.

Here, too, there are a variety of places to stay, eat and shop, as well as several provincial parks with picnic facilities, hiking trails and beautiful views. Sandwell Provincial Park offers petroglyphs for view at low tide. Drumberg Provincial Park has interesting sculptured sandstone formations.

MAYNE ISLAND

Gold Rush miners stopped at Mayne Island in the mid-1800s en route to B.C.'s mainland goldfields. Later the island was a major fruit producer; orchards are still to be found everywhere, reminding visitors of an earlier time. Although one of the earliest islands to be settled, with deeds dating back to 1859, the population today is only about 900. With nearly two dozen different accommodation facilities, the residents are a hospitable group. Locales such as Georgina Point Lighthouse Park, Bennett Bay, Campbell Bay, Oyster Bay and Piggott Bay make staying on worthwhile.

SATURNA ISLAND

GABRIOLA ISLAND'S DRUMBERG PROVINCIAL PARK

With a choice of eighteen places to stay, visitors to Saturna Island can cycle, hike or paddle past galleries of sandstone sculptures. Scenic walks may lead to glimpses of abundant wildlife. East Point Park has a lovely swimming beach ideally situated to view whales from the shore while Winter Cove Provincial Park features a beach and a tidal marsh popular among bird watchers. Think Saturna, think annual Lamb Barbecue each July 1, Canada's birthday. The entire population of about 350 residents work together tirelessly to invite the world at large to come and celebrate with them.

SUNSHINE COAST

KEVIN BARKER

SECHELT FROM THE AIR

The misty fiords immediately north of Greater Vancouver have endured many misconceptions since old George Gibson first weighed anchor in Gibsons Harbour some 100 years ago. But none is more enduring than the mistaken belief of just about everyone that the Sunshine Coast is an island.

Although a forty-minute ferry ride from Horseshoe Bay to Langdale is required to reach it, the Sunshine Coast is not an island but part of mainland British Columbia. It is, in fact, a highly recommended day-trip along a ribbon of highway that winds past seaside communities like Gibsons, Roberts Creek and Sechelt. When you finally reach the rocky shores of Jervis Inlet, you can embark on yet another ferry to Powell River and the northern terminus of Highway 101. Add another day for the extension.

Sunshine is indeed more plentiful on the Sunshine Coast. Unspoiled beaches like Bonniebrook and Davis Bay are in abundance, along with excellent hiking trails such as Cliff Gilker Park. Fishing, diving, canoeing, sailing and kayaking attract visitors to both the Lower and Upper Sunshine coasts. Not that culture doesn't get a nod: Gibsons' Elphinstone Pioneer Museum brings an old-time lifestyle of logging, fishing and farming to life while the *tems swiya* Museum at the east entrance to Sechelt is a showcase for the *shishalh* nation's culture, art and artifacts.

Many visitors are sufficiently enamoured of the seaside town of Gibsons, located about two kilometres (one and a quarter miles) from the Langdale ferry dock, to talk about house prices with the several realtors who work along Marine Drive. Before you move on, check out Molly's Lane for antique stores and the Sunshine Coast Maritime History Museum. It's right behind Molly's Reach, an ancient maritime hotel that was the setting for a long-running television series, The Beachcombers.

167

SECHELT AND SURROUNDING AREA

A few kilometres past Gibsons is Cliff Gilker Park, with an excellent network of trails adjacent to the 18-hole Sunshine Coast Golf & Country Club. In Roberts Creek, turn left on Roberts Creek Road and drive to the The Gumboot Garden Café at the crossroad of Lower Road for a delectable lunch. For a lively evening, join in on the rather frequent hometown dances at the Roberts Creek Hall located near the corner of Roberts Creek Road and Highway 101.

Travelling northwest from "The Creek" one crosses a series of rivers before arriving in the mid-coast town of Sechelt, a narrow isthmus separating the Strait of Georgia from Sechelt Inlet. Downtown fronts a lovely sandy beach, with Snickett Park forming the west perimeter. Rockwood Lodge is a restored heritage house on Cowrie Street that hosts the annual Festival of the Written Arts in mid-August. The Sunshine Coast Arts Centre at the nearby corner of Trail and Medusa has local and off-coast visual arts. Local authors read from their works here. Note the unusual log construction of the building designed by pioneer builder Clarke Stebner.

Further up the road, Halfmoon Bay's rustic General Store suggests an earlier time when steamers made daily stops at the pier to drop off mail and pick up passengers. Situated on a picturesque bay, it is reached from Redroofs Road, which detours off the highway and winds past Sargeant Bay and Coopers Green (great picnicking) before meeting the highway a stone's throw from the bay itself. Homesite Road, farther along, features an old growth forest and great hikes.

The coastline gets progressively rockier towards Secret Cove and finally Pender Harbour, where communities lie clustered in tiny coves linked by secondary roads and the meandering coastline. The popular Pender Harbour Jazz Festival, held in September, draws a laid-back crowd. Madeira Park, Garden Bay and Irvines Landing are centered around the waters of Pender Harbour itself. The Ruby Lake Resort enroute to Earls Cove is ideal for boating and fishing.

If weather permits, take the Egmont turnoff just before Earls Cove and hike to Skookumchuk Narrows, where tidal forces weave the placid waters into gigantic eddies and whirlpools. Check the tide table for the best viewing times.

ISLAND ALTERNATIVES

Foot passengers arriving at the Langdale ferry dock are welcome to board the tiny *Dogwood Princess* to visit Keats or Gambier islands across Howe Sound. Both offer daytrippers excellent trails, beaches and kayaking routes. Keats Island enjoys a commanding view of the Strait of Georgia. Gambier is home to a wonderful general store complete with home-baked goodies, a curlicued façade and a rugged mountain backdrop.

Boaters should try to arrive at dusk when the harbours and coves are at their most exquisite. Keats Island has excellent moorage at Plumpers Cove on the northwest side.

CONTENTS

GETTING THERE

VANCOUVER
On the brink of the Pacific Ocean, at the foot of the Coast Mountains, Vancouver is well-served by air, land and sea routes.

BY AIR
Vancouver International Airport (YVR) is located south of Vancouver, approximately 15 minutes away in Richmond. A new international terminal was opened in 1996 as part of an expansion that included a new control tower and third runway. A major upgrade of the domestic terminal was completed in 2002. YVR serves 38 major carriers, and 19 regional and local airlines. General inquiries are taken at 604 207-7077. More information about YVR can be found at www.yvr.ca.

An Airport Improvement Fee (AIF) is levied from passengers departing from Vancouver: $5 when travelling within BC and the Yukon Territory, $10 when travelling to other North American destinations, and $15 when travelling to destinations outside North America. Children under two and passengers on same-day connecting flights are exempt.

From the airport, buses, shuttles, taxis and limousines are available curbside. TransLink, the city's public transit system (604 953-3333, www.translink.bc.ca), provides a connection from the airport into Vancouver and suburbs ($2 to $4 depending on distance and time of day). Take the #424 from the airport for the five-minute ride to Airport Station, then transfer to the limited-stop 98B-Line into downtown Vancouver 30 minutes away. Bus service to major downtown hotels is available via the Airporter ($12 one way, $18 return), 604 946-8866, 1-800-668-3141. Scheduled bus service is also available to Whistler, Victoria, Nanaimo, and Seattle, USA.

Courtesy shuttles are available to many local hotels. Taxis and limousines (Limojet Gold, 604 273-1331) picking up at the airport are regulated by the airport and are onsite 24 hours per day. Black Top and Checker Cabs (604 731-1111), MacLure's Cabs (604 683-6666),

Vancouver Taxi (604 871-1111) and Yellow Cab Company (604 681-1111 or 1-800-898-8294) are the main taxicab companies. A typical trip downtown would cost $30 by taxi and $39 by limousine. Car rental companies operating from YVR include Avis, Alamo, Budget, Hertz, National and Thrifty, plus several local enterprises.

BY SEA
BC Ferries (250 386-3431 in Victoria and outside BC; other parts of BC call 1-888-223-3779) offers year-round passenger and vehicle service from Vancouver Island, the Gulf Islands and many other parts of BC. Vehicle reservations can be made for an additional fee. Peak season fares (subject to change) are $10.25 adult, $5.75 child 5-11 years, $35.75 per car. See www.bcferries.com for information on sailing and fares.

BY CAR
Three major highways connect Greater Vancouver to the rest of British Columbia, Canada and the United States. Highway 99 connects the north end of the city to Whistler before joining Highway 97, BC.'s main north-south highway. To the south, Highway 99 also connects Vancouver to Washington's Interstate 5 and Seattle. The TransCanada Highway (Highway 1) runs into Vancouver through the Lower Mainland and Fraser River Valley from the rest of Canada, where its feeders include Highway 97 and various connectors and highways from the US.

BY BUS
Pacific Central Station (1150 Station St.) is Vancouver's bus station. Visitors from many US and Canadian cities can get to Vancouver on Greyhound buses (604 482-8747 or 1-800-661-8747 in Canada, 1-800-231-2122 in the US). Seattle travellers can catch Quick Shuttle Bus Service (604 940-4428 or 1-800-665-2122).

BY RAIL
Pacific Central Station is also the city's train station. VIA Rail (1-888-842-7245, www.viarail.ca) offers Canadian transcontinental service

three days a week. Travellers from Seattle may choose Amtrak (1-800-872-7245, www.amtrak.com), which operates one round-trip per day between Seattle and Vancouver.

VICTORIA

Three main options are available to the traveller:
- Fly to Victoria International Airport
- Fly to Vancouver, then transfer to a plane or a bus plus a ferry.
- Fly to Seattle, then transfer to a plane or a ferry.

BY AIR FROM VANCOUVER

Thirty-five minute flights to Victoria from Vancouver are offered by the following:
- Harbour Air Seaplanes (250 384-2215 in Victoria, 604 274-1277 in Vancouver, 1-800-665-0212 toll-free). Twin Otter seaplane service from downtown Vancouver and YVR to Victoria's Inner Harbour.
- Helijet International Incorporated (250 382-6222 in Victoria, 1-800-665-4354 in Vancouver). Helicopter service from downtown Vancouver or YVR to Victoria's Ogden Point, a five-minute drive from the Inner Harbour.
- West Coast Air (250 388-4521 in Victoria, 604 606-6888 in Vancouver, 1-800-347-2222). Float plane service from downtown Vancouver to Victoria's Inner Harbour.
- Air Canada (1-800-247-2262). Flights on small planes from airport to airport.

BY AIR FROM SEATTLE

- Horizon Air (1-800-547-9308). Flights to Victoria International Airport.
- Kenmore Air (425 486-1257 in Seattle, 1-800-543-9595 in the US and Canada). Fifty-five minute seaplane flights from downtown Seattle (shuttles from Seattle-Tacoma Airport available in summer) to Victoria's Inner Harbour.

The Victoria International Airport is located near Sidney, about 30 minutes from the downtown area. From the airport, the AKAL Victoria International Airporter (250 386-2525) runs to all hotels, motels and downtown on the half-hour, for $13

one way. Taxis are run by Victoria Taxi (250 383-7111), Empress Taxi (250 381-5577) and Blue Bird Cabs (250 384-1155). Fares are about $40.

BY SEA FROM VANCOUVER

BC Ferries (250 386-3431 in Victoria, 1-888-223-3779 toll-free) crosses the Strait of Georgia between Vancouver and Victoria. Ferries make the journey from Tsawwassen (Vancouver) to Swartz Bay (Victoria) in approximately 95 minutes. The drive into Victoria is 32 kilometres (20 miles). Board as a walk-on passenger ($10.25 in peak season) or by car ($35.75 in peak season for car, passengers extra). Different rates apply to motorcycles, bicycles and oversized vehicles. Pacific Coach Lines runs buses directly from YVR and downtown Vancouver onto the ferry and into downtown Victoria. Call 1-800-661-1725, 604 662-8074 (Vancouver), or 250 385-4411 (Victoria) for rates and more information.

BY SEA FROM SEATTLE AND PORT ANGELES

- From Pier 69 in Seattle, Victoria Clippers' high-speed catamarans make the trip to Victoria in 2 to 2.5 hours. Rates and information can be found at 1-800-888-2535, 206-448-5000 (Seattle) and 250 382-8100 (Victoria).
- The MV Coho offers daily Port Angeles, Washington, ferries to Victoria on a no-reservations system. Call 250 361-9144 (Canada), 1-800-633-1589 or 360 452-8088 (US), www.victoriaexpress.com.

BY CAR

Driving to Victoria from any place off the Island involves taking a ferry. Allow extra time to make your selected sailing in peak season. From the Swartz Bay Ferry Terminal (and the Victoria International Airport) take Highway 17 south into the city.

BY BUS

Pacific Coach Lines runs buses directly from YVR and downtown Vancouver onto the ferry and into downtown Victoria. Call 1-800-661-1725, 604 662-8074 (Vancouver) or 250 385-4411(Victoria) for rates and more information.

TRAVEL ESSENTIALS

MONEY

Canadian cash consists of $1 (loonie) and $2 (toonie) coins, 1 cent, 5 cent, 10 cent and 25 cent coins and differently-coloured $5, $10, $20, $50, $100 and $1000 bills. Main branches of Canadian chartered banks can exchange foreign currency, although small local branches may not exchange currency other than US dollars directly. Several foreign banks have offices in Vancouver, and will handle some foreign currencies directly. Banking hours in general are 9:30 a.m. to 4:30 p.m., Monday to Friday, with extended hours and weekends at some branches. Most banks have automatic teller machines posted in locations around the city, accessible 24 hours a day with bank cards on international banking networks such as Cirrus, Plus and Interac. Currency can also be exchanged at the many commercial money exchange outlets in each city.

Most businesses accept all major credit cards such as American Express, Diners Club, EnRoute, MasterCard and Visa. Smaller businesses, however, may accept only one or two of these cards. Traveller's cheques can be cashed in major hotels, some restaurants and large stores.

PASSPORTS

To enter Canada, citizens and permanent residents of the United States require a US birth certificate, US passport or green card. Proof of residence, such as a driver's licence, should also be carried. However, this is not accepted as proof of citizenship. All other international visitors must have a valid national passport and, in some cases, a visa. Check with the nearest Canadian Consulate or Embassy well in advance of travel.

CUSTOMS

Arriving

Travellers entering Canada must declare all goods. Reasonable amounts of personal effects and food are admitted free of duty. Special restrictions or quotas apply to certain specialty goods, especially to plant-agricultural- and animal-related materials. Each visitor over the age of 19 may bring into Canada, duty free, up to 40 ounces (1.1 litres) of liquor or wine, or 228 ounces (8 litres or 24 bottles) of beer. Visitors over the age of 19 may also bring up to 50 cigars, 200 cigarettes and 8 ounces (200 grams) of tobacco. Revolvers, pistols, and fully automatic firearms are not allowed into Canada. All other weapons (such as hunting rifles and shotguns) must be declared. For more information contact:

Canada Customs – Pacific Region
Third Floor 333 Dunsmuir Street,
Vancouver, BC,
V6B 5R4 Canada
Fax 604 666-3144
1-800-461-9999 – automated in Canada
Outside Canada: 1-204-983-3500
8 a.m. - 4:15 p.m., Monday - Friday

Departing

Before visiting BC, contact a US Customs office, where copies of the US customs information brochure "Know Before You Go" are available, to find out customs rules for entering or re-entering the United States. Visitors from other countries should check their own customs regulations before leaving home as well.

TAXES

The Federal Goods and Services Tax (GST) of 7% is applied to most goods and services whether the buyer is a resident of Canada or a visitor. Those from outside of Canada can obtain a GST rebate on most goods taken out of Canada within 60 days of purchase, and on accommodation of less than 30 days. Some restrictions apply. Detailed information is available in the Tax Refund for Visitors to Canada publication. Forms can be obtained within the city at major hotels and information centres and online at ww.rc.gc.ca/visitors. To order forms: 1-800-267-5177 (from US) or 1-613-952-3741 (outside Canada). For more information or assistance, call 902 432-5608 (outside Canada) or 1-800-668-4748 (within Canada). Visitors departing by air, rail, charter-bus or ferry must include boarding passes or a carrier ticket with the claim.

A non-refundable provincial sales tax (PST) of 7.5% applies to all retail purchases except liquor, which is taxed at 10%.

GETTING ACQUAINTED

TIME ZONE
Vancouver and Victoria are in the Pacific Standard Time Zone.

CLIMATE
These are the average high and low temperatures in Vancouver (source Environment Canada):

January	5.7°C to 0.1°C	42°F to 32°F
February	8.0°C to 1.4°C	46°F to 34°F
March	9.9°C to 2.6°C	50°F to 37°F
April	12.7°C to 4.9°C	55°F to 41°F
May	16.3°C to 7.9°C	61°F to 46°F
June	19.3°C to 11.0°C	67°F to 52°F
July	21.7°C to 12.7°C	91°F to 55°F
August	21.7°C to 12.9°C	71°F to 55°F
September	18.4°C to 10.1°C	65°F to 50°F
October	13.5°C to 6.4°C	56°F to 44°F
November	9.0°C to 3.0°C	48°F to 37°F
December	6.1°C to 0.8°C	43°F to 33°F

Average temperatures are:
12.0°C (54°F) in spring
16.3°C (61°F) in summer
6.5°C (44°F) in fall
4.7°C (40°F) in winter
Average annual rainfall:
1117.2 mm (44.0 inches)
Average annual snowfall:
54.9 cm (21.6 inches)
The average high and low temperatures in Victoria, near the water are (source Environment Canada, based on data from 1967 to 1990):

January	6.7°C to 1.6°C	44°F to 35°F
February	8.4°C to 2.4°C	47°F to 36°F
March	10.1°C to 3.0°C	50°F to 37°F
April	11.9°C to 4.3°C	53°F to 40°F
May	14.2°C to 6.7°C	58°F to 44°F
June	16.4°C to 8.8°C	62°F to 48°F
July	18.2°C to 9.9°C	65°F to 50°F
August	18.6°C to 10.1°C	65°F to 50°F
September	17.1°C to 8.8°C	63°F to 48°F
October	13.1°C to 6.2°C	56°F to 43°F
November	9.3°C to 3.8°C	49°F to 39°F
December	6.9°C to 2.0°C	44°F to 36°F

Average temperatures are:
10.4°C (51°F) in spring
14.0°C (57°F) in summer
6.9°C (44°F) in fall
5.4°C (42°F) in winter
Average annual rainfall:
1197.7 mm (47.2 inches)
Average annual snowfall:
29.3 cm (11.5 inches)

GUIDES AND INFORMATION SERVICES
BC has established a Visitor's Info Network with Visitor Info Centres in many communities to assist travellers throughout the province. Tourism BC's official website can be found at www.hellobc.com. Visitors can call 1-800-435-5622 in North America, 604 435-5622 in Vancouver and 250 387-1642 internationally, for reservations and help with accommodations and other travel plans.

VANCOUVER
• Vancouver Tourist Info Centre, Plaza Level, 200 Burrard St., Vancouver BC V6C 3L6, 604 683-2000, Fax: 604 682-6839, www.tourismvancouver.com. Source for current information on the Greater Vancouver area, guides and maps. Visitors can make reservations for many accommodations, sightseeing, transportation and outdoor adventures.

VICTORIA

- Tourism Victoria Visitor Info Centre, 812 Wharf St., Victoria BC V8W 1T3, 250 953-2033, 1-800-663-3883, Fax: 250 382-6539, www.tourismvictoria.com. Source for current information on seeing Victoria, with guides, maps and other travel services.
- Tourism Vancouver Island, Suite 203-335 Wesley Street, Nanaimo, BC V9R 2T5, (250 754-3500, Fax: 250 754-3599, www.seetheislands.com). Source for travel information and reservations for Vancouver Island and Gulf Islands.

GETTING AROUND

PUBLIC TRANSIT

VANCOUVER

The TransLink public transit system is a network of buses, SeaBus ferries and light rapid transit (SkyTrain). Fares for buses, SkyTrain and SeaBus are the same: travel in one zone costs $2 for adults and $1.50 for concession (teenagers, children over five and seniors), travel in two zones costs $3/$2, and in three zones, $4/$3. Discount fares (single-zone amount for all zones) apply after 6:30 p.m. weekdays and all day weekends and holidays. Daypasses cost $8/$6. Faresaver books of 10 tickets ($18/one zone, $27/2 zone, $36/3 zone, $15/concession) are available at many convenience stores. Schedules can be found at the Vancouver Tourist Info Centre, public libraries, SkyTrain stations and City Hall.

Buses on most routes run until approximately 1 a.m., with some major routes running until 4 a.m. Drivers carry no change, so bring exact fare. A transfer is given as proof of payment and allows passengers to transfer between buses, SkyTrain and SeaBus until the time shown (90 minutes). Blue Buses serve West Vancouver and leave downtown at the corner of Granville and Georgia. The same fares and transfers apply. Call 604 985-7777 for more information on the Blue Buses.

SkyTrain is an automated rapid-transit line that runs on mostly elevated tracks from Vancouver's westernmost Waterfront Station through the municipalities of Burnaby and New Westminster to Surrey, as well from Sapperton Station to Commercial Station. These operate from downtown from 5 a.m. to 1:15 a.m., Monday through Saturday and on Sunday to 12:15 a.m. Tickets can be purchased or validated at machines in each station. SkyTrain carries bikes from 9:30 a.m. to 3:30 p.m. daily and after 6:30 p.m.

SeaBus carries passengers (and bikes) only. Leaving Waterfront Station every 15-30 minutes, the ferry crosses Burrard Inlet and arrives 12 minutes later at Lonsdale Quay in North Vancouver.

Most buses (except for trolleys) are wheelchair lift-equipped or have low floors for easy access. SkyTrains, SeaBuses and Seabus terminals are wheelchair accessible. All SkyTrain stations except Granville Station have elevators.

For route and schedule information, call TransLink at 604 953-3333, or visit www.translink.bc.ca.

VICTORIA

The Victoria Regional Transit System operates over two zones. Adult fares are $1.75 for one zone; $2.50 for two zones, concession fares for seniors, children over five years of age and students are $1.10 for one zone, $1.75 for two zones. Exact change must be given on buses, and transfers are valid for one-way travel only. Sheets of 10 tickets may be purchased in advance from many stores. Daypasses are also available.

The majority of the Victoria Regional Transit System buses are wheelchair accessible with low-floor buses. For route and schedule information, call the 24-hour information line at 250 382-6161 or visit the website at www.bctransit.com.

CARS AND RENTALS

Most foreign drivers' licences are valid in British Columbia. Check with a BC Motor Vehicle Branch to find out specific requirements. Visiting motorists should bring registration documents and have insurance in place before driving. Insurance is available as an option in most car rental contracts, and Visitor to Canada Insurance can be purchased through the British Columbia Automobile Association (BCAA). United States motorists should have a Canadian Non-Resident Interprovince Motor Vehicle Liability Insurance Card, available only in the US. For more information or to obtain a copy of BC's "rules of the road," contact Driver Services Centre, 254-800 Hornby St., Vancouver, BC, 1-800-950-1498 (within North America), www.icbc.com.

Speed limits within Vancouver and Victoria are 50 km/h (30 mph) unless otherwise posted. The use of seat belts, child restraints and motorcycle helmets is mandatory. Vancouverites and Victoria residents believe in the pedestrian's right of way.

Distances, speed limits and fuel measurements are indicated in metric units. To convert kilometres to miles, multiply by 0.6; to convert miles to kilometres, multiply by 1.6. One litre equals about 1/3 of an American gallon or 1/5 of an Imperial gallon.

VANCOUVER

- Alamo Rent A Car, 1132 West Georgia St., 604 684-1401, 1-800-462-5266 or 1-800-327-9633, Vancouver International Airport, 604 231-1400, 1-800-462-5266 or 1-800-327-9633, www.alamo.com.
- Avis, 757 Hornby St., 604 606-2869, 1-800-272-5871, Vancouver International Airport, 604 606-2847, 1-800-272-5871, www.avis.com.
- Budget Rent A Car, 501 West Georgia St., 604 668-7000, 1-800-268-8900, Vancouver International Airport, 604 668-7000, 1-800-268-8900, www.bc.budget.com.
- EZ Car and Truck Rentals, 1281 East Hastings St., 604 806-6210, 1-888-806-6210, 1-888-806-6210, www.ez-car.com.
- Hertz, 1128 Seymour St., 604 606-4711, 1-800-263-0600, Vancouver International Airport, 604 606-3700, 1-800-263-0600, www.hertz.com.
- Lo-Cost Rent-A-Car Ltd., 1105 Granville St., 604 689-9664, 1-888-377-2277, www.locost.com.
- National Car Rental — Downtown, 1130 West Georgia St., 604 609-7150, 1-800-227-7368, Vancouver International Airport, 604 207-

3730, 1-800-227-7368, www.nationalcar.com.
- Rent-A-Wreck, 1349 Hornby St., 604 688-0001, 1-888-665-3777, www.rentawreckvancouver.com.
- Thrifty Car Rentals, Century Plaza Hotel, 1015 Burrard St., 604 606-1666, 1-800-847-4389, Empire Landmark Hotel, 1400 Robson St., 604 681-4869, 1-800-847-4389, Vancouver International Airport, 604 606-1655, 1-800-847-4389, www.thrifty.com.

VICTORIA

- Avis, 1001 Douglas St., 250 386-8468, Victoria International Airport, 250 656-6033, www.avis.com.
- Budget Rent A Car, 757 Douglas St., 250 953-5300, 1-800-268-8900, Victoria International Airport, 250 953-5300, 1-800-268-8900, www.budget.com.
- Enterprise Rent-A-Car, Victoria International Airport, 250 656-4808, 1-800-325-8007.
- Hertz, 655 Douglas St., 250 360-2822, Victoria International Airport, 250 656-2312, www.hertz.com.
- National, 767 Douglas St., 250 386-1213 or 250 381-1115, Victoria International Airport, 250 386-1213 or 250 381-1115, www.nationalvictoria.com.
- Thrifty Car Rentals, 625 Frances Ave., 250 383-3659, 1-800-847-4389, www.thrifty.com.

Check the Telus Yellow Pages for more listings under Automobile renting.

TOURS

VANCOUVER

- AAA Horse and Carriage (Stanley Park horse-drawn tours). One-hour narrated, horse-drawn tours. Stanley Park, 604 681-5115, www.stanleyparktours.com.
- Accent Cruises. Yachts for charter cruises and special occasions. 100-1676 Duranleau St., 604 688-6625, www.accentcruises.ca.
- Gastown Business Improvement Society. Summer walking tours of Gastown. 207 Abbott St., 604 683-5650, www.gastown.org.
- Gray Line of Vancouver. A wide

variety of sightseeing packages. 255 East 1st Ave., 604 879-3363, 1-800-667-0882, www.grayline.ca.

- Harbour Cruises. Sunset dinner cruises, harbour tours, luncheon cruises, day trips. North foot of Denman St., 604 688-7246, 1-800-663-1500, www.boatcruises.com.
- Landsea Tours. Guided tours of Vancouver, Victoria, Whistler and the North Shore. 875 Terminal Ave., 604 255-7272, www.vancouvertours.com.
- Pride of Vancouver Charters. Charters for luncheons, tours, carol ship dinners, fireworks viewing. Barbary Coast Marine, 604 687-5533, www.vancouvercharters.com.
- Rockwood Adventures. Walking tours of Chinatown and North Shore. 839-Unit C, West 1st St., North Vancouver, 604 980-7749, www.rockwoodadventures.com.
- Vancouver Trolley Company. A loop of 16 attractions in Vancouver with on/off privileges. 875 Terminal Ave., 604 801-5515, www.vancouvertrolley.com.
- Vancouver Yacht Charters. Yacht touring and cruises. 750 Pacific Blvd., 604 682-2070, www.boatcharters.net.
- Walkabout Historic Vancouver. Downtown, Gastown and Granville Island walks. 342-6038 Imperial St., 604 439-0448 or 604-720-0006, www.walkabouthistoricvancouver.com.
- West Coast City and Nature Sightseeing. Tours of Vancouver, Grouse Mountain, Whistler and Victoria in mini-coaches. 3945 Myrtle St., Burnaby, 604 451-1600, www.vancouversightseeing.com.

VICTORIA

- Fantasea Charters. Luxurious covered yacht for whale-watching or sightseeing. 1243 Miramar Dr., 250 658-6052, www.boatchartersvictoria.com.
- Gray Line of Victoria. Popular tours include Butchart Gardens and Whale Watching and Nature Tour. 700 Douglas St., 250 388-6539, 1-800-663-8390, www.grayline.ca/Victoria.
- Kabuki Kabs. Pedicabs with friendly and knowledgeable drivers. Generally downtown tours, but some operators have specialized

tours. 613 Herald St., 250 385-4243, www.kabukikabs.com.
- Tallyho Tours. Horse-drawn carriage tours of up to 20 people as well as small private carriages. 7450 Veyaness Rd., Saanich, 250-383-5067, www.tallyhotours.com.
- Black Beauty Carriages. Private horse-drawn tours for six. Corner of Belleville and Menzies, 250 361-1220.
- Victoria Harbour Ferries. Full tours of the Gorge and Inner Harbour, evening cruises or short hops. Board at any one of 10 stops on the Inner Harbour, 250 708-0201, www.harbourferry.com.
- Victoria Bobby Walking Tours. One and a quarter hours of talk and touring of old-town Victoria. 414-874 Fleming St., 250 995-0233, www.walkvictoria.com.
- Victoria's Secret Gardens. A guided look into private gardens in Oak Bay. 3150 Midland Rd., 250 595-5333.

ACCOMMODATION

In both Vancouver and Victoria, a multitude of lodgings has evolved, both to accommodate the varied tastes of world travellers and to showcase the allure of the West Coast. The major and minor hotels and motels, most located in the downtown areas, put the traveller in each city's heart, while a host of charming bed and breakfasts beckon from quieter residential streets.

What follows is a cross-section of the hotels, bed and breakfasts, and budget establishments to be found in each city. Maps are provided at the beginning of this book. Prices indicated are approximate, based on the costs quoted at the time of publishing, for two people staying in a double room (excluding taxes) during peak season: $ = $50-$90, $$ = $90-$180, $$$ = above $180. Except for campgrounds and houseboats, rates quoted are subject to an 8% provincial hotel and motel room tax. Where approved, an additional 2% tourism tax is levied by the local municipal government. GST (7%) is also applied. Many establishments offer special Internet rates and online reservation services.

HELLO BC (1-800-435-5622, www.hellobc.com) is a free service providing access to over 700 Tourism BC-approved lodgings and trip planning services.

VANCOUVER

HOTELS: VANCOUVER INTERNATIONAL AIRPORT

Most of Vancouver's hotels are within a short drive of the airport. The following, however, are considered the closest:

- Accent Inns, 10551 St. Edwards Dr., Richmond BC V6X 3L8, 604 273-3311, Fax: 604 273-9522, www.accentinns.com. Well kept and comfortable. Exterior corridors, restaurant. Welcomes small pets. $$.
- Best Western Abercorn Inn, 9260 Bridgeport Rd., Richmond BC V6X 1S1, 604 270-7576, 1-800-663-0085, Fax: 604 270-0001, www.albercorn-inn.com. Styled as a Scottish country inn, with antiques and fresh flowers. Spacious rooms, restaurant. $$.
- Best Western Richmond Hotel, 7551 Westminster Hwy., Richmond BC V6X 1A3, 604 273-7878, 1-800-663-0299, Fax: 604 278-0188, www.richmond-hotel.ca. Two restaurants, four nightspots. Welcomes pets. $$.
- Comfort Inn, 3031 #3 Rd., Richmond BC V6X 2B6, 604 278-5161, 1-800-663-0974, Fax: 604 207-2380. www.comfortinnvancouver.com. Location allows easy access to casino, Fraser River trails and malls. Welcomes pets. $$.
- Delta Vancouver Airport Hotel, 3500 Cessna Dr., Richmond BC V7B 1C7, 604 278-1241, 1-800-268-1133, Fax: 604 276-1975, www.deltavancouverairport.com. Older hotel on nine landscaped acres overlooking the Fraser River. Heated pool. Welcomes small pets. $$.
- Executive Airport Plaza Hotel, 7311 Westminster Hwy., Richmond BC V6X 1A3, 604 278-5555, 1-800-663-2878, Fax: 604 278-0255, www.executivehotels.net. Large rooms and suites. Heated pool, whirl-pool. Two restaurants, lounge.$$.
- Fairmont Vancouver Airport, 3111 Grant McConachie Way, PO Box 23798, Vancouver BC V6X 1A1, 604 207-5200, www.fairmont.com. Newly opened, world-class hotel brings sophistication to the concept of airport accommodation. Globe@YVR Restaurant, Jetside Lounge, pool, fitness centre. Offers in-room airline check-in service. Welcomes pets. $$-$$$.
- Four Points by Sheraton Vancouver Airport, 8368 Alexandra Rd., Richmond BC V6X 4A6, 604 214-0888, 1-888-281-8888, Fax: 604 214-0887, www.fourpoints.com. Modern hotel in Richmond's shopping and entertainment district. Heated pool, restaurant, lounge. $$.
- Hilton Vancouver Airport, 5911 Minoru Blvd., Richmond BC V6X 4C7, 604 273-6336, 1-800-445-8667, Fax: 604 273-6337, www.vancouverairport.hilton.com. Restaurant, lounge, pool, fitness centre, tennis courts. $$.
- Holiday Inn Vancouver Airport, 10720 Cambie Rd., Richmond BC V6X 1K8, 604 821-1818, Fax: 604 821-1819, www.hi-airport.bc.ca. Suites include themed, kid-friendly suites with bunkbeds, video games. $$.
- Quality Inn Airport, 725 S.E. Marine Dr., Vancouver BC V5X 2T9, 604 321-6611, 1-800-663-6715, Fax: 604 327-3570, www.qualityinnvancouverairport.com. Casino, bowling alley, liquor store and sports bar onsite. $$.
- Radisson President Hotel and Suites, 8181 Cambie Rd., Richmond BC V6X 3X9, 604 276-8181, 1-800-333-3333, Fax: 604 279-8381, www.radisson.com. Home to Western-style and Chinese seafood restaurants. Heated pool, whirlpool. Welcomes small pets. $$$.
- Ramada Plaza and Park Plaza Vancouver Airport Conference Resort, 10251 St. Edwards Dr., Richmond BC V6X 2M9, 604 278-9611, 1-866-482-8444, Fax: 604 276-1121, www.vacr.bc.ca. Three towers of rooms. Pools, tennis, kids' centre. Welcomes pets (per day charge). $$.
- Travelodge, 3071 St. Edwards Dr., Richmond BC V6X 3K4, 604 278-5155, 1-888-515-6375, Fax: 604 278-5125, www.travelodge.com. Comfortable setting. Heated pool,

whirlpool, restaurant, lounge. $$.
- Vancouver Airport Marriott, 7571 Westminster Hwy., Richmond BC V6X 1A3, 604 276-2112, 1-877-323-8888, Fax: 604 273-0112, www.marriott.com. Caters to corporate travellers, with spacious desks in comfortable rooms. Heated pool. Welcomes small pets. $$.

HOTELS: DOWNTOWN VANCOUVER
In downtown Vancouver, over 10,000 rooms, from budget hostels to luxury hotels, can be found amid a myriad of shops, restaurants and a bustling business district:
- Best Western Chateau Granville Hotel, 1100 Granville St., Vancouver BC V6Z 2B6, 604 669-7070, 1-800-663-0575, Fax: 604 669-4928, www.chateaugranville.com. Downtown hotel bordering the business and shopping districts. Wheelchair access, babysitting, restaurant and lounge. Complimentary passes to nearby health club. $$$.
- Best Western Downtown Vancouver, 718 Drake St., Vancouver BC V6Z 2W6, 604 669-9888, 1-888-669-9888, Fax: 604 669-3440, www.bestwesterndowntown.com. Great views. Rooftop fitness centre, sauna, Jacuzzi. Complimentary downtown shuttle. $$$.
- Blue Horizon Hotel, 1225 Robson St., Vancouver BC V6E 1C3, 604 688-1411, 1-800-663-1333, Fax: 604 688-4461, www.bluehorizonhotel.com. Distinctive comfort with oversized corner rooms and private balconies in all rooms. Harbour and city views, heated pool. $$$.
- Bosman's Hotel, 1060 Howe St., Vancouver BC V6Z 1P5, 604 682-3171, 1-888-267-6267, Fax: 604 684-4010, www.bosmanshotel.com. Newly upgraded older hotel. Dining room, piano lounge, outdoor pool. $$.
- Century Plaza Hotel & Spa, 1015 Burrard St., Vancouver BC V6Z 1Y5, 604 687-0575, 1-800-663-1818, Fax: 604 687-0578, www.century-plaza.com. Oversized suites with panoramic ocean, mountain and city views. Seafood restaurant, lounge, cappuccino bar and day spa, steam room, pool. $$-$$$.
- Crowne Plaza Hotel Georgia, 801 West Georgia St., Vancouver BC V6C 1P7, 604 682-5566, 1-800-663-1111, Fax: 604 642-5579, www.hotelgeorgia.bc.ca. Magnificently restored to reflect its 1920s roots. Full service, with dining room serving afternoon tea. Lounge, fitness centre. Multilingual staff. $$$.
- Days Inn Vancouver Downtown, 921 West Pender St., Vancouver BC V6C 1M2, 604 681-4335, 1-877-681-4335, Fax: 604 681-7808, www.daysinnvancouver.com. 1914 English-style heritage building, renovated 1998. Views restricted by neighbouring buildings. Restaurant, lounge. $$.
- Empire Landmark Hotel – Downtown Vancouver, 1400 Robson St., Vancouver BC V6G 1B9, 604 687-0511, 1-800-830-6144, Fax: 604 687-2801, www.asiastandard.com. Vancouver's tallest, featuring the Cloud Nine Revolving Restaurant and Lounge. Sauna and whirlpool, fitness room, business centre and convention space. $$$.
- Executive Hotel Downtown Vancouver, 1379 Howe St., Vancouver BC V6Z 2R5, 604 688-7678, 1-800-570-3932, Fax: 604 688-7679, www.executivehotels.net. Contemporary deluxe rooms and fully-furnished condos. $$-$$$.
- Fairmont Hotel Vancouver, 900 West Georgia St., Vancouver BC V6C 2W6, 604 684-3131, 1-866-540-4452, Fax: 604 662-1929, www.fairmont.com/hotelvancouver. Heritage landmark that is home to the renowned restaurant 900 West. Beautiful guestrooms and suites. Indoor pool, healthclub, spa, business centre, free local calls. $$$.
- Fairmont Waterfront Centre Hotel, 900 Canada Place Way, Vancouver BC V6C 3L5, 604 691-1991, Fax: 604 691-1999, Email: thewaterfronthotel@fairmont.com, www.fairmont.com. Waterfrontage, terraced gardens. Enclosed walkway links hotel to Vancouver Convention and Exhibition Centre

and cruise ship terminal. Heated pool. Welcomes small pets. $$$.

- Four Seasons Hotel Vancouver, 791 West Georgia St., Vancouver BC V6C 2T4, 604 689-9333, 1-800-819-5053, Fax: 604 684-4555, www.fourseasons.com/vancouver. Luxurious hotel with the exclusive Chartwell Restaurant atop the shops of Pacific Centre. $$$.
- Georgian Court Hotel, 773 Beatty St., Vancouver BC V6B 2M4, 604 682-5555, 1-800-663-1155, Fax: 604 682-8830, Email: info@georgiancourt.com, Website: www.georgiancourt.com. Intimate, European-style hotel, well-known William Tell Dining Room. Deluxe guestrooms and suites. Welcomes small pets. $$$.
- Greenbrier Hotel, 1393 Robson St., Vancouver BC V6E 1C6, 604 683-4558, 1-888-355-5888, Fax: 604 669-3109, www.greenbrierhotel.com. Smallish hotel. Business centre, full kitchens in suites. $$.
- Hampton Inn & Suites – Vancouver Downtown, 111 Robson St., Vancouver BC V6B 2A8, 604 602-1008, 1-877-602-1008, Fax: 604 602-1007, www.hamptoninnvancouver.com. New, West-Coast themed hotel. Breakfast buffet, daily newspaper, local calls, rooftop entertainment and exercise facilities. $$$.
- Holiday Inn Hotel & Suites Vancouver Downtown, 1110 Howe St., Vancouver BC V6Z 1R2, 604 684-2151, 1-800-663-9151, Fax: 604 684-4736, www.hivancouverdowntown.com. Offers some suites with extra-long beds. Unsupervised Kids PlayCentre with video games, jungle gym. Welcomes small pets. $$$.
- Howard Johnson Hotel, 1176 Granville St., Vancouver BC V6Z 1L8, 604 688-8701, 1-888-654-6336, Fax: 604 688-8335, www.hojovancouver.com. Beautifully renovated boutique hotel. Swing bar, continental breakfast. Free fitness passes. $$.
- Hyatt Regency Vancouver, 655 Burrard St., Vancouver BC V6C 2R7, 604 683-1234, 1-800-233-1234, Fax: 604 689-3707, www.vancouver.hyatt.com. Luxury

tower connected to Royal Centre plaza. Two restaurants, coffee bar and lounge, health club, outdoor pool. Multilingual staff. $$$.
- Listel Vancouver, 1300 Robson St., Vancouver BC V6E 1C5, 604 684-8461, 1-800-663-5491, Fax: 604 684-7092, www.listelvancouver.com. Features two Gallery floors showcasing original work by regional and international artists. Restaurant and bar with live jazz on weekends. $$$.
- Lord Stanley Suites on the Park, 1889 Alberni St., Vancouver BC V6G 3G7, 604 688-9299, 1-888-767-7829, Fax: 604 688-9297, Location at entrance to Stanley Park offers unobstructed views of the water, mountains, and the city. Private workrooms, washer and dryer available. $$$.
- Marriott Pinnacle Hotel, 1128 West Hastings St., Vancouver BC V6E 4R5, 604 684-1128, Fax: 604 298-1128, www.vancouvermarriott pinnacle.com. Sauna, whirlpool, indoor pool. $$$.
- Metropolitan Hotel, 645 Howe St., Vancouver BC V6C 2Y9, 604 687-1122, Fax: 604 643-7267, www.metropolitan.com. Sumptuous surroundings, full-service rooms. Hosts elegant Diva at the Met Restaurant. Sports court. Welcomes small pets. $$$
- Opus Hotel, 322 Davie St., Vancouver BC V6B 5Z6, 604 642-6787, 1-866-642-6787, Fax: 604 642-6780, www.opushotel.com. Modern, stylish hotel with French brasserie Elixir and eclectic Opus Bar.$$$.
- Pacific Palisades Hotel, 1277 Robson St., Vancouver BC V6E 1C4, 604 688-0461, Fax: 604 688-4374, www.pacificpalisadeshotel.com. All-suite hotel. Kitchens in some suites, health club with pool, sauna. Complimentary shoe shine and daily newspaper. Welcomes small pets. $$$.
- Pan Pacific Hotel Vancouver, 300-999 Canada Place, Vancouver BC V6C 3B5, 604 662-8111, 1-800-663-1515, Fax: 604 685-8690, www.panpacific.com. One of the city's best luxury hotels. Part of a complex shared by the cruise ship terminal, convention centre and the celebrated Five Sails Restaurant.

Racquetball court, harbour and mountain views, full service. Welcomes small pets. $$$.

- Quality Hotel Downtown, 1335 Howe St., Vancouver BC V6Z 1R7, 604 682-0229, 1-800-663-8474, Fax: 604 662-7566, www.qualityhotel.ca. Sante Fe atmosphere. Heated outdoor pools, complimentary access to nearby fitness centre. Offers excellent "passport" featuring 50% savings at 35 Vancouver attractions, restaurants and entertainment. $$-$$$.

- Ramada Inn & Suites Downtown Vancouver, 1221 Granville St., Vancouver BC V6Z 1M6, 604 685 1111, 1-888-835-0078, Fax: 604 685-0707, www.ramadavancouver.com. Situated in the Granville Entertainment district, with Granville Island just an Aquabus ferry away. Restaurant, lounge, airport shuttle. $$-$$$.

- Renaissance Vancouver Hotel Harbourside, 1133 West Hastings St., Vancouver BC V6E 3T3, 604 689-9211, 1-800-468-3571, Fax: 604 689-4358, www.renaissancevancouver.com. Guestrooms and suites with harbour and city views. Restaurant, heated pool, convention space. Welcomes small pets. $$$.

- Robsonstrasse Hotel, 1394 Robson St., Vancouver BC V6E 1C5, 604 687-1674, 1-888-667-8877, Fax: 604 685-7808, www.robsonstrassehotel.com. Studio and deluxe suites with kitchennette. Personalized voice mail, modem hookup, free covered parking. $$$.

- Rosedale on Robson, 838 Hamilton St., Vancouver BC V6B 6A2, 604 689-8033, 1-800-661-8870, Fax: 604 689-4426, www.rosedaleonrobson.com. Vancouver's newest all-suite hotel offers one- or two-bedroom suites. Recreation facilities, restaurant, lounge. $$$.,

- Sheraton Vancouver Wall Centre Hotel, 1088 Burrard St., Vancouver BC V6Z 2R9, 604 331-1000, 1-888-625-5144, Fax: 604 893-7200, www.sheratonvancouver.com. Luxurious guestrooms and suites, first-class service. $$$.

- St. Regis Hotel, 602 Dunsmuir St., Vancouver BC V6B 1Y6, 604 681-1135, 1-800-770-7929, Fax: 604 683-1126, www.stregishotel.com. A boutique-style hotel. Steakhouse, bar and grill, breakfast lounge. $$.

- Sutton Place Hotel, 845 Burrard St., Vancouver BC V6Z 2K6, 604 682-5511, 1-800-961-7555, Fax: 604 642-2926, www.suttonplace.com. Attentive staff, understated elegance. Home to award-winning Fleuri Restaurant. $$$.

- Sylvia Hotel, 1154 Gilford St., Vancouver BC V6G 2P6, 604 681-9321, Fax: 604 682-3551, www.sylviahotel.com. A charming, ivy-covered heritage building immortalized by the children's book *Mister Got To Go*. Welcomes pets. $$.

- Terminal City Tower Hotel, 837 West Hastings St., Vancouver BC V6C 1B6, 604 681-4121, Fax: 604 488-8617, www.tctowerhotel.com. Full-service hotel offers the privileges of the members-only Terminal City Club. Conference facilities, two restaurants, pub, billiards, fitness club, pool. $$$.

- Wedgewood Hotel, 845 Hornby St., Vancouver BC V6Z 1V1, 604 689-7777, 1-800-663-0666, Fax: 604 608-5348, www.wedgewood-hotel.com. Intimate and stylish European boutique hotel. Attentive staff, award-winning Bacchus restaurant. Afternoon tea, lounge, cigar room. $$$.

- Westin Bayshore Resort & Marina Vancouver, 1601 Bayshore Dr., Vancouver BC V6G 2V4, 604 682-3377, 1-800-228-3000, Fax: 604 687-3102, www.westin.com/bayshore. Luxury in a waterfront setting. Two restaurants, two lounges, whirlpool, masseur, pools, some environmentally friendly rooms. Welcomes small pets. $$$.

- YMCA Hotel, 955 Burrard St., Vancouver BC V6Z 1Y2, 604 681-0221, Fax: 604 681-1630, www.vanymca.org. Clean, affordable co-ed accommodations. Daily maid service, shared bathrooms, café, complete fitness facility with pools. $.

- YWCA Hotel, 733 Beatty St., Vancouver BC V6B 2M4, 604 895-5830, 1-800-663-1424, Fax: 604

681-2550, www.ywcahotel.com.
Built in 1995 for women and men.
Air-conditioning, private, shared or
hall bathrooms, shared kitchen,
laundry room. Complimentary
access to YWCA Health and
Wellness Centre with pool, steam
room whirlpool, gym, fitness and
aquatics drop-in classes. $-$$.

BED AND BREAKFASTS

Bedding down in one of Vancouver's
bed and breakfasts gives travellers a
glimpse of the enviable, everyday
lifestyle of the West Coast.
The following reservations services
can be of great help:
- Best Canadian Bed and Breakfast
  Reservations (free service, 604
  738-7207).
- Canada-West Accommodations
  B&B Registry (604 990-6730 or 1-
  800-561-3223).
- Old English B&B Registry (604
  986-5069)
Vancouver B&Bs include:
- Anthem House/O Canada House,
  1114 Barclay St., Vancouver BC
  V6E 1H1, 604 688-0555, 1-877-
  688-1114, Fax: 604 488-0556,
  www.ocanadahouse.com. Five
  rooms in a beautifully restored
  1897 home, where the national
  anthem O Canada was written in
  1909. Fans, designated smoking
  area, breakfast. Wheelchair
  accessible. $$-$$$.
- Camilla House Bed & Breakfast,
  2538 West 13th Ave., Vancouver
  BC V6K 2T1, 604 737-2687, Fax:
  604 737-2586. Five rooms in a
  private home with oriental touches
  in public areas. Breakfast plan. $$.
- Cherub Inn, 2546 West 6th Ave.,
  Vancouver BC V6K 1W5, 604 733-
  3166, 1-877-733-3166, Fax: 604
  733-3106, www.cherubinn.com.
  Four rooms in a restored and
  updated 1913 Craftsman house.
  Anaglyphic wallpaper, stained
  glass, high ceilings, wood
  panelling, English and Belgian
  antiques. Chocolates and morning
  paper, full breakfast. $$.
- Columbia Cottage, 205 West 14th
  Ave., Vancouver BC V5Y 1X2, 604
  874-7787, www.columbiacottage-
  .com. Five rooms in a 1929
  Tudor-style cottage, Fairview area
  close to City Hall. Full breakfast,
  no smoking. $$.

- Johnson Heritage House Bed and
  Breakfast, 2278 West 34th Ave.,
  Vancouver BC V6M 1G6, 604 266-
  4175, Fax: 604 266-4175,
  www.johnsons-inn-vancouver.com.
  Three rooms in a 1920s home
  restored in the Craftsman style.
  Lots of whimsy in antique
  furniture, Persian carpets, carousel
  horse, gramophone and themed
  bathrooms. Breakfast plan. No
  smoking, no pets. $-$$.
- Penny Farthing Inn, 2855 West 6th
  Ave., Vancouver BC V6K 1X2, 604
  739-9002, Fax: 604 739-9004,
  www.pennyfarthinginn.com. Two
  rooms, two suites in a renovated
  1912 house. Guest living room,
  guest fridge, guest business room
  with computer, scanner, printer,
  email connection, fax, photocopier.
  Full breakfast. The four resident
  cats aren't permitted in guest rooms
  or suites. $$.
- West End Guest House, 1362 Haro
  St., Vancouver BC V6E 1G2, 604
  681-2889, Fax: 604 688-8812,
  www.westendguesthouse.com.
  Eight period rooms in a pink
  Victorian-era home. Resident ghost,
  designated smoking areas, breakfast
  plan. $$-$$$.
- Windsor House, 325 West 11th
  Ave., Vancouver BC V5Y 1T3, 604
  872-3060, Fax: 604 873-1147. Ten
  rooms, simple décor. Designated
  smoking areas, breakfast plan. $-$$.

HOSTELS AND EDUCATIONAL RESIDENCES

Hostels offer spartan but economical
alternatives for accommodation. In
the summer, a few educational
institutes open their residences to
travellers as well.
- C & N Backpackers Hostel, 927
  Main St. and 1038 Main St.,
  Vancouver BC V6A 2V8 and V6A
  2W1, 604 682-2441 and 604 681-
  9118, 1-888-434-6060, Fax: 604
  682-2441 and 604 681-9118,
  www.cnnbackpackers.com. A 1926
  heritage building with renovated
  interior near public transit. Staff
  speak many languages. Fully
  equipped kitchen, several showers
  per floor, laundry facility. Internet,
  guest phones, fax. $.
- Cambie International Hostel, 300
  Cambie St., Vancouver BC V6B
  2N3, 604 684-6466, Fax: 604 687-

5618, www.cambiehostels.com. Gastown hostel features a pub, general store and bakery/café. Full laundry, bike storage, email and Internet. Shuttle bus to bus station and airport. $.

- Cambie International Hostel (Seymour), 515 Seymour St., Vancouver BC V6B 2H6, 604 684-7757, Fax: 604 687-5618, www.cambiehostels.com. Downtown location. Features a pub, general store and bakery/café. Full laundry, bike storage, email and Internet. Shuttle bus to bus station and airport. $.
- Hostelling International — Vancouver Central, 1025 Granville St., Vancouver BC V6Z 1L4, 604 685-5335, 1-888-203-8333, Fax: 604 685-5351, www.hihostels.ca. Renovated hostel offering private and dormitory rooms. Popular pub The Royal onsite. $.
- Hostelling International — Vancouver Downtown, 1114 Burnaby St., Vancouver BC V6E 1P1, 604 684-4565, 1-888-203-4302, Fax: 604 684-4540, www.hihostels.ca. Shared and private rooms with fully equipped kitchens. Internet, TV room, game room and organized activities. Library/reading room, laundry room, bike rental/storage, limited parking. $.
- Hostelling International - Vancouver Jericho Beach, 1515 Discovery St., Vancouver BC V6R 4K5, 604 224-3208, 1-888-203-4303, Fax: 604 224-4852, www.hihostels.ca. Shared and private rooms with fully equipped kitchens. Internet, laundry, licensed cafeteria. Free shuttle makes loop from Jericho Beach to Pacific Centre, bus and train stations, to downtown HI hostel. $.
- UBC Conference Centre, 5961 Student Union Blvd., Vancouver BC V6T 2C9, 604 822-1000, Fax: 604 822-1001, www.ubcconferences.com. Arranges accommodations at four on-campus residences. $-$$.

VICTORIA

HOTELS: VICTORIA INTERNATIONAL AIRPORT

Because the Victoria International Airport is located on the Saanich Peninsula away from the city, Victoria itself has no "airport hotels." However, the towns bordering the airport extend a number of lodgings to serve travellers too tired to make the 30-minute drive to the core of Victoria:

- Best Western Emerald Isle Motor Inn, 2306 Beacon Ave., Sidney BC V8L 1X2, 250 656-4441, 1-800-315-3377, Fax: 250 655-1351, www.bwemeraldisle.com. Huge guest rooms. Sauna, whirlpool, restaurant. $$.
- Sidney Waterfront Hotel and Suites, 2537 Beacon Ave., Sidney BC V8L 1Y3, 250 656-1131, 1-888-656-1131, Fax: 250 656-9396, www.hotelsidney.com. The hotel's location on the Sidney Harbour means access to whale-watching, fishing and other water-related activities. Some rooms with harbour views, kitchens. $$.
- Super 8 Motel Victoria/Saanichton, 2477 Mt. Newton X Road, Saanichton BC V8M 2B7, 250 652-6888, 1-800-800-8000, Fax: 250 652-6800, www.super8.com. Modern comfort, economically styled. Restaurant. Welcomes pets. $$.
- Travelodge Victoria Airport Sidney, 2280 Beacon Ave., Sidney BC V8L 1X1, 250 656-1176, 1-888-515-6375, Fax: 250 656-7344, www.travelodge.com. Older but remodelled digs. Courtyard, heated outdoor pool. Welcomes small pets. $$.

HOTELS: DOWNTOWN VICTORIA AND INNER HARBOUR

Victoria's downtown and Inner Harbour hotels perfectly situate the traveller in the thick of the city's attractions:

- Admiral Inn, 257 Belleville St., Victoria BC V8V 1X1, 250 388-6267, 1-888-823-6472, Fax: 250 388-6267, www.admiral.bc.ca. Well-equipped rooms and suites in a harbourside hotel-class accommodation. Complimentary local calls, parking, continental breakfast and coffee. English and French-speaking staff. Welcomes pets. $$-$$$.
- Bedford Regency Hotel, 1140

Government St., Victoria BC V8W 1Y2, 250 384-6835, 1-800-665-6500, Fax: 250 386-8930, www.bedfordregency.com. Architectural details lend old-world charm to this small but elegant 1800s hotel. Wood-burning fireplaces in some suites. Off-site parking only. Restaurant serving breakfast only. $$-$$$.

- Best Western Carlton Plaza, 642 Johnson St., Victoria V8W 1M6, 250 388-5513, 1-800-663-7241, Fax: 250 388-5343, www.bestwesterncarltonplazahotel. com. Refurbishing has made for bright and spacious rooms. Air conditioning, restaurant. $$-$$$.
- Best Western Inner Harbour, 412 Quebec St., Victoria BC V8V 1W5, 250 384-5122, 1-800-383-2378, Fax: 250 384-5113, www.bwinnerharbour.com. Spacious, renovated rooms, all with private balconies. Jacuzzi, sauna, heated outdoor pool. $$-$$$.
- Chateau Victoria Hotel, 740 Burdett Avenue, Victoria BC V8W 1B2, 250 382-4221, 1-800-663-5891, Fax: 250 380-1950, www.chateauvictoria.com. Full-service boutique hotel hosting Victoria's only rooftop restaurant. English, Chinese, German, Portuguese, Spanish and Swiss spoken. Lounge, heated pool. $$-$$$.
- Coast Victoria Harbourside Hotel and Marina, 146 Kingston St., Victoria BC V8V 1V4, 250 360-1211, 1-800-663-1144, Fax: 250 360-1418, www.coasthotels.com. Waterfrontage with indoor/outdoor pools, health club. Award-winning Blue Crab Bar and Grill, lounge. $$$.
- Crystal Court Motel, 701 Belleville St., Victoria BC V8W 1A2, 250 384-0551, Fax: 250 384-5125, martin.scott@crystalcourt.ca. Well-kept, older budget motel with mix of room size and style. Exterior corridors. $.
- Days Inn on the Harbour, 427 Belleville St., Victoria BC V8V 1X3, 250 386-3451, 1-800-665-3024, Fax: 250 386-6999, www.daysinnvictoria.com. Restaurant, lounge, heated pool, whirlpool. $$-$$$.
- Delta Victoria Ocean Pointe Resort

Hotel and Spa, 45 Songhees Road, Victoria BC V9A 6T3, 250 360-2999, 1-800-667-4677, Fax: 250 360-1041, www.oprhotel.com. Casually elegant with heated pool, sauna, whirlpool, racquetball and tennis courts, European spa. Home to The Victorian Restaurant. Welcomes small pets. $$-$$$.
- Executive House Hotel, 777 Douglas St., Victoria BC V8W 2B5, 250 388-5111, 1-800-663-7001, Fax: 250 385-1323, www.executivehouse.com. Older hi-rise hotel with spacious rooms and suites. Sauna, steam room, whirlpool, restaurants. Welcomes small pets. $$.
- The Fairmont Empress Hotel, 721 Government St., Victoria BC V8W 1W5, 250 384-8111, 1-866-540-4452, Fax: 250 389-2747, www.fairmont.com/empress. Elegance and service in a restored heritage setting as regal as the name implies. Restaurant and lounge, fitness facilities. World-famous afternoon tea. $$-$$$.
- Harbour Towers Hotel, 345 Quebec St., Victoria BC V8V 1W4, 250 385-2405, 1-800-663-5896, Fax: 250 385-4453, www.harbourtowers.com. Spacious rooms. Indoor pool and fitness centre. Restaurant and lounge. $$$.
- Hotel Grand Pacific, 463 Belleville St., Victoria BC V8V 1X3, 250 386-0450, 1-800-663-7550, Fax: 250 380-4475, www.hotelgrandpacific.com. Rooms all have private balconies, air conditioning. Pool, whirlpool, sauna, workout facilities, squash and racquetball courts. Chinese, English, French, German, Spanish, Punjabi spoken. $$$.
- Laurel Point Inn, 680 Montreal St., Victoria BC V8V 1Z8, 250 386-8721, 1-800-663-7667, Fax: 250 386-9547, www.laurelpoint.com. Resort-style downtown hotel with indoor pool, sauna, Jacuzzi. Free local calls and parking. Two restaurants, lounge, business centre. English, French and Japanese spoken. $$$.
- The Magnolia Hotel and Spa, 623 Courtney St., Victoria BC V8W 1B8, 250 381-0999, 1-877-624-6654, Fax: 250 381-0988, www.magnoliahotel.com. Opulent

boutique hotel with floor-to-ceiling windows and lavish bathrooms. Family suites available. Restaurant, brew pub. $$$.

- Quality Inn Green Gables, 850 Blanshard St., Victoria BC V8W 2H2, 250 385-6787, 1-800-661-4115, Fax: 250 385-5800, www.victoriaqualityinn.com. Comfortable and cheerful. English-style pub, restaurant. $$.

- Queen Victoria Hotel & Suites, 655 Douglas St., Victoria BC V8V 2P9, 250 386-1312, 1-800-663-7007, Fax: 250 381-4312, www.qvhotel.com. Heated outdoor pool, sauna, restaurant. $$-$$$.

- Ramada Huntingdon Manor, 330 Quebec St., Victoria BC V8V 1W3, 250 381-3456, 1-800-663-7557, Fax: 250 382-7666, www.bellevillepark.com. Full-service hotel with English-style interiors. Sauna, whirlpool, aromatherapy. Restaurant, bar and grill, ice-cream parlour. Home to Artisans Lane. $$-$$$.

- Strathcona Hotel, 919 Douglas St., Victoria BC V8W 2C2, 250 383-7137, 1-800-663-7476, Fax: 250 383-6893, www.strathconahotel.com. A 1913 building recently refurbished with charisma. Victorian-era pub, nightclub. Rooftop lounge and volleyball court. $-$$.

- Swans Suite Hotel, 506 Pandora St., Victoria BC V8W 1N6, 250 361-3310, 1-800-668-7926, Fax: 250 361-3491, www.swanshotel.com. Restored heritage building with art collection in Olde Towne. Onsite brew pub, restaurant, club, beer and wine store. $$.

- Travellers Inn Downtown, 1850 Douglas St., Victoria BC V8T 4K6, 250 381-1000, 1-888-254-6476, Fax: 250 381-1001, www.travellersinn.com. Spacious rooms. Top floor rooms with small patio deck. Some rooms with kitchen, whirlpools. No pets. $.

- Victoria Plaza Hotel, 603 Pandora Ave., Victoria BC V8W 1N8, 250 386-3631, 1-800-906-4433, Fax: 250 386-9452. Modern and clean rooms with fine service. $.

- Victoria Regent Hotel, 1234 Wharf St., Victoria BC V8W 3H9, 250 386-2211, 1-800-663-7472, Fax: 250 386-2622, www.victoriaregent.com.

Condominium-style accommodations with sundecks, kitchens and dining areas. English and French spoken. $$-$$$.

BED AND BREAKFASTS

More than any other, the bed-and-breakfast experience evokes the graciousness and hospitality of a bygone era.

The following reservations services can be of great help:

- AA-Accommodations West Reservation Agency (250 479-1986).

- Western Canada B&B Innkeepers Association (250 388-6669).

The following are but a few of the many bed and breakfasts that dot the Victoria area:

- A B&B at Swallow Hill Farm, 4910 William Head Rd., Victoria BC V9C 3Y8, 250 474-4042, Fax: 250 474-4042, www.swallowhillfarm.com. Two suites with private baths on an apple farm on the southwest coast. Ocean and mountain views. Wildlife viewing. Farm breakfast served. No pets (resident dog), no smoking. $$.

- Abigail's Hotel, 906 McClure St., Victoria BC V8V 3E7, 250 388-5363, 1-800-561-6565, Fax: 250 388-7787, www.abigailshotel.com. Twenty-two rooms on four floors in a Tudor-style country bed and breakfast inn. Antique furniture, no elevator. Breakfast served, hors d'oeuvres and sherry in library. German spoken. No smoking, no pets. $$$.

- Andersen House B&B, 301 Kingston St., Victoria BC V8V 1V5, 250 388-4565, Fax: 250 721-3938, www.andersenhouse.com. Four suites in 1897 house with high ceilings, stained glass, built for a sea captain. Additional suite in a classic, 50-foot motor yacht moored five minutes away. Full breakfast. $$-$$$.

- Beaconsfield Inn, 998 Humboldt St., Victoria BC V8V 2Z8, 250 384-4044, 1-888-884-4044, Fax: 250 384-4052, www.beaconsfieldinn.com. Six rooms, three suites in a 1905 manse. Edwardian atmosphere, beamed ceilings and leaded glass windows. Gourmet breakfast, afternoon tea and sherry served. No pets, no smoking, no elevator (four stories). $$$.

- Cartref Bed and Breakfast, 1345 Readings Dr., Sidney BC V8L 5K7, 250 656-1247, Fax: 250 656-1247, www.islandnet.com/~cartref. Two rooms, shared and private bathrooms, in a new country-style home. Landscaped rock garden, sunny hillside, especially appealing for gardeners. Full or light breakfasts. No smoking, no pets. $$.

- Gatsby Mansion Bed & Breakfast & Restaurant, 309 Belleville St., Victoria BC V8V 1X2, 250 388-9191, 1-800-563-9656, Fax: 250 920-5651, www.bellevillepark.com. A collection of 18 suites in Belleville Park in a restored Queen Anne mansion (1877) and smaller house, both with ocean view. Main house has antiques and large verandah. Licensed lounge, restaurant, gift shop. Full breakfast. No smoking, no pets. $$-$$$.

- Haterleigh Heritage Inn, 243 Kingston St., Victoria BC V8V 1V5, 250 384-9995, Fax: 250 384-1935, www.haterleigh.com. Six rooms in a 1901 Victorian heritage mansion. Restored, with mix of modern and antique furnishings. Private Jacuzzis, gourmet breakfast. No smoking, no pets. $$$.

- Hidden Garden, 1326 Manor Rd., Victoria BC V8S 2A2, 250 595-2625, 1-877-595-2625, Fax: 250 595-2645, www.ahiddengarden.com. Four-star self-contained suites with bathrooms in a 1922 home, 15 minutes from city centre. Breakfast served. No smoking, no pets. $$.

- Humboldt House Bed and Breakfast, 867 Humboldt St., Victoria BC V8V 2Z6, 250 383-0152, 1-888-383-0327, Fax: 250 383-6402, www.humboldthouse.com. Five romantic rooms in authentic Victorian-era house. Large whirlpool, wood burning fireplaces. Sherry served in sitting room. Gourmet champagne breakfast delivered to rooms. No smoking. $$$.

- Iris Garden Country Manor Bed and Breakfast, 5360 West Saanich Rd., Victoria BC V9E 1J8, 250 744-2253, 1-877-744-2253, Fax: 250 744-5690, www.irisgardenvictoria.com. Four rooms with vaulted ceilings in an elegant country retreat. Three acres of irises, Douglas firs surround the 1960s character home. Guest living room. Full breakfast served. No smoking. $$.

- Oak Bay Guest House, 1052 Newport Ave., Victoria BC V8S 5E3, 250 598-3812, 1-800-575-3812, Fax: 250 598-0369, www.oakbayguesthouse.com. Eleven rooms in a restored manor previously owned by an eccentric Oak Bay philosopher. Charming décor, lush landscape reflecting gentility of the Oak Bay suburb. Compact bathrooms. No smoking. $$.

- Orchard House Bed and Breakfast, 9646 Sixth St., Sidney BC V8L 2W2, 250 656-9194 www.gerrymartin.com. Four rooms in a historic house built in 1914 by Sidney founding family. Close to airport and Vancouver ferries. Full breakfast served. Smoking outdoors, no pets. $.

- Prior House B&B Inn, 620 St. Charles St., Victoria BC V8S 3N7, 250 592-8847, 1-877-924-3300, Fax: 250 592-8223, www.priorhouse.com. Six rooms and suites in a restored 1912 manor house built originally for the lieutenant-governor. Lush land-scaped grounds, gracious interior, wood-burning fireplace. No elevator, smoking outdoors. Breakfast and High Tea served. $$-$$$.

- Rosewood Victoria Inn, 595 Michigan St., Victoria BC V8V 1S7, 250 384-6644, 1-800-335-3466, Fax: 250 384-6117, www.rosewoodvictoria.com. Seventeen rooms in a 1930s residence. Relaxed elegance, country antique items, charming library/lounge with open-log fire. No elevator, no pets, designated smoking area. Breakfast served. $$-$$$.

- Ryan's Bed and Breakfast, 224 Superior St., Victoria BC V8V 1T3, 250 389-0012, 1-877-389-0012, Fax: 250 389-2857, www.ryansbb.com. Six rooms in 1892 restored home. Lace curtains, china cabinets, oil paintings in heavy gilded frames. Designated smoking area, small

pets only. Breakfast served. $$-$$$.
- White Heather Cottage, 626 Simcoe St., Victoria BC V8V 1M4, 250 383-0152, 1-888-383-0327, Fax: 250 383-6402, www.whiteheathercottage.com. Two guestrooms in beautiful 1925 English Cottage. Pine beds, ensuite baths with deep soaking or Jacuzzi tubs. Gourmet breakfast served with champagne and chocolate truffles. No pets. $$-$$$

HOSTELS AND EDUCATIONAL RESIDENCES

For the budget-conscious traveller not looking for pampering, hostels and schools are the accommodation of choice:
- Backpackers Hostel Turtle Refuge, 1608 Quadra St., Victoria BC V8W 2L4, 250 386-4471, Fax: 250 386-4471. Dorm-style and private rooms. Four shared bathrooms, full kitchen facility, laundry room. Parking available. English and French spoken. $.
- Hostelling International Victoria, 516 Yates St., Victoria BC V8W 1K8, 250 385-4511, 1-888-883-0099, Fax: 250 385-3232, www.hihostels.ca. Shared and private rooms. Equipment storage, self-service kitchen, laundry room. Hostel-based activities and tours. Games/TV room, Internet access. $.
- Ocean Island Backpacker's Inn, 791 Pandora Ave., Victoria BC V8W 1N9, 250 385-1788, 1-888-888-4180, Fax: 250 385-1750, www.oceanisland.com. Spacious dorms with kitchen facilities. Licensed café, music room, Internet access. Pub crawl, parties, day trips organized. $.
- St. Margaret's School, 1080 Lucas Ave., Victoria BC V8X 3P7, 250 479-7171, Fax: 250 479-8976. Modern hotel-like accommodations on 22-acre property. Various meal plans available. $.
- University of Victoria Student Residences, PO Box 1700, Stn CSC, Victoria BC V8W 2Y2, 250 721-8395, Fax: 250 721-8390, housing.uvic.ca/Housing.htm. Available May to August. Single and double rooms with shared bath, coin-operated laundry, pay phones, lounge. Seven suites (Craigdarroch

House) with private bath, desk, TV, phone, complimentary breakfast. Fully-furnished townhouses also available at higher rates. $.

DINING

Vancouver and Victoria restaurants take full advantage of their setting, poised on the edge of an ocean and surrounded by wilderness. Fresh flavours incorporating indigenous ingredients mark each restaurant, as do the creativity of each chef and the diverse origins of the people they serve. Smoking in Vancouver and Victoria restaurants is prohibited by law. Please smoke in designated areas only. Tips are not usually added to a restaurant bill. Tipping a server is standard practice at the rate of 15% to 20%. The following lists a select number of the multitude of restaurants in each city. Each listing includes the approximate price range for dinner for two, including a bottle of wine (where served), taxes and gratuity: $ = under $45, $$ = $45-$80, $$$ = $80-$120, $$$$ = $120-$180, $$$$$ = over $180. Keep in mind that many fine restaurants make a wide selection of wines available by the glass as well. Meals served are indicated as: B = breakfast, L = lunch, D = dinner, G = grazing, T-O = take-out, Late = open past midnight. The credit cards accepted by each establishment are also listed: AX = American Express, V = Visa, MC = Mastercard, DC = Diners Club.

VANCOUVER

ASIAN
Chinese
Most restaurants represent the Cantonese and Mandarin regions. Many other styles, however, are showing up at diverse locations. Dim sum is available at most establishments, with the exception of noodle houses.
- Floata Seafood Restaurant, 400-180 Keefer St., 604 602-0368. Sets a standard for good food and strong service in a huge venue. Additional location at 1425-4380 #3 Rd., Richmond, 604 270-8889. L/D/T-O, $$$, AX/V/MC/DC.
- Grand King Seafood Restaurant, Holiday Inn, 705 West Broadway Ave., 604 876-7855. A small hotel

restaurant with a huge Chinese following. L/D, $$$$, AX/V/MC.

- Hon's Wun Tun House, 1339 Robson St., 604 685-0871. An institution for fast, cheap rice and noodles, potstickers, wun tun, and vegetarian dim sum. Multiple locations: 108-268 Keefer St., 604 688-0871; 280 Keefer St., 604 688-0871; 288 East Pender St., 604 681-8842; 310-3025 Lougheed Hwy., Coquitlam, 604 468-0871; 408 6th St., New Westminster, 604 520-6661; 101-4600 #3 Rd., Richmond, 604 273-0871. L/D/T-O, $, AX/V/MC/DC.

- Imperial Chinese Seafood Restaurant, 355 Burrard St., 604 688-8191. Elevated Chinese Dining. L/D, $$$$, AX/V/MC.

- Kirin Mandarin Restaurant, 102-1166 Alberni St., 604 682-8833. Refined dining from China's northern regions. L/D, $$$$, AX/V/DC.

- Pink Pearl Chinese Restaurant, 1132 East Hastings St., 604 253-4316. Come early for the dim sum, come late if you want to see a Chinese wedding banquet. L/D/T-O, $$$, AX/V/MC/DC.

- Richmond Mandarin Chinese Restaurant, 2200-8181 Cambie Rd., 604 270-3003. A hotel restaurant in Richmond's Asia West just has to have authenticity, and it doesn't disappoint. L/D, $$$, AX/V/MC.

- Shanghai Chinese Bistro, 1124 Alberni St., 604 683-8222. Chinese food, Shanghai-style and a dinner show in the form of noodle-pulling demonstration. L/D/Late, $$, AX/V/MC.

- Sun Sui Wah Restaurant, 3888 Main St., 604 872-8822. Every visiting food writer makes this stop for seafood and dim sum. Additional location in Richmond at 102-4940 #3 Rd., 604 273-8208. L/D, $$$-$$$$, AX/V/MC.

- Szechuan Chongqing Seafood Restaurant, 1668 West Broadway Ave., 604 734-1668. Showcases Chongqing regional cooking style. Additional location at 4519 Kingsway, Burnaby, 604 434-1668. L/D, $$-$$$, AX/V/MC.

- Won More Szechuan Cuisine, 201-1184 Denman St., 604 688-8856. Mainly spicy dishes in a crowded, upstairs space. Bigger version at 1944 West 4th Ave., 604 737-2889. D, $$, V/MC.

Japanese

- Ezogiku Noodle Café, 5-1329 Robson St., 604 685-8606. For ramen in all its forms (and more). An additional location is under the Rosedale Hotel at 270 Robson, 604 685-9466. L/D/T-O, $, no credit cards.

- Gyoza King, 1508 Robson St., 604 669-8278. Gyozas galore: meat-based, vegetable-based, seafood-based. Noodle and rice dishes, too. D/Late, $, V/MC.

- Musashi Japanese Restaurant, 780 Denman St., 604 687-0634. The West End's answer to sensibly-priced sushi. D, $, AX/V/MC.

- Suehiro Japanese Restaurant, Delta Pacific Resort, 10251 St. Edwards Dr., Richmond, 604 276-1163. For the teppan-yaki experience. L/D, $$$$, AX/V/MC/DC.

- Tojo's Restaurant, 202-777 West Broadway Ave., 604 872-8050. The ultimate in sushi springs from the hands of chef Hidekazu Tojo. Closed Sunday. D, $$$$, AX/V/MC/DC.

- Yuji's Japanese Tapas, 2059 West 4th Ave., 604 734-4990. Appetizer dishes, sashimi, sushi. Open nightly and weekends, closed Monday. D, $$, AX/V/MC.

South Asian

- Heaven & Earth India Curry House, 1754 West 4th Ave., 604 732-5313. Hot (and not so hot) curries and more in a warm, relaxed setting. D, $$, AX/V/MC.

- Maurya, 1643 West Broadway Ave., 604 742-0622. Modern fine dining. Indian. L/D/T-O, $$$, AX/V/MC.

- Rubina Tandoori, 1962 Kingsway, 604 874-3621. Deceptively plain exterior hides a sophisticated and skillful kitchen. Closed Sundays, no lunch Saturday. L/D/T-O, $$$, AX/V/MC.

- Vij's Restaurant, 1480 West 11th Ave., 604 736-6664. Expect lineups (no reservations are taken) for Vij's BC-influenced Indian dishes. Closed Sunday. D, $$$, AX/V/MC/DC.

Thai
- Montri's Thai Restaurant, 3629 West Broadway Ave., 604 738-9888. Authentically hot, in every sense of the word. D, $$$, V/MC.

Other Asian
- Phnom Penh, 244 East Georgia St., 604 682-5777. A Vietnamese-Cambodian-Chinese mix of dishes in a family-run establishment. L/D, $$, AX/MC.
- Singapore Restaurant, 546 West Broadway Ave., 604 874-6161. Bargain-priced dishes, spice-rated, and a cozy atmosphere. L/D, $-$$, V/MC.

FRENCH AND ITALIAN
- Beach Side Café, 1362 Marine Dr., West Vancouver, 604 925-1945. Light, subtle food and stunning views. Brunch on weekends. L/D, $$$$, AX/V/MC.
- Bistro Pastis, 2153 West 4th Ave., 604 731-5020. Satisfying bistro classics. Closed Monday. L/D, $$$, AX/V/MC.
- Café de Paris, 751 Denman St., 604 687-1418. Both the setting and fare bring to mind the classic Paris bistro. No lunch weekends. L/D, $$$, AX/V/MC.
- Cioppino's Mediterranean Grill, 1133 Hamilton St., 604 688-7466. Light, fresh dishes melding Italian, French and Spanish flavours. L/D, $$$-$$$$, AX/V/MC.
- Il Giardino di Umberto, 1382 Hornby St., 604 669-2422. A seaside villa recreated, serving excellent pasta and game. Closed Sunday, no lunch Saturday. L/D, $$$$, AX/V/MC/DC.
- La Régalade, 103-2232 Marine Dr., West Vancouver, 604 921-2228. Country French at bistro prices. L/D, $$, V/MC.
- Le Crocodile, 909 Burrard St., 604 669-4298. Offers the full, real Alsace experience. Closed Sundays, no lunch Saturday. L/D, $$$$, AX/V/MC.
- Piccolo Mondo, 850 Thurlow St., 604 688-1633. Traditional cooking from Northern Italy. Closed Sunday, no lunch Saturday. L/D, $$$$, AX/V/MC/DC.
- Quattro on Fourth, 2611 West 4th Ave., 604 734-4444. Additional location at Gusto di Quattro, North Vancouver, 604 924-4444. Mosaic and mahogany and marvellous food. D, $$$-$$$$, AX/V/MC/DC.
- Smoking Dog Bar and Grill, 1889 West 1st Ave., 604 732-8811. Simple French fare in the perfect people-watching place. No lunch weekends. L/D, $$-$$$, AX/V/MC.
- Villa Del Lupo, 869 Hamilton St., 604 688-7436. Generous and contemporary cooking in a charming old house. D, $$$$, AX/V/MC/DC.

PACIFIC NORTHWEST
- Liliget Feast House, 1724 Davie St., 604 681-7044. A rarity: original First Nations cuisine in a fabulous longhouse setting. D, $$$, AX/V/MC/DC.
- Rodney's Oyster House, 405-1228 Hamilton St., 604 609-0080. Oysters are the main attraction here, but other seafoods are popular too. L/D, $$$, AX/V/MC/DC.
- The Beach House, 150 25th St., West Vancouver, 604 922-1414. Strong on seafood. By Dundarave Beach, it's a great spot for Sunday brunch. L/D, $$$$, AX/V/MC/DC.
- The Cannery Seafood Restaurant, 2205 Commissioner St., 604 254-9606. Promises good seafood, and delivers. No lunch weekends. L/D, $$$$, AX/V/MC/DC.
- The Fish House in Stanley Park, 8901 Stanley Park Dr., 604 681-7275. Bold and creative seafood. Sunday brunch. L/D, $$$-$$$$, AX/V/MC/DC.
- The Pear Tree, 4120 Hastings St., Burnaby, 604 299-2772. Inventive food, reasonable prices. Closed Sunday. D, $$$, AX/V/MC/DC.
- Raincity Grill, 1193 Denman St., 604 685-7337. Ever-changing menu based on what's fresh. Weekend brunch. L/D, $$$$, AX/V/MC/DC.
- Seasons in the Park Restaurant, Queen Elizabeth Park, Cambie St. and West 33rd Ave., 604 874-8008. Good, conservative food in an intoxicating garden setting. Weekend brunch. L/D, $$$-$$$$, AX/V/MC.

FINE DINING AND HOTEL DINING
- 900 West Sea & Steakfood Restaurant and Wine Bar (Fairmont Hotel Vancouver), 900 West Georgia St., 604 684-3131. Steak,

seafood, wine and a beautiful setting. D, $$$$, AX/V/MC/DC.

- Bacchus Ristorante, Wedgewood Hotel, 845 Hornby St., 604 689-7777. Small, exclusive room with unfailingly good food. Afternoon tea served. B/L/D/Late (lounge), $$$$, AX/V/MC/DC.
- Bishop's Restaurant, 2183 West 4th Ave., 604 738-2025. Flawlessly prepared food, understated elegance and superb service. No lunch weekends. L/D, $$$$, AX/V/MC/DC.
- C, 2-1600 Howe St., 604 681-1164. Intriguing dishes and a million-dollar marina view. D, Lunch in summer months. $$$$-$$$$$, AX/V/MC/DC.
- Chartwell, Four Seasons Hotel, 791 West Georgia St., 604 689-9333. The classic dining choice. D, $$$$-$$$$$, AX/V/MC/DC.
- Diva at the Met, Metropolitan Hotel, 645 Howe St., 604 602-7788. Airy space with multi-tiered seating and stylish food preparation. Weekend brunch. B/L/D, $$$$, X/V/MC/DC.
- Feenie's, 2563 West Broadway Ave., 604 739-7115. Casual Canadian bistro cooking with flare includes burgers and speghettini with prawns and scallops. B/L/D/, $$$, AX/V/MS/DC.
- Five Sails Restaurant, Pan Pacific Hotel, 300-999 Canada Place, 604 662-8111. Imaginative orchestration of flavours and breathtaking views. D, $$$$, AX/V/MC/DC.
- Fleuri Restaurant, Sutton Place Hotel, 845 Burrard St., 604 642-2908. A hidden treasure. Afternoon tea, Sunday brunch, Chocoholic Bar. No lunch Saturday. B/L/D, $$$$, AX/V/MC/DC.
- Lumière, 2551 West Broadway Ave., 604 739-8185. Classic French preparation with contemporary flair. Tasting menus are superb. Closed Mondays. D, $$$$-$$$$$, AX/V/MC/DC.
- West, 2881 Granville St., 604 738-8938. Regional, seasonal fare. L/D. $$$$, AX/V/MC/DC.

SPECIALTY
Heritage
- Hart House on Deer Lake, 6664 Deer Lake Ave., Burnaby, 604 298-

4278. The Tudor-style setting embraces both traditional and more daring fare. L/D, $$$-$$$$, AX/V/MC/DC.
- Teahouse at Ferguson Point, 7501 Stanley Park Dr., 604 669-3281. Former officers' mess perfectly situated in the midst of one of the world's best and biggest urban parks. Weekend brunch. L/D, $$$$, AX/V/MC.

Vegetarian
- Habibi's, 7-1128 West Broadway Ave., 604 732-7487. Bargain-priced, vegetarian Lebanese fare makes for both a healthy body and a happy wallet. No lunch weekends, closed Sundays. L/D, $, no credit cards.
- The Naam, 2724 West 4th Ave., 604 738-7180. Vancouver's oldest vegetarian restaurant offers dishes from around the world. B/L/D/G/Late, $, AX/V/MC.
- Planet Veg, 1941 Cornwall Ave., 604 734-1001. A warning: lineups form fast for the Indian, Mexican and Mediterranean vegetarian fast foods. L/D/T-O, $, no credit cards.

Tapas
- Bin 941 Tapas Parlour, 941 Davie St., 604 683-1246. Generously filled tasting bowls. D/Late, $$-$$$, V/MC.
- Bin 942 Tapas Parlour, 1521 West Broadway Ave., 604 734-9421. Much like Bin 941, but bigger. D/Late, $$-$$$, V/MC.

CASUAL DINING AND BAKERIES
- Dockside Brewing Company, 1253 Johnston St., 604 685-7070. Pub, casual restaurant, microbrewery and smashing patio, all in one. B/L/D, $$, AX/D/V/MC.
- Earl's Restaurants, 1601 West Broadway Ave., 604 736-5663. Fresh and healthy food that's fast, for parents travelling with children. Various additional locations: 901 West Broadway Ave., 604 734-5995 and 1185 Robson St., 604 669-0020 in Vancouver. L/D, $$, AX/V/MC.
- Patisserie Lebeau, 1728 West 2nd Ave., 604 731-3528. Fine Belgian waffles and jewel-like pastries and French breads, freshly baked. Eat-

in or take-out. Closed Monday, Tuesday, AX/V/MC.

- Les Amis Du Fromage, 1752 West 2nd Ave., 604 732-4218. Say cheese and comfort take-out at Vancouver's best cheese shop. T-O, $, AX/V/MC.
- Memphis Blues Barbeque House, 1465 West Broadway Ave., 604 738-6806. Additional location at 1342 Commercial Dr., 604 215-2599. Southern baah-be-cue with all the Memphis favourites. L/D/T-O, $, AE/MC/V.
- Notte's Bon Ton Bakery and Confectionary, 3150 West Broadway Ave., 604 681-3058. While the tea quenches your thirst and the pastries sate your hunger, the cards reveal your fate. Closed Sunday and Monday. G/T-O, $, V/MC.
- Solly's Bagelry, 189 East 28th Ave., 604 872-1821. Order from the bagelry and deli, or sit with a coffee and something sweet (the best cinnamon bun in town, perhaps). Additional location at 2873 West Broadway Ave., 604 738-2121. B/L/G/T-O, $, V.
- Steamworks Brewing Company, 375 Water St., 604 689-2739. Some say the best beer in town is found in Steamworks' onsite brewery. B/L/D/Late, $$, AX/V/MC.
- Subeez, 891 Homer St., 604 687-6107. Popular industrial-style bistro. B/L/D, $$-$$$, V/MC.
- Tomato Fresh Food Café, 3305 Cambie St., 604 874-6020. Distinctively healthy and colourful comfort food, with the same food available for takeout around the corner at Tomato to Go, 530 West 17th Ave., 604 873-4697. B/L/D/T-O, $$, AX/V/MC.
- Waazubee Café, 1622 Commercial Dr., 604 253-5299. Casual and upbeat spot on The Drive. B/L/D, $$, V/MC.
- White Spot Triple O, 1881 Cornwall Ave., 604 738-3888. The express version of Nat Bailey's famous White Spot. Fries, milkshakes and Vancouver's favourite burgers with legendary Triple O sauce are served fast. Other Vancouver locations: 805 Thurlow St., 604 609-7000, 1455 Quebec St. (Science World), 604 647-0003. B/L/D/T-O, $, V/MC.

VICTORIA

FINE DINING

- Aerie Resort, 600 Ebadora Lane, Malahat, 250 743-7115. French class and quality well worth the price. L/D, $$$$-$$$$$, AX/V/MC/DC.
- Café Brio, 944 Fort St., 250 383-0009. Contemporary Pacific Northwest creations in a lively, art-filled room. No lunch weekends. L/D, $$$-$$$$, AX/V/MC.
- Deep Cove Chalet, 11190 Chalet Road, Deep Cove, Sidney, 250 656-3541. Exceptional French cuisine, specializing in local seafood. L/D, $$$$, AX/V/MC.
- Sooke Harbour House, 1528 Whiffen Spit Rd., Sooke, 250 642-3421. Innovative, even eccentric, one of Canada's gastronomic treasures. D, $$$$$, V/MC/DC.
- Victorian Restaurant, Ocean Pointe Resort and Spa, 45 Songhees Rd., 250 360-2999. Sleek and contemporary, with impeccable service. D, $$$$, AX/V/MC/DC.

BISTROS AND CAFÉS

- Barb's Fish & Chips, 310 St. Lawrence St., 250 384-6515. Look inside the blue-painted shack for authentic halibut fish and chips. Closed November to March. L/D/G/T-O, $, no credit cards.
- Bond Bond's, 1010 Blanshard St., 250 388-5377. The city's top bakery makes lunch items, too. Closed Sunday. G/T-O, $, no credit cards.
- Brasserie L'Ecole, 1715 Government St., 250 475-6260. Classic French bistro dishes using Vancouver Island ingredients. D, $$$, MC/V.
- Bravo Restaurant, 1218 Wharf St., 250 386-2900 Popular contemporary bistro with great prices. L/D, $$$, MC/V/AX/DC.
- La Collina Bakery, 3115 Cedar Hill Rd., 250 595-2624. Italian bakery featuring pastries, breads and small dinner menu in the evening. L/D, $$$, MC/V.
- Foster's Eatery, 753 Yates St., 250 382-1131. Designer sandwiches for a quick lunch. B/L/D, $, AX/V/MC.

- Ottavio Gastronomia, 2272 Oak Bay Ave., 250 592-4080. Italian bakery specializing in cheese, pastries, organic gelato and sandwiches. L/D, $$, V.
- Paprika Bistro, 2524 Estevan Ave., 250 592-7424. Vivid, yet light dishes with a Hungarian history. Closed Sunday. D, $$$, AX/V/MC.
- Paradiso di Stelle, 10 Bastion Sq., 250 920-7266. The place to go for a gelato fix. Open 7 days. V/MC.
- Rebar Modern Foods, 50 Bastion Sq., 250 361-9223. Inventive, delicious, healthy food. Kid-friendly. B/L/D, $$, AX/V/MC/DC.
- Suze Restaurant and Lounge, 515 Yates St., 250 383-2829. The place to go for people-watching and international fare. Sunday brunch. L/D/Late/T-O, $$$, AX/V/MC.
- The Temple, 525 Fort St., 250 383.2313. Contemporary regional cuisine in cosmopolitan ambience. L/D, $$$, MC/V/AX.
- Zambri's, 110-911 Yates St., 250 360-1171. Best Italian café in town. L/D, $$, AX/V/MC.

SEAFOOD
- Blue Crab Bar and Grill, Coast Victoria Harbourside Hotel, 146 Kingston St., 250 480-1999. Look for Pacific Northwest casual and look out for dessert. B/L/D, $$$, AX/V/MC/DC.
- Dock 503 Waterfront Café, 2320 Harbour Rd., Sidney, 250 656-0828. Zeroes in on the freshest seafood in Sidney. Breakfast, weekend brunch in summer. B/L/D/G, $$$, AX/V/MC/DC.
- Marina Restaurant, 1327 Beach Dr., 250 598-8555. The natural setting for a nautical meal. Sunday Brunch. L/D, $$$-$$$$, AX/V/MC/DC.

BREWPUBS
- Canoe Brewpub, Marina and Restaurant, 450 Swift St., 250 361-1940. Historic waterfront brewpub with modern food. L/D, $$-$$$, MC/V/AX/DC.
- Harbour Canoe Club, 450 Swift St., 250 361-1940. A prize location in a restored 1894 heritage powerhouse, homemade brews and a continental menu besides. L/D/Late, $$, V/MC.
- Hugo's Grill and Brewhouse, Magnolia Hotel, 625 Courtney St.,

250 920-4846. Hotel brewpub worth a visit. L/D/Late, $$-$$$.
- The Penny Farthing Olde English Pub, 2228 Oak Bay Ave., 250 370-9008. Lively pub that appeals to all ages. L/D, $$-$$$, MC/V/AX.
- Spinnakers Brewpub, 308 Catherine St., 250 384-2739. Traditional brewery, sausage kitchen, smokehouse and bakery. B/L/D, $$, AX/V/MC.
- Swans Brewpub, Swans Suite Hotel, 506 Pandora St., 250 361-3310. In-house brews and reasonably priced food makes this a popular hangout. B/L/D/Late, $$, AX/V/MC.

TEA
While in Victoria, one must have tea. Keep in mind that many places make a distinction between "Afternoon" or "Light" Tea — small sandwiches, scones, clotted cream, jam, berries and coffee or tea — and High Tea, a more substantial tea with trifles and more of the above.
- Blethering Place Tea Room and Restaurant, 2250 Oak Bay Ave., 250 598-1413. A cozy place in Oak Bay Village. Light Tea, Full Tea, $$, AX/V/MC.
- Butchart Gardens, 800 Benvenuto Ave., Central Saanich, 250 652-8222. Tea in the garden, a fine idea. Afternoon Tea, $$, AX/V/MC.
- Empress Room, The Fairmont Empress Hotel, 721 Government St., 250 384-8111. Afternoon tea served as it should be. Reserve ahead. Dress code in Tea Lobby. High Tea, $$$$, AX/V/MC/DC.
- James Bay Tearoom and Restaurant, 322 Menzies St., 250 382-8282. A favourite for friendliness and prices. Afternoon Tea, High Tea Sunday, $, AX/V/MC.
- Point Ellice House, 2616 Pleasant St., 250 380-6506. Tea served out on the lawn, complete with white wicker, against a heritage house setting overlooking the Gorge. Light Tea, High Tea, $$ per person. AX/V/MC.

ETHNIC
- J & J Won Ton Noodle House, 1012 Fort St., 250 383-0680. Savory noodles, soups, mein, fun, simply served. L/D, $, V/MC.

TOP ATTRACTIONS

VANCOUVER

The list that follows gives the sights that define Vancouver to the rest of the world. Travellers who spend even a weekend here, however, will agree there's much more to see and do.

- Vancouver Museum. Fronted by Vancouver's pet stainless steel Crab, this odd structure encloses Vancouver's past. Also hosts visiting and temporary exhibits. 1100 Chestnut St., 604 736-4431, www.vanmuseum.bc.ca.
- H. R. MacMillan Space Centre. Space comes to Earth with the Space Centre's hands-on galleries, interactive computer displays, multimedia and laser shows and live demonstrations, while the H. R. MacMillan Planetarium snares the stars on a 20-metre dome. 1100 Chestnut St., 604 738-7827, www.hrmacmillanspacecentre.com
- Vancouver Maritime Museum. A historic ship, Heritage Harbour, the Children's Maritime Discovery Centre and permanent as well as temporary exhibits pay tribute to Vancouver's seagoing heritage. 1905 Ogden Ave., 604 257-8300, www.vmm.bc.ca.
- Vancouver Aquarium Marine Science Centre. Brings the denizens of different sea habitats into close focus through displays of 60,000 aquatic creatures. Also features special events, behind-the-scenes tours, sleepovers and animal encounters. Stanley Park, 845 Avison Way, 604 659-3474, www.vanaqua.org.
- Canada Place/CN IMAX Theatre. Five white sails hover over the Canada Place convention centre with its wraparound outdoor walkway and stunning views of Vancouver harbour. Included is the CN IMAX Theatre, where the steeply pitched amphitheatre seating, a five-story screen and six-channel IMAX Digital wraparound sound make film-viewing an intense experience. 999 Canada Place Way, 604 682-4629, www.imax.com/vancouver.
- Science World/Alcan OMNIMAX Theatre. Science and entertainment merge in creative, hands-on exhibits inside the mirrored geodesic dome. The Alcan OMNIMAX Theatre runs documentaries to tremendous effect. 1455 Quebec St., 604 443-7440, www.scienceworld.bc.ca.
- Grouse Mountain/The Peak of Vancouver. Hike up Grouse or take the Skyride aerial tram for panoramic views, fine and casual dining and winter and summer sports at the top. 6400 Nancy Greene Way, North Vancouver, 604 984-0661, www.grousemountain.com.
- Capilano Suspension Bridge and Park. A structure of sturdy steel cables sways high above the forested Capilano River canyon. 3735 Capilano Rd., North Vancouver, 604 985-7474, www.capbridge.com.
- Vancouver Art Gallery. The neo-classical building is a permanent home to a collection of works by Emily Carr, among others, and hosts touring exhibitions, demonstrations and lunch-hour concerts. 750 Hornby St., 604 662-4700, www.vanartgallery.bc.ca.
- UBC Museum of Anthropology. Research and teaching museum-cum-gallery, with artifacts from around the world and one of the world's finest collections of Northwest Coast First Nations art. Free outdoor sculpture garden with totem poles and Haida houses. 6393 N.W. Marine Dr. (University of British Columbia campus), 604 822-5087, www.moa.ubc.ca.
- Stanley Park. One thousand acres of urban wilderness. While its rim has been adapted for recreation, its centre is untamed. 604 257-8400, www.parks.vancouver.bc.ca.
- Dr. Sun Yat-Sen Classical Chinese Garden. A serene garden set in the heart of Chinatown reflects perfect equilibrium in all elements, from design through use. 578 Carrall St., 604 662-3207, www.vancouverchinesegarden.com.

VICTORIA

- Parliament Buildings. The seat of the Provincial Legislature. Free tours and a live "performance" when the house is in session. 501 Belleville St., 250 387-3046, www.legis.gov.bc.ca.

- Inner Harbour and Fisherman's Wharf. Outdoors where buskers and artisans offer their talents against a view of the harbour. On one side is Fisherman's Wharf, where commercial fishing boats dock. In front of The Fairmont Empress Hotel and Parliament Buildings.
- The Fairmont Empress Hotel. Grand, chateau-style heritage hotel. Famed Afternoon Tea. 721 Government St., 250 384-8111, www.fairmont.com/empress.
- Chinatown. Two crammed blocks' worth of browsing, shopping and eating almost hides narrow Fan Tan Alley, current home to artist studios and boutiques, former haven for opium dens. Fisgard and Government streets.
- Emily Carr House. Artist and writer Emily Carr's family home, restored and updated with computerized information centre and Canadian artists' gallery. 207 Government St., 250 383-5843, www.heritage. gov.bc.ca/emily/emily.htm.
- Helmcken House. Oldest house in BC still on its original site. Douglas and Belleville Streets, 250 361-0021, www.heritage.gov.bc.ca/ helm/helm.htm.
- Point Ellice House. Meticulously restored house and garden with unusual collection of Victoriana. 2616 Pleasant St., 250 380-6506, www.heritage.gov.bc.ca/point/point. htm.
- Craigdarroch Castle. Monumental Dunsmuir family stone mansion. 1050 Joan Crescent, 250 592-5323, www.craigdarrochcastle.com.
- The Art Gallery of Greater Victoria. 1889 mansion attracting internationally-renowned exhibits and housing contemporary BC and other Canadian art, North American, European, Japanese and Chinese works. Moss Street Paint-In festival every August. 1040 Moss St., 250 384-1531 or 250-4101, www.aggv.bc.ca.
- Royal British Columbia Museum. Three permanent galleries — Natural History Gallery, Open Ocean Gallery and The First Peoples and Modern History Gallery — plus multiple exhibits and the National Geographic IMAX Theatre. 675 Belleville St.,

250 356-7226, 1-888-447-7977, www.royalbcmuseum.bc.ca.
- Maritime Museum of British Columbia. Original 1889 provincial courthouse houses artifacts documenting the province's oceangoing history. Treasure hunt for kids. 28 Bastion Sq., 250 385-4222, www.mmbc.bc.ca.

GALLERIES AND MUSEUMS

VANCOUVER
Vancouver's galleries now number approximately 150 and cover a wide range of expressions: historic art, contemporary, avant garde and traditional. The art is made by First Nations people, Canadians, Asians and Europeans. Check the Thursday editions of *The Georgia Straight* and *Queue Magazine* in the *Vancouver Sun* for details of current shows. *Preview: The Gallery Guide* listings and maps are also useful. An online version can be found at www.preview-art.com.

GALLERIES
- Access Gallery. New art installations. 206 Carrall St., 604 689-2907.
- Appleton Gallery. Northwest Coast art. 1451 Hornby St., 604 685-1715.
- Art Beatus. International and Chinese art. M1-888 Nelson St., 604 688-2633.
- Art Emporium. Canadian art. 2928 Granville St., 604 738-3510.
- Artspeak. Phototext and interactive video. 233 Carrall St., 604 688-0051.
- Atelier Gallery. Contemporary art. 2421 Granville St., 604 732-3021.
- Bau-Xi Gallery. Contemporary art. 3045 Granville St., 604 733-7011.
- Bfly Gallery. Curated exhibits. 2nd floor, 341 Water St., 604 647-1019.
- Buschlen Mowatt Gallery. International art. 1445 West Georgia St., 604 682-1234.
- Catriona Jeffries Gallery. Emphasis is on avant garde Canadian art. 3149 Granville St., 604 736-1554.
- Le Centre Culturel Francophone de Vancouver. Shows by French-speaking artists. 1551 West 7th Ave., 604 736-9806.

- Centre A. Shows of Asian art. 849 Homer St., 604 683-8326.
- Charles H. Scott Gallery. Located in the Emily Carr Institute of Art and Design. 1399 Johnston St., Granville Island, 604 844-3809.
- Circle Craft Gallery. Jury-selected works by BC craft artists. 1-1666 Johnston St., Granville Island, 604 669-8021.
- Crafthouse. 1386 Cartwright St., Granville Island, 604 687-7270.
- Coastal People's Fine Arts. Northwest Coast, Inuit and Plains art. 1024 Mainland St., 1-888-686-9298.
- Contemporary Art Gallery. Vanguard works. 555 Nelson St., 604 681-2700.
- Crafthouse Gallery. Non-profit gallery showcases BC craftspeople. 1386 Cartwright St., Granville Island, 604 687-6511.
- Diane Farris Gallery. Contemporary art. 1590 West 7th Ave., 604 737-2629.
- Doctor Vigari Furniture & Art. 1312 Commercial Dr., 604 255-9513.
- Dorian Rae. African and Asian collections. 410 Howe St., 604 874-6100.
- Douglas Udell. Western contemporary. 1558 West 6th Ave., 604 736-8900.
- Douglas Reynolds Gallery. Northwest Coast art and jewellery. 2335 Granville St., 604 731-9292.
- Dundarave Print Workshop. Limited edition prints. 1640 Johnston St., Granville Island, 604 689-1650.
- Eagle Spirit Gallery. Northwest Coast art including masks. 1803 Maritime Mews, Granville Island, 604 801-5205.
- Elfsar Collection. Animation cells. 1007 Hamilton St., 604 688-5922.
- Elissa Cristall. Contemporary art. 2245 Granville St., 604 730-9611.
- Equinox Gallery. Contemporary Canadian works. 2321 Granville St., 604 736-2405.
- Exposure Gallery. Photography. 851 Beatty St., 604 888-9501.
- Gallery of BC Ceramics. Talented local potters. 1359 Cartwright St., Granville Island, 604 669-5645.
- grunt Gallery. First Nations and avant garde art. 116-350 East 2nd Ave., 604 875-9516.
- Harrison Galleries. Traditional Canadian. 2932 Granville St., 604 732-5217.
- Havana Gallery. Emerging artists. 1212 Commercial Dr., 604 253-9119.
- Heffel Gallery. Group of Seven and 19th-century artists. 2247 Granville St., 604 732-6505.
- Helen Pitt Gallery. Emerging artists. 882 Homer St., 604 681-6740.
- Honjo Gallery. Contemporary Japanese. 506-55 Water St., 604 688-2605.
- Howe Street Gallery of Fine Art/Soul of Africa Collection. Contemporary. 555 Howe St., 604 681-5770.
- Images for a Canadian Heritage. Northwest Coast, Inuit and wildlife art. 164 Water St., 604 685-7046.
- Industrial Artifacts. Sculptural furniture. 49 Powell St., 604 874-7797.
- Inuit Gallery. Museum-quality Inuit art. 206 Cambie St., 604 688-7323.
- The Ironworks. Warehouse gallery. 235 Alexander St., 604 681-5033.
- Jacana. Oriental furniture and contemporary art. 2435 Granville St., 604 879-9306.
- Kurbatoff Gallery. International art. 2427 Granville St., 604 736-5444.
- Leona Lattimer Gallery. Northwest Coast artists. 1590 West 2nd Ave., 604 732-4556.
- Malaspina Printmakers Gallery. Limited edition prints. 1555 Duranleau St., Granville Island, 604 688-1827.
- Marion Scott Gallery. Inuit art. 481 Howe St., 604 685-1934.
- Monte Clark Gallery. Contemporary photography. 2339 Granville St., 604 730-5000.
- Morris and Helen Belkin Gallery at the University of British Columbia. Exhibitions of international and Canadian art. 1825 Main Mall, 604 681-6730.
- New-Small and Sterling Studio Glass. Hot glass blowing and glass works. 1440 Old Bridge St., Granville Island, 604 681-6730.
- onepointsix. Photobased works. 878 Homer St., 604 684-0478.
- Or Gallery Society. Conceptual art. 103-480 Smithe St., 604 683-7395.
- Petley Jones Gallery. 2235 Granville St., 604 732-5353.
- Pendulum Gallery. Community art

shows. 885 West Georgia St., HSBC foyer, 604 879-7714.
- Phthalo Gallery. International and local art. 1068 Homer St., 604 689-2787.
- Romanov Gallery. Realist art. 1590 Harbour Quay, 604 687-6987.
- Simon Patrich Gallery. Some Latin-American art. 2329 Granville St., 604 733-2662.
- Sharing the Spirit Gallery. Northwest Coast art. 232-757 West Hastings St., 604 438-1111.
- Sopel Gallery. Jade sculpture. 327 Howe St., 604 689-8844.
- Spirit Wrestler Gallery. First Nations works. 8 Water St., 604 669-8813.
- Spirits of the North. First Nations works. 2327 Granville St., 604 733-8516.
- Tensho Gallery. Oriental and international. 2243 Granville St., 604 738-8876.
- Third Avenue Gallery. Exhibits recent art grads and emerging artists in various genres. 1725 West 3rd Ave., 604 738-3500.
- Tracey Lawrence Gallery. Contemporary art. 105-1529 West 6th Ave., 604 730-2875.
- Uno Langmann. Antiques. 2117 Granville St., 604 736-8825.
- Vancouver Art Gallery. Traditional and contemporary Canadian and European art. 750 Hornby St., 604 662-4719.
- VOX. Contemporary art. 1839 Commercial Dr., 604 253-1013.
- Waterfall Building. Four galleries under one roof. 1540 West 2nd Ave., no telephone.
- Winsor Gallery. Contemporary South East Asian art. 667 Howe St., 604 681-4870.

MUSEUMS
- BC Sports Hall of Fame and Museum. Chronicles BC's professional and amateur sports and recreation history through displays, hands-on exhibits and multimedia. Gate A, BC Place Stadium, 777 Pacific Blvd. S., 604 687-5520, www.bcsportshalloffame.com.
- Burnaby Village Museum. A turn-of-the-century town with authentically costumed "residents" and restored 1912 carousel called the "Carry-Us-All." 6501 Deer Lake Ave., Burnaby, 604 293-6501.

- Chinese Cultural Centre Museum and Archives. Temporary exhibits Chinese artists, archive of Chinese history in BC. 555 Columbia St., 604 658-8880.
- Granville Island Museums. Three international collections: Sport Fishing Museum, Model Trains Museum, Model Ships Museum. 1502 Duranleau St., Granville Island, 604 683-1939, www.sportfishingmuseum.bc.ca.
- Hastings Mill Store Museum. A charmingly cluttered museum inside Vancouver's oldest building shelters items such as muskets, Native baskets, period clothes, clocks and a coach. 1575 Alma St., 604 734-1212.
- UBC Museum of Anthropology. Research and teaching museum-cum-gallery, with artifacts from around the world and Northwest Coast First Nations art. Outdoor sculpture garden with totem poles and Haida houses. 6393 N.W. Marine Dr. (University of BC campus), 604 822-5087, www.moa.ubc.ca.
- Vancouver Maritime Museum. A historic ship, Heritage Harbour, the Children's Maritime Discovery Centre and permanent as well as temporary exhibits pay tribute to Vancouver's seagoing heritage. 1905 Ogden Ave., 604 257-8300, www.vmm.bc.ca.
- Vancouver Museum. Vancouver's past plus visiting and temporary exhibits. 1100 Chestnut St., 604 736-4431, www.vanmuseum.bc.ca.
- Vancouver Police Centennial Museum. Crime and crime-fighting paraphernalia, including old photos, gambling displays, artifacts and accounts of ancient unsolved murders. 240 East Cordova St., 604 665-3346.

VICTORIA MUSEUMS
- Maritime Museum of British Columbia. The original 1889 provincial courthouse houses artifacts documenting British Columbia's oceangoing history. Treasure hunt for kids. 28 Bastion Sq., 250 385-4222, www.mmbc.bc.ca.
- Royal British Columbia Museum. Three permanent galleries (Natural History Gallery, Open Ocean Gallery and The First Peoples and Modern

History Gallery) plus multiple exhibits and the National Geographic IMAX Theatre. 675 Belleville St., 250 356-7226, 1-888-447-7977, www.royalbcmuseum.bc.ca.
• Royal London Wax Museum. Wax figures of famous and infamous characters in history, show business and literature. 470 Belleville St., 250 388-4461, www.waxworld.com.

VANCOUVER ENTERTAINMENT

In addition to a well-known film and television production industry, entertainment in Vancouver can be found live at clubs, theatres and arts centres around town. The Vancouver Cultural Alliance's website (www.vcn.bc.ca/vca) is a valuable resource, and *The Georgia Straight* publishes weekly events listings as well. Ticketmaster operates an Arts Line at 604 280-3311. Note that those under 19 years of age are not allowed in nightclubs serving alcohol.

CLUBS
• Au Bar, 647 Seymour St., 604 647-2227. Popular, chic dance club.
• Body Perve Social Club, Lotus Sound Lounge 455 Abbott St., 604 685-7777. Fetish.
• Cabbages & Kinx, 315 West Hastings St., 604 669-4238. Fetish.
• The Gérard Lounge (Sutton Place Hotel), 845 Burrard St., 604 682-5511. Attracts celebrities and a moneyed crowd.
• Honey Lounge, 466 Abbott St., 604 685-7777. Elegant mixed club that is lesbian friendly.
• Lick, 455 Abbott St., 604 685-7777. Women only.
• MOR Rubber, 1263 Homer St., 604 683-2667. Fetish.
• Numbers Cabaret, 1098 Davie St., 604 685-4077. Four split-levels and a pair of bars are crammed with a regular gay clientele.
• Odyssey, 1251 Howe St., 604 689-5256. Caters to a loyal gay crowd, features alternative dance music.
• Pumpjacks, 1167 Davie St., 604 685-3417. Gay club
• Richard's On Richards, 1036 Richards St., 604 687-6794. Posh club with local bands, international recording acts and DJ dance music.

• Sin City, 23 West Cordova, 604 662-3277. Fetish.
• Skybar, 615-938 Howe St., 604 697-9199. Three levels with open rooftop.

THEATRE
• Arts Club Mainstage and Revue Theatre, 1585 Johnston St., Granville Island, 604 687-1644. Western Canada's largest regional theatre and a local institution.
• Firehall Arts Centre, 280 East Cordova St., 604 689-0926. Converted fire station specializing in alternative theatre, performance art and dance.
• Metro Theatre Centre, 1370 S.W. Marine Dr., 604 266-7191. Attracts a loyal, mature audience looking for British comedy.
• Norman Rothstein Theatre, 950 West 41st Ave., 604 257-5111. State-of-the-art theatre in the Jewish Community Centre.
• Presentation House Arts Centre, 333 Chesterfield Ave., North Vancouver, 604 990-3473. Terrific community theatre.
• Queen Elizabeth Theatre. 600 Block Hamilton St., 604 665-3050. Glitzy, glamorous Broadway-style productions.
• St. Andrew Wesley's Church (Tony & Tina's Wedding), 1012 Nelson St., 604 280-3311 (Ticketmaster). Dinner theatre that begins in a real church and ends with the reception a short distance away.
• Stanley Theatre, 2750 Granville St., 604 687-1644. The Arts Club's third stage in a former vaudeville venue and movie theatre.
• Urban Well Restaurant & Lounge, 1516 Yew St., 604 737-7770. Adult improv comedy.
• Vancouver Playhouse. 600 Block Hamilton St., 604 873-3311. One of the best regional theatres in Canada.
• Waterfront Theatre, 1410 Cartwright St., Granville Island, 604 685-6217. Big stage in a small theatre where many Canadian works debut.
• The Centre in Vancouver for Performing Arts, 777 Homer St., 604 602-0616.

MUSIC
• Chan Centre for the Performing Arts, 6265 Crescent Rd., University

of BC, 604 822-9197. Best acoustics in town.
- The Commodore Ballroom, 868 Granville St., 604 739-7469. Hosts an eclectic range of artists.
- Orpheum Theatre, 884 Granville St., 604 665-3050. Old-time, elegant home of the Vancouver Symphony Orchestra.
- Performance Works, 1218 Cartwright St., 604 687-3020. A Granville Island stage for the popular KISS Project, among others.
- The Purple Onion Jazz Cabaret, 15 Water St., 604 602-9442. Best place for jazz, with both lounge and large dance room.
- Vancouver East Cultural Centre (The Cultch), 1895 Venables St., 604 251-1363. BC's most diverse performance space.
- Vogue Theatre, 918 Granville St., 604 331-7909. Hosts top musical acts and film screenings during the Vancouver International Film Festival.
- The Yale, 1300 Granville St., 604 681-9253. One of the world's best blues bars.

PARKS AND GARDENS

Mild in climate and outdoors-oriented, Vancouver and Victoria are rife with gardens. The following lists a few that shouldn't be missed:
- Beacon Hill Park, bounded by Dallas Rd. and Douglas, Southgate and Heywood Streets, 250 361-0600. Victoria's oldest and largest park with wading pool, swans, ducks, English-style rose garden and exotic trees.
- Butchart Gardens, 800 Benvenuto Ave., Central Saanich, Vancouver Island, 250 652-4422, www.butchartgardens.com. Fifty acres (20 hectares) of garden on the former site of a rock quarry.
- Century Gardens at Deer Lake Park, 6344 Deer Lake Ave., Burnaby, www.city.burnaby.bc.ca. Rhododendrons are Burnaby's official flower, and flourish on the grounds of the Burnaby Art Gallery.
- Dr. Sun Yat-Sen Garden, 578 Carrall St., 604 662-3207, www.vancouverchinesegarden.com.

Authentic, full-scale classical Chinese garden offering tours and a popular summertime evening concert series.
- Park & Tilford Gardens, 440-333 Brooksbank Ave., North Vancouver, 604 984-8200. A garden oasis on the edge of a shopping centre.
- Queen Elizabeth Park and Bloedel Floral Conservatory, West 33rd Ave. and Cambie St., 604 257-8570, www.parks.vancouver.bc.ca. Quarry garden atop Little Mountain offers showy natural surroundings and a view of the city. The Conservatory, Canada's largest triodetic dome, encloses tropical birds and plants as well as desert and exotic trees.
- Riverview Lands Davidson Arboretum, 500 Lougheed Hwy., Coquitlam, 604 290-9910. Free spring to fall tours are offered by the Riverview Horticultural Society of the more than 1,800 trees on the Riverview Hospital grounds.
- Stanley Park's gardens. Stanley Park, 604 257-8400 or 604 257-8544 for nature walks, www.parks.vancouver.bc.ca. Gardens flourishing in heavily forested Stanley Park include the Rose Garden and the Ted and Mary Grieg Rhododendron Garden.
- UBC Botanical Garden, 6804 S.W. Marine Dr., 604 822-9666, www.ubcbotanicalgarden.org. A living teaching and research library spread over 30 hectares (74 acres). UBC also includes Alpine, Asian, Japanese Nitobe Memorial and BC native gardens with unusual and new locally developed plants. Parking is free.
- VanDusen Botanical Garden, 5251 Oak St., 604 878-9274, www.vandusengarden.org. Themed gardens on 22 hectares (55 acres) of former golf course include Asian, Children's, Fragrance, Meditation, and Canadian Heritage gardens, a maze and fern dell.

SPORTS AND ACTIVITIES

Vancouver is host to professional and amateur sports, as well as a wide range of year-round outdoor activities.

SPORTS

- Alcan Dragon Boat Festival. Colourful dragon boats compete as part of the Alcan Dragon Boat Festival. False Creek, 604 688-2382, www.adbf.com.
- BC Lions Football. Canadian Football League franchise. BC Place Stadium, 765 Pacific Blvd., 604 661-7373 or 604 589-7627, www.bclions.com.
- BC Sports Hall of Fame and Museum. Gate A, BC Place Stadium, 604 687-5520, www.bcsportshalloffame.com.
- Fraser Downs Racecourse. Harness racing from October to April. 17755 60th Ave., Surrey, 604 576-9141, www.fraserdowns.com.
- Hastings Racecourse. Thoroughbred racing live or via satellite. Located in Hastings Park, off Renfrew, Gate 6. 604 254-1631, www.hastingsracecourse.com.
- Molson Indy Vancouver. July championship auto races in downtown Vancouver. 765 Pacific Blvd., 604 684-4639, www.molsonindy.com.
- Vancouver Canadians. Minor league affiliate of Oakland Athletics. Nat Bailey Stadium, 4601 Ontario St., 604 872-5232, www.canadiansbaseball.com.
- Vancouver Canucks. National Hockey League franchise. General Motors Place, 800 Griffiths Way, 604 899-4610, www.canucks.com.
- Vancouver Giants. Western Hockey League team. Pacific Coliseum, 100 North Renfrew St., 604 444-2687, www.vancouvergiants.com.
- Vancouver Whitecaps/Whitecaps Women. Professional men's and women's soccer, Swanguard Stadium, Central Park, Burnaby, 604 669-9283, www.whitecapsfc.com.
- Western Lacrosse Association. 604 421-9755, www.theboxrocks.com. Six BC teams (five local) compete in this fast-paced, all-Canadian game at several venues in the Lower Mainland.

OUTDOOR ACTIVITIES

Cycling, hiking, swimming and lying on the beach can be done at will, almost anywhere. Beaches and parks in the city are the responsibility of the Vancouver Board of Parks and Recreation (604 257-8400). The following list provides useful information for a number of other recreational activities.

CYCLING

- Cycling British Columbia, 1367 West Broadway Ave., 604 737-3034, www.cycling.bc.ca. Information on BMX, road and track and mountain biking competitions.

SKIING AND SNOWBOARDING

- Cypress Mountain. Great place for toboggans and inner tubes, with groomed trails for skiing. West Vancouver. Weather and trail information: 604 926-6007. Programs: 604 926-5612. www.cypressmountain.com.
- Grouse Mountain. Sleigh rides and outdoor ice-skating as well as downhill and cross-country skiing and snowboarding. 6400 Nancy Greene Way, North Vancouver. Snow reports: 604 986-6262. Programs: 604 984-0661. www.grousemountain.com.
- Mount Seymour. Backcountry and downhill skiing, toboggans and inner tubes. 1700 Mount Seymour Rd., North Vancouver. Weather and conditions: 604 718-7771. Programs and special events: 604 986-2261. www.mountseymour.com.

BIRDWATCHING

- Reifel Bird Sanctuary, 5191 Robertson Road on Westham Island, Ladner, 604 946-6980, www.reifelbirdsanctuary.com. Wetlands environment is especially attractive to shorebirds and migrating birds.

CANOEING, KAYAKING, WINDSURFING

- Canoeing, whitewater kayaking and sea kayaking information is available from the Outdoor Recreation Council of British Columbia, at 604 737-3058, www.orcbc.ca.

GOLFING

- Fraserview Golf Course, 7800 Vivian Dr., 604 257-6923 (Pro Shop) or 604 280-1818 (Tee Time), www.parks.vancouver.bc.ca. A busy South Vancouver course.

- Furry Creek Golf and Country Club, 150 Country Club Rd., Furry Creek, 604 896-2224, www.golfbc.com.. For water views and a course carved from a mountainside.
- Langara Golf Course, 6706 Alberta St., 604 713-1816 (Pro Shop) or 604 280-1818 (Tee Time). Popular city golf course. www.parks.vancouver.bc.ca.
- Mayfair Lakes Golf & Country Club, 5460 #7 Rd., Richmond, 604 276-0585, www.golfbc.com. Challenges the golfer with many water hazards.
- Stanley Park Pitch & Putt, 2099 Beach Ave., 604 681-8847 (seasonal). City-operated course in park setting. www.parks.vancouver.bc.ca.
- Queen Elizabeth Park Pitch & Putt, 33rd Ave. and Cambie St., 604 874-8336. Scenic park setting. www.parks.vancouver.bc.ca.
- University Golf Club, 5185 University Blvd., 604 224-1818. Beautiful, well-maintained course on the UBC grounds. www.universitygolf.com.

SWIMMING
- Kitsilano Pool, 2305 Cornwall Ave., 604 731-0011. Gigantic outdoor saltwater pool on Kitsilano Beach, www.parks.vancouver.bc.ca. Open May to Aug.
- Vancouver Aquatic Centre, 1050 Beach Ave., 604 665-3424, www.parks.vancouver.bc.ca.
- Vancouver beaches, www.parks.vancouver.bc.ca.

KIDS' STUFF

INDOORS
- Alcan OMNIMAX Theatre, Science World. Runs documentaries to tremendous effect. 1455 Quebec St., 604 443-7440, www.scienceworld.bc.ca.
- CN IMAX Theatre, Canada Place. Film-viewing becomes an intense experience with big sound and bigger screens. Check with staff to determine if the film is too intense for young children. 999 Canada Place Way, 604 682-4629, www.imax.com/vancouver.

- H. R. MacMillan Space Centre and Planetarium. Hands-on galleries, interactive computer displays, multimedia and laser shows and live demonstrations bring space and the stars down to Earth. 1100 Chestnut St., 604 738-7827, www.hrmacmillanspacecentre.com.
- Science World. Science and entertainment merge in creative, hands-on exhibits inside the mirrored geodesic dome. 1455 Quebec St., 604 443-7440, www.scienceworld.bc.ca.
- Vancouver Aquarium Marine Science Centre. Brings the denizens of different dark sea habitats into close focus through aquatic displays, live shark dives, feedings and dolphin shows. Also features the new Pacific Canada Pavilion, behind-the-scenes tours, sleepovers and special animal encounters. Stanley Park, 845 Avison Way, 604 659-3474, www.vanaqua.org.

OUTDOORS
- Capilano Suspension Bridge. Hang high above the forested Capilano River canyon on a swaying structure of sturdy steel cables, visit the totem poles and exhibits. 3735 Capilano Rd., North Vancouver, 604 985-7474, www.capbridge.com.
- Reifel Bird Sanctuary. Feed the birds or view a wetlands ecosystem. 5191 Robertson Rd., Ladner, 604 946-6980, www.reifelbirdsanctuary.com.
- Greater Vancouver Zoo. Home to 93 animal species. 5048 264th St., Aldergrove, 604 856-6825, www.greatervancouverzoo.com.
- Lynn Canyon Park. Begin a hike in Lynn Headwaters Regional Park with a visit to the Ecology Centre and brave the swinging footbridge high above the rapids of Lynn Creek. Lynn Canyon entrance on Park Rd., 604 981-3103.
- Maplewood Farm. Small petting farm with seasonal special events and weekend pony rides. 405 Seymour River Pl., North Vancouver, 604 929-5610, www.maplewoodfarm.bc.ca.
- Pacific Spirit Regional Park. Experience BC's coastal cedar and fir forests firsthand with an easy hike through the many trails. West

16th Ave. and Blanca (Visitor Centre), 604 224-5739.
- Playland. Outdoor amusement park rides, midway games and cotton candy from April to Labour Day. Pacific National Exhibition Park, 604 253-2311, www.pne.bc.ca.
- Stanley Park. Kids' attractions include the Children's Farm Yard and Miniature Railway, and the totem poles at Lower Brockton Oval. 2099 Beach Ave., 604 257-8400.
- VanDusen Botanical Garden. Themed gardens on 55 acres include Children's Garden and Heritage and Elizabethan Hedge Maze. Many popular special events. 5251 Oak St., 604 878-9274, www.vandusengarden.org.

WATERPLAY
- Canada Games Pool and Fitness Centre. Olympic-size pool and teaching/toddler pool. 65 East 6th Ave., New Westminster, 604 526-4281.
- Eileen Dailly Leisure Pool and Fitness Centre. Burnaby's best indoor pool and community centre. 240 Willingdon Ave., Burnaby, 604 298-7946.
- Granville Island Water Park. Wet adventure playground with water cannons, spouts, waterslide and wading areas. Near Sutcliffe Park, Granville Island, 604 666-5784.
- Kitsilano Pool. Gigantic outdoor saltwater pool. 2305 Cornwall Ave., 604 731-0011. (May-Aug)
- Newton Wave Pool. Metre-high waves for bodysurfing and waterslides. 13730 72nd Ave., Surrey, 604 501-5540, 604 594-7873.
- Second Beach Pool. Features three small waterslides. Stanley Park, 604 783-8535 (mid-May to mid-October).
- Splashdown Park. Twisting waterslides, hot tubs and smaller sized equipment for little kids. 4799 Nu Lelum Way, Tsawwassen, 604 943-2251.
- Stanley Park Water Park. Wet adventure playground with equipment suitable for children with physical disabilities. Near Lumberman's Arch, Stanley Park, 604 257-8400.
- Vancouver Aquatic Centre.

Olympic-size indoor and outdoor pools and toddler pool. 1050 Beach Ave., 604 665-3424.
- Vancouver beaches. Second and Third Beach, English Bay, Sunset Beach, Kits Beach, Jericho Beach, Locarno Beach and Spanish Banks. Beach Information: 604 665-3418, mid-May to mid-September.

CHILDREN'S CULTURE
- Arts Umbrella. Classes in dance, acting, animation and filmmaking for those on longer stays. 1286 Cartwright St., Granville Island, 604 681-5268, www.artsumbrella.com.
- Buschlen Mowatt Gallery. Hosts annual visual art show by budding artists in spring. 1445 West Georgia St., 604 682-1234.
- Spring Break Theatre Festival for Young Audiences. March performances at five locations: New Revue Stage, 1601 Johnston St., Granville Island, 604 687-1644; Granville Island Stage, 1585 Johnston St., Granville Island, 604 687-1644; Evergreen Cultural Centre, 1205 Pinetree Way, Coquitlam, 604 927-6555; Shadbolt Centre for the Arts, 6450 Deer Lake Ave., Burnaby, 604 205-3000; Surrey Arts Centre, 13750 88th Ave., Surrey, 604 205-3000.
- Vancouver Art Gallery Super Sunday. Experiences in art for school age children on the third Sunday of each month. 750 Hornby St., 604 662-4719, www.vanartgallery.bc.ca.
- Vancouver East Cultural Centre Kids Series. Saturday afternoon musical or dramatic performances monthly. Also a Youth Program discounting admission for youth to $2. 1895 Venables St., 604 251-1363, www.vecc.bc.ca.
- Vancouver International Children's Festival. Week-long event featuring quality performances, roving entertainers, face painters and a multicultural community stage. Vanier Park, 1100 Chestnut St., 604 708-5655, www.childrensfestival.ca.
- Vancouver Public Library. Children's floor has CD-ROM stations, videos, books and displays of children's art. 350 West Georgia St., 604 331-3600.
- Vancouver International Comedy Festival. Free and funny street

entertainment and some ticketed family-oriented events. Granville Island, 604 683-0883, www.comedyfest.com.

- Vancouver International Writers (and Readers) Festival. Mid-October writers' festival has three days of children's events. Granville Island, 604 681-6330, www.writersfest.bc.ca.
- Vancouver Kidsbooks. Readings, book launches and book signings complement the huge variety of children's books. 3083 West Broadway Ave., 604 738-5335, www.kidsbooks.ca.

HISTORY AND LIVING CULTURE

- BC Sports Hall of Fame and Museum. BC's past professional and amateur sports and recreation history. Displays, a Participation Gallery and multimedia. Gate A, BC Place Stadium, 765 Pacific Blvd. S., 604 687-5520, www.bcsportshalloffame.com.
- Burnaby Village Museum and Carousel. Recreation of a 1920s village with hands-on activities, restored carousel and special events. 6501 Deer Lake Ave., Burnaby, 604 293-6501.
- Cedar Cottage/Trout Lake Pow Wow. Mother's Day event featuring intertribal dancing, drumming, hoop dancing, pageant and displays presents the cultural traditions of Canada's First Nations people. Trout Lake Community Centre, 3350 Victoria Dr., 604 874-4231.
- Fort Langley National Historic Park. Sample life as it was in the last century in this reconstructed Hudson's Bay Company post. 23433 Mavis, Fort Langley, 604 513-4777.

VANCOUVER ANNUAL EVENTS

January
- Polar Bear Swim. A New Year's Day plunge into the Pacific Ocean on English Bay, Glenn Schultz, Vancouver Aquatic Centre, 604 665-3418.
- Brackendale Winter Eagle Festival and Count. Just after the New Year begins, an eagle count is taken, and related events are hosted all month. Squamish-Brackendale area, 604 898-3333.
- Chinese New Year's Festival. Chinatown greets the first day of the lunar year (in January or February) with festivals and events, 604 273-1655.

February
- Vancouver International Boat Show. Consumer show featuring the latest in boating. BC Place Stadium, Coal Harbour Marina, 604 678-8820.
- BC Home and Garden Show. The largest consumer home show in Western Canada. BC Place Stadium, 604 433-5121.

March
- Festival du bois. Maillardville celebrates voyageur traditions and French-Canadian music, dance and food. Maillardville, Coquitlam.
- Vancouver Playhouse International Wine Festival. Week-long fund-raising celebration of good wine and food. Vancouver Convention and Exhibition Centre, 604 872-6622, www.playhousewinefest.com.

May
- Vancouver International Marathon. Canada's largest marathon. Starts at the Plaza of Nations, 604 872-2928, www.vanmarathon.bc.ca.
- Vancouver International Children's Festival. A week of quality performances, roving entertainers, face painters and a multicultural community stage, all for kids. Vanier Park, 604 708-5655, www.youngarts.ca.

June
- Alcan Dragon Boat Festival. Dragon boats race in the largest dragon boat festival in North America. False Creek, 604 688-2382, www.adbf.com.
- Vancouver International Jazz Festival. Something for every jazz lover in the 400 or so performances held downtown, 604 872-5200, www.jazzvancouver.com.
- Bard on the Beach. Shakespeare is staged in a backless tent to take advantage of the magical natural backdrop. Shows from June to

September. Vanier Beach, 604 739-0559 or 737-0625, www.bardonthebeach.org.

July

- Vancouver International Comedy Festival. Performances from a diverse mix of comic artists. Granville Island, 604 683-0883, www.comedyfest.com.
- Celebration of Light Fireworks. Pyrotechnicians from different countries set fireworks to music in a four-day competition from late July to early August. English Bay, www.celebration-of-light.com.
- Festival Vancouver. Two-week long festival featuring an array of classical, jazz and world music. Various venues throughout the city, 604 688-1152, www.festivalvancouver.bc.ca.
- Vancouver International Folk Music Festival. Hugely popular annual celebration of folk music. Jericho Beach, 604 602-9798, www.thefestival.bc.ca.
- Molson Indy Vancouver. Championship Auto Racing in Vancouver. False Creek area, 604 684-4639, www.molsonindy.com.

August

- Abbotsford International Airshow. Aerial displays and aerobatics. Abbotsford Airport, 604 852-8511.
- Pacific National Exhibition. Demolition derby, petting farm, Superdogs show, exhibits, midway games and amusement park rides. Win a house, win a car, eat candy floss and corndogs. Pacific National Exhibition Park, 604 253-2311, www.pne.bc.ca.
- Powell Street Festival. A celebration of Japanese-Canadian history and traditional Japanese food, music and entertainment. Oppenheimer Park, Powell Street, 604 682-4335.
- Squamish Nations Pow Wow, Aboriginal Cultural Festival. Traditional dancing and drumming and cuisine. Capilano Reserve, Squamish Territory, North Vancouver, 604 986-2120, www.squamish.net.

September

- Chilliwack Bluegrass Festival. Camp out for the bluegrass performances, 604 792-2069.
- Vancouver Fringe Festival. Alternative theatre performances by emerging and established companies, 604 257-0350, www.vancouverfringe.com.
- Vancouver International Film Festival. Over 250 innovative and accessible films from around the world. Various venues, 604 685-0260, www.viff.org.

October

- Vancouver International Writers (and Readers) Festival. One week of readings, talks and other events surrounding local and international writers. Granville Island, 604 681-6330, www.writersfest.bc.ca.

December

- Christmas Carol Ships Parade. Carollers sail on ships decked out with lights. Vancouver Harbour, 604 682-2007.

EXCURSIONS

WHISTLER

- Whistler Activity and Information Centre. 4010 Whistler Way, Whistler BC V0N 1B4, 604 938-2769, 1-877-991-9988, www.mywhistler.com.
- Whistler's Central Reservations Service. Official central reservations for Whistler Resort. 604 664-5625 in Vancouver;1-800-944-7853 in Canada and the US; 604 664-5625 direct; Fax: 604 938-5758, www.mywhistler.com.
- Resort Reservations Whistler. Intrawest's accommodations and activities centre also books customized vacation packages. 604 932-3434, 1-866-218-9690, www.whistlerblackcomb.com.
- Vancouver/Whistler 2010 Olympic and Paralympic Winter Games. www.winter2010.com.

THE GULF ISLANDS

- Tourism Vancouver Island, Old City Square, 203-335 Wesley St., Nanaimo BC V9R 2T5, 250 754-3500, Fax: 250 754-3599, www.islands.bc.ca

THE SUNSHINE COAST

- Big Pacific, Lower Coast Visitor Info, 604 885-0662, Upper Coast

Visitor Info, 604 485-4701,
www.bigpacific.com. Provides
information on the Sunshine Coast
and helps visitors find
accommodations, dining and
entertainment.

SHOPPING

VANCOUVER

NEIGHBOURHOODS
Georgia and Granville
- The Bay, Georgia & Granville streets, 604 681-6211.
- Bentall Centre, Burrard and Dunsmuir streets, 604 661-5656.
- Cadillac Fairview Pacific Centre, 700 West Georgia St., 604 688-7236.
- Brookfield Royal Centre, 1055 West Georgia St., 604 689-1711.
- Vancouver Art Gallery Shop, 750 Hornby St., 604 662-4706.

Robson Street
- Banana Republic, 1098 Robson St., 604 331-8285.
- The Gap, 9-1121 Robson St., 604 683-0906.
- Mexx, 1119 Robson St., 604 801-6399.
- Roots, 1001 Robson St., 604 683-4305.

Gastown
- Deluxe Junk, 310 West Cordova St., 604 685-4871.
- Hill's Native Art, 165 Water St., 604 685-4249.
- Inuit Gallery, 206 Cambie St., 604 688-7323.
- Salmegundi West, 321 West Cordova St., 604 681-4648.
- The Edinburgh Tartan Gift Shop, The Landing, 375 Water St., 604 646-3915.

Granville Island
- Edie's Hats, 11-1666 Johnston St., 604 683-4280.
- El Greco Jewellery, 1660 Johnston St., 604 681-0942.
- Granville Island Public Market, 1689 Johnston St., 604 666-6477.
- Kids Only Market (Kids Market) 1496 Cartwright St., 604 689-8447.
- Nancy Lord, 4-1666 Johnston St., 604 633-9377.

ANTIQUES AND COLLECTIBLES
- Ages Ago Used Furniture and Antiques, 4373 Main St., 604 876-3055.
- Baker's Dozen, 3520 Main St., 604 879-3348.
- Blue Heron, 3516A Main St., 604 874-8401.
- Canada West Antique Co., 4430 West 10th Ave., 604 222-9190.
- Farmhouse Collections, 2915 Granville St., 604 738-0167 and 1098 S.W. Marine Dr. SW, 604 261-3681.
- Folkart Interiors, 3651 West 10th Ave., 604 731-7576.
- Small Comforts Antiques, 1525 West 6th Ave., 604 222-4992.
- Hampshire Antiques, 3007 Granville St., 604 733-1326.
- Second Time Around, 4428 Main St., 604 879-2313.
- William Robert Antiques, 1529 West14th Ave., 604 731-0808.

BOOK STORES
- Banyen Books and Sound, 3608 West 4th Ave., 604 732-7912.
- Chapters, 788 Robson St., 604 682-4066. Additional locations: 4700 Kingsway, Burnaby, 604 431-0463 and 2505 Granville St., 604 731-7822 and 8171 Ackroyd Rd., Richmond, 604 303-7392.
- Duthie Books, 2239 West 4th Ave., 604 732-5344.
- Granville Book Company, 850 Granville St., 604 687-2213.
- Kidsbooks, 3083 West Broadway Ave., 604 738-5335. Additional location: 3040 Edgemont Blvd., North Vancouver, 604 986-6190.
- Little Sister's Book Store, 1238 Davie St., 604 669-1753, 1-800-567-1662.

CANADIAN CLOTHING DESIGNERS
- A-Wear Clothing, 757 West Hastings St., 604 685-9327.
- Dorothy Grant, 1656 West 75th Ave., 604 681-0201.
- Jacqueline Conoir Boutique, 46 West 6th Ave., 604 688-5222.
- Margareta Design, 2448 West 41st Ave., 604 264-4625.
- Nancy Lord Couture, 1672 West 2nd Ave., 604 689-3972.
- Tilley Endurables, 2401 Granville St., 604 732-4287.

- Zonda Nellis Design, 2203 Granville St., 604 736-5668.

CHILDREN'S STORES
- Bobbit's for Kids, 2935 West 4th Ave., 604 738-0333.
- Isola Bella Design, 5692 Yew St., 604 266-8808.
- Kaboodles Toy Store, 4449 West 10th Ave., (604) 224-5311 and 1496 Cartwright St., Granville Island, 604 684-0066.
- Kidsbooks, 3083 West Broadway Ave., 604 738-5335. Additional location: 3040 Edgemont Blvd., North Vancouver, 604 986-6190.
- Kids Only Market (Kids Market), 1496 Cartwright St., Granville Island, 604 689-8447.
- Please Mum, 2041 West 41st Ave., 604 264-0366 and 2951 West Broadway Ave., 604 732-4574. Also in many malls.
- The Toybox, 3002 West Broadway Ave., 604 738-4322.
- Toys R Us, 1154 West Broadway Ave., 604 733-8697.

CHINA AND CRYSTAL
- Atkinson's, 1501 West 6th Ave., 604 736-3378.
- Chintz and Company, 950 Homer St., 604 689-2022.
- W.H. Puddifoot & Co., 2375 West 41st Ave., 604 261-8141.

DESIGNER BOUTIQUES
- Bacci Design, 2788 Granville St., 604 733-4933.
- Boboli, 2776 Granville St., 604 257-2300.
- Cabbages & Kinx, 315 West Hastings St., 604 669-4238.
- Chanel, 900 West Hastings St., 604 682-0522.
- Dyanna's, 355 Howe St., 604 685-4225.
- Edward Chapman's Ladies Shops, 2596 Granville St., 604 732-3394. Also at 750 West Pender St., 604 688-6711 and Oakridge Centre, 604 261-8161.
- Enda B Fashion, 4346 West 10th Ave., 604 228-1214 and 2625 Granville St., 604 733-2000.
- Gianni Versace Boutique, 757 West Hastings St., 604 683-1131.
- Leone Fashions, 757 West Hastings St., 604 683-1133.
- Plaza Escada, 757 West Hastings St., 604 688-8558.

FIRST NATIONS ART AND JEWELLERY
- Eagle Spirit Gallery, 1803 Maritime Mews, Granville Island, 604 801-5205.
- Hill's Native Art, 165 Water St., 604 685-4249.
- Inuit Gallery, 206 Cambie St., 604 688-7323.
- Lattimer Gallery, 1590 West 2nd Ave., 604 732-4556.
- Marion Scott Gallery, 481 Howe St., 604 685-1934.
- Museum of Anthropology, 6393 N.W. Marine Dr. (University of BC campus), 604 822-5087.

GIFT SHOPS
- Bookmark — Vancouver Public Library Gift Shop, 350 West Georgia St., 604 331-4040.
- Chachkas Design, 1075 Robson St., 604 688-6417.
- Circle Craft Co-op, 1-1666 Johnston St., Granville Island, 604 669-8021.
- Lightheart and Co., 100-535 Howe St., 604 684-4711.
- Moulé, 1944 West 4th Ave., 604 732-4066.
- The Museum Company, 53D-701 West Georgia St., 604 688-1502.
- Vancouver Art Gallery Shop, 750 Hornby St., 604 662-4706.

HOME FURNISHINGS
- Country Furniture, 3097 Granville St., 604 738-6411.
- Industrial Revolution, 2306 Granville St., 604 734-4395.
- Jordan's Interiors, 1470 West Broadway Ave., 604 733-1174.
- Koolhaus, 2199 West 4th Ave., 604 875-9004.
- Sofa So Good, 2219 Cambie St., 604 879-4878.
- Upholstery Arts, 2430 Burrard St., 604 731-9020.

JEWELLERY
- Birks Jewellers, 698 West Hastings St., 604 669-3333 and 118-650 West 41st Ave., 604 266-2301.
- Karl Stittgen Goldsmiths, 2203 Granville St., 604 737-0029.
- Martha Sturdy Originals, 3039 Granville St., 604 737-0037.
- Tiffany & Co at Holt Renfrew, 633 Granville St., 604 681-3121.

LEATHER

- Castle Milano, 248-757 West Hastings St., 604 647-0202.
- Danier Leather, 1018 Robson St., 604 689-7330. Also in Pacific Centre, 604 683-6846 and Oakridge, 604 266-0775. Factory outlet, 3003 Grandview Hwy., 604 432-6137.
- Mack's Leathers, 1043 Granville St., 604 688-6225.
- Marquis of London Manufacturing Ltd., 526 Beatty St., 604 688-2201.
- French Laundry By Neto , 252 East 2nd Ave., 604 875-8474.

MALLS

- Aberdeen Centre, 4400 Hazelbridge Way, Richmond, 604 273-1234.
- Arbutus Village Square, 4255 Arbutus St., 604 732-4255.
- Bentall Centre, Burrard and Dunsmuir Sts., 604 661-5656.
- Brookfield Royal Centre, 1055 West Georgia St., 604 689-1711.
- Cadillac Fairview Pacific Centre, 700 West Georgia St., 604 688-7236.
- Central City Shopping Centre, 102 Ave. and King George Hwy., Surrey, 604 588-6431.
- City Square, 555 West 12th Ave., 604 876-5165.
- Guildford Town Centre, 2695 Guildford Town Centre, Surrey, 604 585-1565.
- Lougheed Mall Shopping Centre, 9855 Austin, 604 421-2882.
- Metropolis at Metrotown, 4700 Kingsway, Burnaby, 604 438-4715.
- Oakridge Centre, 650 West 41st Ave., 604 261-2511.
- Park Royal Shopping Centre, 2002 Park Royal South, West Vancouver, 604 925-9576.
- Richmond Centre, 6551 #3 Rd., Richmond, 604 713-7467.
- Vancouver Centre, 650 West Georgia St., 604 688-5658.
- Yaohan Centre, 3700 #3 Rd., Richmond, 604 231-0601.

MUSIC

- A & B Sound, 556 Seymour St., 604 687-5837. Also at 3433 East Hastings St., 604 298-0464, 3434 Cornett Road, 604 430-2999, and 732 S.W. Marine Dr., 604 321-5112.
- Black Swan Records, 3209 West Broadway Ave., 604 734-2828.
- D & G Collectors Records, 3580 East Hastings St., 604 294-5737.

- Highlife Records & Music, 1317 Commercial Dr., 604 251-6964.
- HMV Canada, 1160 Robson St., and Metropolis at Metrotown, 604 430-1699.
- Magic Flute Record Shop, 2203 West 4th Ave., 604 736-2727.
- Virgin Megastore, 788 Burrard St., 604 669-2289.
- Zulu Records, 1972 West 4th Ave., 604 738-3232.

MEN'S CLOTHING

- Boboli, 2776 Granville St., 604 257-2300.
- Boys' Co., 1044 Robson St., 604 684-5656. Also at Oakridge Centre, 604 266-0388, 910 Richards St., 604 687-2221, Metrotown Centre, 604 431-1866 and Richmond Centre, 604 303-0374.
- Chevalier Creations, 620 Seymour St., 604 687-8428 or 604 687-4643.
- E.A. Lee, 1050 West Pender St., 604 683-2457.
- Eddie Bauer, Oakridge Centre, 604 261-2621, Pacific Centre, 604 683-4711, Park Royal Centre, 604 925-0858.
- Enda B Fashion, 4346 West 10th Ave., 604 228-1214 and 2625 Granville St., 604 733-2000.
- Harry Rosen Men's Wear, 700 West Georgia St., 604 683-6861 and Oakridge Centre, 604 266-1172.
- Holt Renfrew, 633 Granville St., 604 681-3121.
- Leone Fashions, 757 West Hastings St., 604 683-1133.
- Mark James, 2941 West Broadway Ave., 604 734-2381.
- Roots, 1001 Robson St., 604 683-4305, Metropolis at Metrotown, 604 435-5554, Guildford Town Centre, 604 583-0689, Grandview Factory Outlet, 3695 Grandview Hwy., 604 433-4337, Oakridge Centre, 604 266-6229, Richmond Centre, 604 244-9113, Park Royal Shopping Centre, 604 925-2166.
- S. Lampman, 2126 West 41st Ave., 604 261-2750.
- Tilley Endurables Adventure Clothing, 2401 Granville St., 604 732-4287.

SECOND-HAND CLOTHING

- The Comeback, 3122 Edgemont Blvd., North Vancouver, 604 984-2551.
- Kisa's of Kerrisdale Consignment

Boutique, 2352 West 41st Ave., 604 266-2885.
- Nipper's Tog 'n Toy, 3712 West 10th Ave., 604 222-4035.
- Turnabout Collections, 3121 Granville St., 604 732-8115.
- Value Village, 1820 East Hastings St., 604 254-4282 and 6415 Victoria Dr., 604 327-4434.

SHOE STORES
- Dayton Boots, 872 Granville St., 604 682-2668 and 2250 East Hastings St., 604 253-6671.
- Ingledew's Shoes 535 Granville St., 604 687-8606
- John Fluevog Boots and Shoes, 837 Granville St., 604 688-2828.
- Salvatore Ferragamo, 918 Robson St., 604 669-4495 or 604 669-2218.
- Simard & Voyer Shoes, 1047 Robson St., 604 689-2536 and Oakridge Centre, 604 263-1080.
- Stephane de Raucourt Shoes, 1067 Robson St., 604 681-8814 and Oakridge Centre, 604 261-7419.

VICTORIA

FAIRMONT EMPRESS HOTEL AND VICTORIA CONVENTION CENTRE
- Art of Man Gallery, 721 Government St., 250 383-3800.
- Collections by Madison Avenue, 736 Douglas St., 250 380-0697.
- La Cache, 1150 Douglas St., 250 384-6343.
- Stephen Lowe Art Gallery, 752 Douglas St., 250 384-3912.

GOVERNMENT STREET
- British Importers, The Bay Centre, 250 386-1496.
- Christmas House, 1209 Wharf St., 250 388-9627.
- Copithorne and Row, 901 Government St., 250 384-1722.
- The Bay Centre Mall, 1150 Douglas St., 250 952-5680.
- Harbour Trading Company, 811 Wharf St., 250 381-1022.
- Irish Linen Stores, 1019 Government St., 250 383-6812.
- Original Christmas Village, 1323 Government St., 250 380-7522.
- Purdy's Chocolates, The Bay Centre, 250 361-3024.
- Rogers Chocolates, 913 Government St., 250 384-7021, 1-800-663-2220.
- Sydney Reynolds, 801 Government St., 250 383-3931.
- The Spirit of Christmas, 1022 Government St., 250 385-2501.
- W&J Wilson Clothiers, 1221 Government St., 250 383-7177.

YATES STREET AREA
- Cowichan Trading Company, 1328 Government St., 250 383-0321.
- English Sweet Shop, 738 Yates St., 250 382-3325.
- Grandpa's Antique Photo, 1252 Wharf St., 250 920-3800.
- Hill's Native Crafts, 1008 Government St., 250 385-3911.
- Starfish Glassworks, 630 Yates St., 250 388-7827.
- The British Candy Shoppe, 635 Yates St., 250 382-2634.

MARKET SQUARE
- Fat Phege's Fudge Factory, 560 Johnson St., 250 383-3435.
- Foxglove Toys, 162-560 Johnson St., 250 383-8852.
- Marigold Galleria, 101-560 Johnson St., 250 386-5339.
- Out of Hand, 560 Johnson St., 250 384-5221.

CHINATOWN
- Chinatown Trading Company, 551 Fisgard St., 250 381-5503.
- Fan Tan Gallery, 541 Fisgard St., 250 382-4424.
- Quonley's, 1628 Government St., 250 383-0623.

ANTIQUE ROW
- Charles Baird, 1044A Fort St., 250 384-8809.
- Faith Grant, 1156 Fort St., 250 383-0121.
- Old Vogue Shop, 1034 Fort St., 250 380-7551.
- Recollections Antiques and Collectibles Mall, 817A Fort St., 250 385-1902.
- The Glass Menagerie, 1036 Fort St., 250 475-2228.

WHISTLER ACCOMMODATIONS LISTINGS

For two people staying in a double room (excluding taxes) during peak season: $ = $50-$90, $$ = $90-$180, $$$ = $180-$250, $$$$ = above $250. Rates quoted are subject to a 7% federal tax and a 10% hotel tax.

WHISTLER VILLAGE

- Coast Whistler Hotel, 4005 Whistler Way, Whistler BC V0N 1B4, 604 932-2522, 1-800-663-5644, Fax: 604-932-6711, www.coastwhistlerhotel.com. Value and location are very good. Free buffet-style breakfast. Covered pool, hot tub, sauna, exercise room. $$.
- Crystal Lodge, 4154 Village Green, Whistler BC V0N 1B4, 604 932-2221, 1-800-667-3363, Fax: 604 932-2635, www.crystal-lodge.com. Casual, friendly, renovated. Short walk to Whistler Mountain gondolas, good price. Tuck shop, two family restaurants on site (Tex Corleone's and The Old Spaghetti Factory) plus lounge. Up to three bedrooms available. Pool. $$-$$$.
- Delta Whistler Resort, 4050 Whistler Way, Whistler BC V0N 1B4, 604 932-1982, 1-800-515-4050, Fax: 604 932-7332, www.deltawhistler.com. Luxury hotel with big rooms, big beds, great mountain views. Some rooms with double Jacuzzis, dry saunas. Health Club, pool, hot tub, spa. Lounge, restaurant. Pet-friendly. $$$-$$$$.
- Timberline Lodge, 4122 Village Green, Whistler BC V0N 1B4, 604 932-5211, 1-866-580-6649, Fax: 604 932-2306, www.whistler-timberline.com or www.whistlerlodgingco.com. Smaller hotel, European-style, some rooms with lofts/dens. Full kitchens. Hot tub, saunas. $$$.
- The Westin Resort & Spa, 4090 Whistler Way, Whistler BC V0N 1B4, 604 905-5000, 1-888-634-5577, Fax: 604 905-5640, www.westinwhistler.com. Condo-style, luxury all-suite hotel, spa, health club, pools, Whistler Kids Club program, lounge, restaurant. Deluxe beds, down duvets. Full kitchen, dining room, living room in all suites. $$$-$$$$.

VILLAGE NORTH

- The Alpenglow, 4369 Main St., Whistler BC V0N 1B4, 604 905-7078, 1-866-580-6642, Fax: 604 905-7053, www.whistler-alpenglow.com. Newer, lodge-style with smaller-size studio, one- and two-bedroom suites. Good value, central location. Fireplaces, full kitchens, air conditioning, fitness facilities with lap pool, hot tub, steam room, sauna. $$$.
- Whistler's Marketplace Lodge, 4360 Lorimer Rd., Whistler V0N 1B4, 604 938-6699, 1-800-663-7711, Fax: 604 932-6622, www.resort-questwhistler.com. Low-frills lodging, good price, full kitchen, living and dining area with gas fireplace. No pool. Free parking. $$.

UPPER VILLAGE

- The Fairmont Chateau Whistler, 4599 Chateau Blvd., Whistler BC V0N 1B4, 604 938-8000, 1-800-441-1414, Fax: 604 938-2291, www.fairmont.com. Rated one of the top ski resort hotels worldwide. Canadian Chateau-style luxury with double queen- and king-size beds and goose-down duvets. Restaurant, lounge, shopping on-site. Ski-in/ski-out Blackcomb Mountain. Pool, spa, sauna, fitness facilities. $$$$.
- Residence Inn by Marriott, 4899 Painted Cliff Rd., Whistler BC V0N 1B4, 604 905-3400, 1-866-580-6648, Fax: 604 905-3432, www.whistler-marriott.com. Ski-in/ski-out location on Blackcomb Mountain. Large rooms, fireplaces, full kitchens, pool, hot tubs. Free shuttle bus to and from Whistler Village. Free breakfast buffet, excellent fitness facilities. Pet-friendly. $$$$.
- Summit Lodge, 4359 Main St., Whistler BC V0N 1B4, 604 932-2778, 1-888-913-8811, Fax: 604 932-2716, www.summitlodge.com. Intimate boutique hotel with exceptional service. All suites have full kitchen and gas fireplaces. Free shuttle to Whistler Village and gondolas. Pool, hot tub. $$$.

CREEKSIDE

- Lake Placid Lodge, 2050 Lake Placid Rd., Whistler BC V0N 1B2, 604 932-6699, 1-800-663-7711, Fax: 604 932-6622, www.resort questwhistler.com. Good value. Ski in/ski out access to Creekside Gondola. Large pool and patio area. One- to three-bedroom suites, gas fireplaces, fully equipped kitchens. Free underground parking. $$-$$$.
- Legends Whistler Creek, 2036 London Lane, Whistler BC V0N 1B2, 1-800-332-3152, Fax: 604 983-9699, www.lodgingovations.com. Ski-in/ski-out access to Creekside Gondola. Opened by Intrawest in 2002, luxury one- to three-bedroom condo-style suites with full kitchens. Family and adult fitness facilities, indoor kids' play area, movie room, two pools, two Jacuzzis. $$$-$$$$.

OTHER LOCATIONS

- Edgewater Lodge and Dining Room, 8841 Hwy. 99. Mailing: Edgewater Lodge, Box 369, Whistler BC V0N 1B0, 604 932-0688, 1-888-870-9065, Fax: 604-932-0686, www.edgewater-lodge.com. Small motel-like lodge in forest setting overlooking Green Lake. Deluxe breakfast, tea and coffee all day, gourmet restaurant. One bedroom units with bathtub and extra pullout twin bed. Shower-only in six units. Free parking. $$-$$$.
- Hostelling International Whistler, 5678 Alta Lake Rd., Whistler BC V0N 1B5, 604 932-5492, Fax: 604 932-4687, www.hihostels.ca. Located in a former fishing lodge on Alta Lake. Wood-burning stove, common kitchen, dining room, sauna. Dorm rooms, private room sleeps up to four (children must stay with family in private room). Reservations recommended. $.
- Riverside RV Resort and Campground and Cabins, 8018 Mons Rd., Whistler BC V0N 1B8, 604 905-5533, 1-877-905-5533, Fax: 604 905-5539, www.whistlercamping.com. Tent camping and RV with amenities in lodge including grocery store and Internet café. Fourteen log cabins

with lofts, showers only in units. Free parking. $$.
- The Shoestring Lodge, 7124 Nancy Greene Dr., Whistler BC V0N 1B0, 604 932-3338, 1-877-551-4954, Fax: 604 932-8347, www.shoestringlodge.com. North of Whistler Village. Dorms sleep four to six people with bunk beds and TV, private double and queen rooms available. Free parking, free bus shuttle in winter. $.

BED & BREAKFAST

For information on more than 25 B&B members, contact Whistler Chamber of Commerce, PO Box 181, Whistler BC V0N 1B0, 604 932-5528, Fax: 604 932-3755, www.whistlerchamber.com.

- Alpine Lodge Pension, 8135 Alpine Way, Whistler BC V0N 1B8, 604 932-5966, Fax: 604 932-1104, www.alpinelodge.com. Casual, European-style pension in a huge cedar lodge. Free hot and cold breakfast, in-house chef, down duvets, steam room, Japanese spoken. Communal kitchen open to guests. Free parking, free shuttle bus to mountains. $$-$$$.
- Cedar Springs Bed & Breakfast Lodge, 8106 Cedar Springs Rd., Whistler BC V0N 1B8, 604 938-8007, 1-800-727-7547, Fax: 604 938-8023, www.whistlerbb.com. Pretty cedar and pine lodge. Gourmet breakfast, dining room has woodburning fireplace, tea and coffee always on. Sauna, hot tub. Showers only in rooms, except family room with soaker tub. Next to Meadow Park and the Valley Trail. Free shuttle in winter. $$.
- Durlacher Hof Pension Inn, 7055 Nesters Rd., Whistler BC V0N 1B7, 604 932-1924, 1-877-932-1924, Fax: 604 938-1980, www.durlacherhof.com. Impressive guest rooms, extra-long twin or queen beds, goose-down duvets, private baths with Jacuzzi tubs or showers. Full breakfast, afternoon tea. No telephone or television in rooms. Free hot breakfast with Austrian sweet pancakes. Whirlpool, sauna. No children. $$$.

WHISTLER — DINING LISTINGS

All major credit cards accepted.

FINE DINING ON THE MOUNTAINS

- Christine's, Blackcomb Mountain, 604 938-7437. Elegant, full-service dining, BC ingredients includes fish and shellfish, pasta specials. L, $$$, V/MC/AX/DC.
- Steeps Grill, Whistler Mountain, 604 905-2379. Alpine bistro at 1,158 meters (3,800 vertical ft.). Seasonal BC fare, includes grilled salmon and chowder. L, $$$, V/MC/AX/DC.

ASIAN

- Amami Restaurant, 4274 Mountain Square, Westbrook Hotel, Whistler Village, 604 932-6431. Japanese and Chinese dishes in a casual setting. L/D, $$, V/MC/AX/DC.
- Mongolie Grill, 201-4295 Blackcomb Way, Upper Village, 604 938-9416. Notable Chinese stir-fry restaurant, including seafood and noodles, 18 gourmet sauces. No reservations accepted. L/D, $$, V/MC/AX.
- Tandoori Grill, 201-4368 Main St., Village North, 604 905-4900. Mild to hot authentic East Indian dishes. Reservations recommended. Take out and delivery available. L/D, $$$, V/AX/MC.
- Teppan Village Japanese Steak House, 4291 Mountain Square, Delta Whistler Resort, Whistler Village, 604 932-2223. Teppan-yaki-style restaurant features steak, also chicken and seafood. Reservations suggested in peak seasons. D, $$$, V/AX/MC/DC.
- Thai One On, 108-4557 Blackcomb Way, Upper Village, 604 932-4822. Hot and not-so-hot gourmet Thai dishes such as coconut prawns and satays. Reservations recommended. Free underground parking. D, $$, V/AX/DC/MC.
- Zen Japanese Restaurant, 2202 Gondola Way, First Tracks Lodge, Creekside, 604 932-3667. Sleek restaurant features traditional Japanese cuisine with West Coast influences. L/D, $$$, V/AX/MC/DC.

CAFÉS

- Chef Bernard's, 1-4573 Chateau Blvd., Whistler Village, 604 932-7051. Tiny café with a great chef and fresh local produce. Soups, salads, cinnamon buns. B/L/D, $, AX/MC/V.
- Esquires Coffee House, 127-4338 Main St., Village North, 604 905-3386. Excellent coffee and teas with quiches, wraps and panini. B/L/D, $, AX/DC/MC/V.
- Southside Deli, 2102 Lake Placid Rd, Creekside, 604 932-3368. Famous for "Beltch" breakfast special of bacon, eggs, cheese and ham, burgers, sandwiches, soups, blackened snapper and BBQ charbroiled pork tenderloin. B/L/D, $$, AX/V.
- Splitz Grill, 4369 Main St., Alpenglow Hotel, Village North, 604 938-9300. Burgers galore including all-beef burger and spicy lentil vegetarian. L/D, $$, V.
- Uli's Flipside, 2021 Karen Cres., Creekside, 604 935-1107. Pasta, pizza, perogies, schnitzel, spicy Italian salsiccia sausage and chicken dishes. Casual atmosphere, children's menu. L/D, $$, V/MC.

ALPINE

- Bavaria Restaurant, 4369 Main St., Village North, 604 932-7518. Traditional fondue, schnitzel and all dishes Austrian from a superb chef. Deserts include home-made apple strudel and Kaiserschmarrn, a caramelized crepe. D, $$$$, AX/MC/V.

FAMILY/CASUAL

- Caramba! Restaurante, 12-4314 Main St., Village North, 604 938-1879. Pizzas, pastas in a cheery, lively setting. New York steak and calamari a la Plancha on the menu. L/D, $$$, AX/MC/V.
- Gaitors Bar & Grill, 7124 Nancy Green Drive, north of Whistler Village, 604 938-5777. Above the Shoestring Lodge, a fun spot for casual fare. Burgers, veggie enchiladas, curried prawns, soups, Mexican food. Sunday brunch buffet. L (weekdays), B/L/D Sat.-Sun, $$, AX/MC/V.
- Old Spaghetti Factory, 4154 Village Green, Crystal Lodge, Whistler Village, 604 938-1081. Adult and

children's menu of soups, salads, pastas, sourdough bread, New York steak, vegetarian lasagna, ice cream. L/D, $$$, AX/MC/V.
- The Original Ristorante, 4270 Mountain Square, Whistler Village, 604 932-6408. Fast-paced service starting with breakfast. Pizzas and pastas. B/L/D, $$, V/AX/MC.
- Tex Corleone's, 4154 Village Green, Crystal Lodge, Whistler Village, 604 932-7427. Chicago-style deep-dish pizza, chicken, Alberta-beef ribs. Breakfast buffet or individual items start the day. Children's coloring activities. B/L/D, $$$, DC/MC/V.

MEDITERRANEAN
- Pasta Lupino Gourmet, 121-4368 Main St., Village North, 604 905-0400. Fresh pasta and sauces in a tiny, popular café. L/D, $$$, MC/V.
- Quattro at Whistler, 4319 Main St., Village North, 604 905-4844. Country Italian cooking and extensive wine list. D, $$$, AX/DC/MC/V.
- Trattoria di Umberto, 4417 Sundial Place, Whistler Village, 604 932-5858. Tuscan cooking features linguine, spaghetti, fettuccine and more. Seafood cioppino is chef Umberto Menghi's specialty. L/D, $$$$, AX/DC/MC/V.
- Zeuski's Taverna, 40-4314 Main St., Village North, 604 932-6009. Lunch, dinner, and children's menus include Greek-style chicken burgers, felafels and wraps, roasted lamb, baklava. L/D, $$$, AX/DC/MC/V.

SEAFOOD & STEAK
- Brewhouse, 4355 Blackcomb Way, Village North, 604 905-2739. Wood-fired pizza and rotisserie-grilled prime ribs and chicken, sandwiches and tuna melts. L/D, $$, AX/MC/V.
- The Crab Shack, 4005 Whistler Way, Whistler Village, 604 932-4451. Casual dining. Features are hand-shucked oysters and steak. Live music at specified times. B/L/D, $$$, DC/MC/V.
- Creekside Grillroom, 2129 Lake Placid Rd., Creekside, 604 932-4424. Friendly ambiance, features 10 variations of Alberta beef, as well as chicken and salmon. D,

$$$, AX/MC/V.
- Rimrock Café, 2117 Whistler Rd., Creekside, 604 932-5565. Seabass, ahi tuna, grilled prawns as well as steak and lobster. Very popular, free parking. D, $$$$, AX/MC/V.

WEST COAST CUISINE
- Araxi Restaurant & Bar, 4222 Village Square, Whistler Village, 604 932-4540. Superb menu and 12,000-bottle wine list. West Coast with Italian and French influences. D, $$$$, AX/DC/MC/V.
- The Aubergine Grille, 4090 Whistler Way, Westin Resort & Spa, Whistler Village, 604 935-4344. Breakfast, lunch, dinner with a mountain view. West Coast seafood and salmon plus rustic pizza, certified Angus Beef, pastas. Dazzling deserts. B/L/D, $$$$, AX/MC/V.
- Edgewater Lodge Lakeside Dining Room, 8841 Hwy 99, north of Whistler Village, 604 932-0688. Secluded waterfront setting offering gourmet locally grown fare. Venison medallions, chicken, steaks. D, $$$$, AX/MC/V.
- Evergreens Restaurant, 4050 Whistler Way, Delta Whistler Resort, Whistler Village, 604 932-7346. Elegant and casual, occasional live piano. Taste of British Columbia Salmon specialty offers three in one. Venison striploin a specialty. B/L/D, $$$$, AX/DC/MC/V.
- La Rua Restaurante, 4557 Blackcomb Way, Upper Village, 604 932-5011. Great food and great wines with six gourmet pasta selections. D, $$$, AX/DC/MC/V.
- The Wildflower, 4599 Chateau Blvd., Fairmont Chateau Whistler, Upper Village, 604 938-2033. Daily breakfast buffet, Sunday brunch, lunches. Dinner includes Fraser Valley duck, rib-eye steak, free-range chicken, venison. Over 2,500 bottles of wine. B/L/D, $$$-$$$$, AX/DC/DISC/MC/V.

INDEX

PHOTO CREDITS

Legend: Top – T; Centre – C; Bottom – B; Left – L: Right - R
Photography by Hamid Attie, except those listed below.

Andy Mons, 42T,B; Appleton Gallery, Vancouver, 63C; Arts Club Theatre, Andrée Lanthier photo, 55BL; Arts Club Theatre, David Cooper photo, 55BR; Arts Club Theatre, Tim Matheson, 56C & B; Ballet British Columbia, David Cooper Photography, 58B, 59T; Bard on the Beach, 83T; Barry Piersdorf, 60 T; Bau-Xi, 61T&B, 62C; Chinese Cultural Centre Museum & Archives, 103T; Chris Nickless, 84T; Courtesy of UBC, 19T; Dan McCormick photographytips.com, 167T; Dr. Sun Yat-Sen Classical Chinese Garden, 67T; Eric Sinclair, 159 T; Grouse Mountain, 37B; Hastings Racecourse, 71B; Jeff Vinnick/Vancouver Canucks, 70B, 71T; Kan Chew, 69, 81T, 82T; Leanna Rathkelly, 75T; Maplewood Farm, 77BPacific National Exhibition, 76B; Paul Morrison, 159B; Perry Danforth, 115, 166T; Robert Kwong, 72; Sharmini Thiagarajah, 115L; Stephen Ruttan (with special thanks), 163, 164, 165, 166; Tourism Vancouver, 13B; Tourism Vancouver/Al Harvey, cover (T),13C, 14B, 20T, 28B, 35B, 41T, 49 ; Tourism Vancouver/Colin Jewall, 83B; Tourism Vancouver/Josef Hanus, 12C, 19B, 168T; Tourism Vancouver/Tom Ryan, 9, 11, 21T, 22C, 23T, 43C, 66T, 86T, 89T, 98T&B, 101, 103C, 111T, 112C, 119B, 167B, 168B; Tourism Whistler/Dean Thompson, 160T; Tourism Whistler/Greg Eymundson, 157, 161T, 162C; Tourism Whistler/Greg Griffith, 158T; Tourism Whistler/Leanna Rathkelly, 161B; Tourism Whistler/Maureen Provençal, 162B; Tourism Whistler/Tim King, 162T; Tourism Whistler/Toshi Kawano, 158B; Vancouver Art Gallery, 30T&C; Vancouver Int'l Writers Festival (Lala Espejo photo), 79B; Vancouver Opera,Tim Matheson Photography, 57 C&B;Vancouver Public Library, 15L, 17C&B, 18T; Vancouver Symphony Orchestra, 57T
Maps, Peggy McCalla, Maritime Mapping, Halifax

Formac Publishing Company Limited acknowledges the support of the Cultural Affairs Section, Nova Scotia Department of Tourism and Culture. We acknowledge the financial support of the Government of Canada through the Book Publishing Industry Development Program (BPIDP) for our publishing activities.